Incorporate!

An Easy Step-by-Step Plan for Entrepreneurs

Karen B. Nathan

Alice H. Magos

McGraw-Hill

New York   Chicago   San Francisco   Lisbon   London
Madrid   Mexico City   Milan   New Delhi   San Juan
Seoul   Singapore   Sydney   Toronto

2 3 4 5 6 7 8 9 0 AGM/AGM 0 9 8 7 6 5 4

ISBN 0-07-140983-1

McGraw-Hill books are available at special quantity discounts to use as premiums and sales promotions, or for use in corporate training programs. For more information, please write to the Director of Special Sales, Professional Publishing, McGraw-Hill, Two Penn Plaza, New York, NY 10121-2298. Or contact your local bookstore.

This book is printed on recycled, acid-free paper containing a minimum of 50% recycled, de-inked fiber.

Library of Congress Cataloging-in-Publication Data

Nathan, Karen B.
    Incorporate! : an easy step-by-step plan for entrepreneurs / by Karen
B. Nathan, Alice H. Magos
        p. cm.
    ISBN 0-07-140983-1 (pbk. : alk. paper)
    1. Incorporation—United States—Popular works. I. Magos, Alice H.
II. Title.
KF1420 .Z9N38 2003
346.73'06622—dc21   2002152448

CONTENTS

ACKNOWLEDGMENTS

This project faced a number of changes in the latter stages, but the ultimate goal remained the same. We wanted to create a book that furthered the founding principle of Business Filings Incorporated—make incorporating a business both easy and easy-to-understand. The pairing of resources from Business Filings with those of CCH Incorporated was natural, since both companies help to make starting and running a business easier for entrepreneurs.

We would like to thank the cofounders of Business Filings, Brian Wiegand and Richard Oster, for their input and guidance. As entrepreneurs who started one of the first online incorporation service companies, their insight and assistance were invaluable throughout this project.

The talented staff of Business Filings now assists hundreds of entrepreneurs each day with their incorporation needs. We would like to thank all the knowledgeable employees of Business Filings, particularly Janet Rubleske, CPA; Megan Rusch; Mary Lou Sharpe; and Vickie Taylor. Your assistance in this project was a tremendous asset. Our gratitude is expressed as well to the Delaware Secretary of State, Division of Corporations, for providing an actual certificate of incorporation for our fictitious company example in Chapter 12.

We would also like to thank Paul Robinson of Digital Zone for his assistance with all of the figures in this book. An additional thank you goes to Michael R. Miller for his suggestions and to Ann Wildman of McGraw-Hill for providing feedback throughout the process.

We must extend a special thank you to the customers of Business Filings Incorporated. Your use of Business Filings' incorporation services has helped the company grow to be a leader in the incorporation industry. We must also thank those entrepreneurs who turn to CCH Incorporated and the CCH Business Owner's Toolkit for information and assistance. The questions these business owners pose continue to provide insight into the unique situations that entrepreneurs face when starting their businesses and evaluating whether to incorporate. Through your feedback Business Filings continues to offer ways to make the incorporation process easier and more affordable, and CCH continues to provide the information and resources that help create successful businesses.

Incorporating a business can seem like an intimidating task. Entrepreneurs who are starting a business often have a number of questions to answer and decisions to make—with whether or not to incorporate being only one of these. Small business owners who have been operating as sole proprietorships or in partnerships also face the option of incorporating. Unfortunately, there are often negative stereotypes associated with incorporating a business—it's too costly, too time-consuming, too much of a hassle. However, with the proper advice and information, none of these have to be the case, and the benefits of incorporating your business far outweigh any potential negatives.

This book is not a legal guideline for incorporating a business. The focus was to make this often complex subject more understandable, and the information included is often general in nature. This book should not serve as a substitute for legal advice regarding your particular situation. It should, however, help to provide insight into all aspects of the incorporation process and provide a practical outline for the steps entrepreneurs should consider, and, in some cases, must undertake.

As you consider whether incorporation is the right step for your business, keep in mind that there are a number of differences between public corporations and small, privately held corporations. Incorporating a business is not synonymous with going public, nor does it mean that your corporation must have millions of shares of stock. This book seeks to help you understand the corporate structure and formalities and how they differ for small businesses.

Through their backgrounds and involvement with companies assisting entrepreneurs, the authors of this book can speak directly to the questions you have about incorporating. They can help not only by making the process easy to understand but also by increasing your comfort level with the decisions before you. Forming your business as a corporation means more than filing the necessary paperwork with the state and paying the necessary fees. There are a number of considerations, details, and choices that must be made both before and after you file your incorporation documents. The more you know about these steps, the easier the entire process will be.

There are three primary phases to the incorporation process: preparing to incorporate, the incorporation process itself, and the requirements after you've incorporated. This book is divided into parts addressing each of these phases.

GETTING READY TO INCORPORATE

What exactly is a corporation? This is a very valid question that many entrepreneurs have. Maybe you know certain things about corporations, but you would like to know more. The first chapter in this section introduces you to the corporate entity. As you start a business, you need to be aware of the different types of business structures that are available for your business. If you are currently a sole proprietor or part of a partnership, you should know how these structures compare to others, particularly those that offer the owners limited liability. Chapter 2 introduces you to the sole proprietorship, partnership, limited partnership, C corporation, S corporation, and limited liability company, and lists the potential advantages and disadvantages of each. When you have information on all your options, it will be easier for you to make an informed decision on the direction you should take.

In Chapter 3, we dive more deeply into the advantages and disadvantages of incorporating your business, and also include basic information on corporate taxation. Taxation is one of the biggest questions in entrepreneurs' minds as they evaluate the different types of business entity.

Once you decide that forming a corporation is the right step for your business, you face the questions of who will incorporate your business and in which state you should incorporate. Chapters 4 and 5 help you analyze the options for who will prepare and file your incorporation paperwork, and provide information on items you should consider when you are deciding whether to incorporate in your home state or in a state such as Delaware. Knowing that many entrepreneurs have a limited amount of capital with which to start and run their businesses, we take particular care to let you know how the options available to you may affect your costs. Finally, Chapter 6 provides you with a pre-incorporation checklist to help you prepare for moving to the next step . . . the incorporation process.

MOVING FORWARD—INCORPORATING YOUR BUSINESS

Well, you've decided to form a corporation. Now what? Have you selected your corporate name? If so, have you checked to ensure that the name you have chosen is available for use in your intended state of incorporation or as a domain name for the World Wide Web? Did you check to ensure that no other company already has trademark rights to that name? There are a number of things that entrepreneurs should consider when they name their businesses, and Chapter 7 helps you understand how these things come together during the incorporation process.

Next, your incorporation documents will have to be prepared and filed. What information is required? What are shares and par value? What is a registered agent, and why do the states require one? Chapter 8 introduces you to the information that is typically required in your articles of incorporation, so that you can make these determinations prior to filing your documents.

How long does incorporating take, and how much does it cost? These questions are answered in Chapter 9. Will you be transacting business in states other than your state of incorporation? If so, there are items you need to consider and steps you need to take in order to legally do business in other states. Chapter 10 helps you to understand these requirements.

Are there other items you should consider when you are incorporating? Absolutely. For instance, do you want your corporation to be taxed as an S corporation, so that the profits and losses of the business are passed through the corporation to your personal income tax return? If so, you need to elect this status with the Internal Revenue Service (IRS). Your corporation needs an employer identification number (EIN) from the IRS, and it may need business licenses to operate in your state, county, city, or all areas. These items and the process for obtaining them are outlined in Chapter 11. How does the whole process come together? For your convenience, we have given two case studies in Chapter 12 that illustrate all the concepts covered in Chapters 1 through 11.

AFTER INCORPORATING

The requirements placed on corporations do not end once you have received your final incorporation documents from the state. Corporations face a number of unique obligations. These post-incorporation steps, some immediate and others ongoing, are important elements that cannot be overlooked. Because many of these are unique to the corporate entity, we devote Part 3 to addressing them.

After your filing has been approved by the state, and your corporation therefore officially exists, an initial meeting of the directors needs to be held to appoint officers, approve the rules for the internal governance of the corporation, and issue stock to the shareholders. An initial meeting of shareholders also needs to be held to ratify the decisions made by the board of directors. Chapter 13 includes information on these meetings and the formalities for calling, holding, and documenting them.

Corporate bylaws are a corporation's second most important document, after the articles of incorporation (the document that forms the corporation). The bylaws are the rules for the corporation's internal governance. Because of the importance of the bylaws and the information they contain, this document warrants its own chapter—Chapter 14. The corporation's shareholders, directors, and officers have already been mentioned. Who are these corporate players, and what are their roles? Chapter 15 answers that question for you.

How to capitalize a company is another question most entrepreneurs have. How do you get money into and out of your corporation? Chapter 16 provides a general look at this complex subject. Entrepreneurs also often have questions on how to open bank accounts, how to set up accounting books, how to establish credit, and how to lease space or equipment. Considering the number of decisions that entrepreneurs face when they start their businesses, some of these general business items may not cross your mind. Chapter 17 outlines a number of them.

Finally, corporations face a number of annual and ongoing corporate compliance requirements. Some of these are unique to corporations, such as annual statements and franchise taxes, whereas others are imposed on most businesses, such as federal and state income taxes. Are you aware that corporations need to hold annual meetings of directors and shareholders and to document all formal decisions made by the directors and shareholders? There are consequences to not honoring your corporate responsibilities, the primary one being that you could lose the benefits, such as limited liability, that the corporate entity provides. Chapter 18 outlines these responsibilities and provides a checklist for use in remembering these steps and their deadlines.

READY, SET, GO

While starting a business or taking your existing business to a new level may feel like a race, remember that there are a number of resources to assist you as you start, run, and grow your business. Attorneys and accountants can provide valuable advice for your specific business situation. The Internet is also a vast resource of information on every facet of owning your own business.

Owning your own business is similar to leaving home. You are now out on your own, and you are excited about the future. You may be cash-strapped, but you envision success being just around the corner. Some bumps in the road are to be expected, but you always plan to have resources to which you can turn for direction. Just as you did when you were growing up, you learn from your mistakes, embrace the challenges, and celebrate the triumphs—no matter how big or how small they may be.

Enjoy learning about all aspects of incorporating a business. For entrepreneurs, this important business step has never been easier than it is today, and we're here to make it even easier for you.

PART ONE

Getting Ready to Incorporate

CHAPTER 1

What Is a Corporation?

Understanding the elements of a corporation is the first step in evaluating whether incorporation is right for your business. This chapter provides basic information on corporations as well as a starting point for each of the steps that will be discussed in this book.

> *Major topics covered: This chapter seeks to answer the following questions: What is a corporation? Who are the important players in a corporation? What are the important documents involved with corporations?*

WHAT IS A CORPORATION?

In the shortest definition possible, a corporation is a legal entity, created by a state filing, that exists separately from its owners. Legally speaking, a corporation is an artificial being, invisible, intangible, and existing only in contemplation of the law (*Dartmouth* v. *Woodward* [1819]). Legal-speak can often be confusing, and that is one of the reasons why many entrepreneurs seek to incorporate their businesses themselves, or at least to research the incorporation process before they meet with an attorney.

A corporation is created when properly completed articles of incorporation (also called a charter or a certificate of incorporation in some states) are filed with and approved by the proper state authority. In many states, it is the secretary of state that processes and approves the articles of incorporation. Each state charges filing fees to form a corporation, which will be discussed in more depth in Chapter 9.

Most people are probably familiar with a different type of business structure, the general partnership. The general partnership is an extension of its owners; it is defined by the Uniform Partnership Act (1994) as "an association of two or more persons to carry on as co-owners of a business for profit." A partnership comes into existence without the need to file any formal papers with any state agency or official. Thus, if Eric and Amy begin to jointly operate a corner store without signing any formal agreement between them and without filing any documents with the state, they will have a general partnership. Chapter 2 includes additional information on partnerships and introduces other types of business structures to which you can compare and contrast the corporation.

As you can see, forming a partnership is much less formal than incorporating a business. However, corporations have distinct advantages that partnerships do not have. A primary advantage of forming a corporation is limited liability, meaning that the owners, who are usually called shareholders, generally are not held responsible for the debts and liabilities of the business. A corporation offers this limited liability protection because it exists separately from its shareholders. Corporations file separate tax returns with the Internal Revenue Service (IRS), thus keeping their profits and losses separate from the shareholders' income; however, profits can be passed on to shareholders in the form of dividends. The concepts of limited liability and corporate taxation will be explained in more depth in Chapter 3.

PUBLICLY HELD VERSUS PRIVATELY HELD CORPORATIONS

There is often confusion regarding the difference between publicly held and privately held corporations. Incorporating your business does not mean "going public" or having your corporation's stock traded on a national exchange, such as the New York Stock Exchange (NYSE) or NASDAQ. Many people automatically assume that the term *corporation* means a large, publicly held company, but that is not the case. In reality, there are fewer publicly held corporations than there are privately held corporations.

In privately held corporations, often also called closely held corporations, the ownership of the company is private, meaning that the stock is not offered for sale to the general public. Private companies generally have relatively few shareholders, as compared to the thousands of shareholders that publicly traded companies have. Most entrepreneurs who incorporate their businesses have closely held corporations, often with as few as one shareholder, and keep their corporations closely held throughout the life of the business. That's not to say that your business cannot grow, go public, and become the next hot stock touted on Wall Street. After all, many successful companies grew out of entrepreneurial dreams and visions put in place in a college dorm room, a basement, or a garage. Hewlett-Packard, Dell, and Apple are examples of companies started by entrepreneurs that grew to be large, multinational, public companies.

WHO ARE THE IMPORTANT PLAYERS IN A CORPORATION?

Corporations have three basic groups of players: shareholders, directors, and officers. Each has a distinct role within the corporation; however, with small corporations these roles may blur to a certain extent.

Shareholders

The shareholders are the owners of the corporation. Shareholders do not oversee or manage the corporation's activities, unless they also act as directors or officers. Having shareholders who also act as directors and officers is fairly common in small businesses, particularly corporations that were started by one person or a small number of people.

A person becomes a shareholder in a corporation when he or she buys or receives shares of that corporation's stock. All corporations, whether publicly or privately held, have stock. The major difference is that the stock of publicly held companies is available for sale to the general public on a major stock exchange. Also, while the number of shareholders a corporation can have is unlimited, closely held companies often have only a small number of shareholders. Public companies often have thousands or tens of thousands of shareholders.

When you file your incorporation paperwork, you must specify the number of shares of stock the corporation is authorized and intends to issue. These shares, which establish a shareholder's ownership in the corporation, can be issued or sold to others throughout the life of the corporation. Stock will be discussed in more depth in Chapter 8, and the roles of shareholders will be discussed in more depth in Chapter 15.

Directors

The directors oversee and direct the affairs of the corporation. As the majority of the corporate authority rests with the directors, they are responsible for the major corporate decisions, but typically they are not responsible for the day-to-day operations of the business. Directors outline corporate policy, approve or reject major corporate actions, and appoint the officers. They also shoulder the responsibility if the management of the business does not run smoothly, since the directors typically oversee the activities of the corporation's officers.

Directors, who are elected by the shareholders, form a governing body called the board of directors. The maximum number of directors is often specified by a corporation's bylaws; however, some states have statutes regarding the minimum number of directors required. Some states require a corporation to have three directors, with the exception that if the number of shareholders is less than three, the number of directors can equal the number of shareholders. For example, if your corporation has only one shareholder, it can have only one director.

The traditional roles of directors are more clearly defined within public companies than within closely held companies. In closely held corporations, the role of directors often merges with the roles of shareholders and officers, since the same person or persons often occupy all three of these positions.

Officers

Officers manage the day-to-day operations of the corporation. The board of directors appoints the officers, whose powers are typically defined in the corporation's bylaws. A closely held corporation's officers usually consist of a president, a vice president, a treasurer, and a secretary. Many states allow one person to hold all of these posts. Publicly held companies often have a number of officers with varying titles, such as chief executive officer, chief financial officer, and chief operating officer.

Officers have substantial authority to make decisions and carry out actions on behalf of the company; however, they ultimately answer to the board of directors. This is also typically the case with closely held corporations, with the primary difference that the officers are also often directors and shareholders of the corporation.

Figure 1-1 illustrates how the roles of shareholders, directors, and officers generally differ between publicly held and closely held corporations. This chapter touches only briefly on these players and their roles. Chapter 15 outlines the roles of shareholders, directors, and officers in more depth.

FIGURE 1-1

Corporate Players in Closely Held Corporations versus Publicly Held Corporations

	Closely Held Corporations	Publicly Held Corporations
Number of Shareholders	One or relatively few	Thousands
Primary Shareholder Roles	• Own the corporation • Often very involved in management of the corporation • Often act as directors and officers as well	• Own the corporation • Not directly involved in management of the corporation • Elect directors
Primary Director Roles	• Oversee and direct the affairs of the corporation, often including day-to-day management, since directors are also frequently officers	• Oversee and direct the affairs of the corporation • Not responsible for day-to-day management • Manage the officers
Primary Officer Roles	• Responsible for day-to-day operations of the corporation • Often are the corporation's shareholders and directors as well	• Responsible for day-to-day operations of the corporation • Often are the corporation's shareholders and directors as well

WHAT ARE THE IMPORTANT DOCUMENTS?

The two most important corporate documents are the articles of incorporation and the bylaws. The articles of incorporation are filed with the state to bring a corporation into existence. The bylaws outline the rules and procedures for the internal governance of the corporation. As an internal document, the bylaws require no external approval or state filing.

Articles of Incorporation

The articles of incorporation are the equivalent of the constitution of the corporation. Chapter 8 outlines and defines the types of information required for the articles of incorporation, but briefly, the articles typically include information such as:

- The name of the corporation
- The business purpose of the corporation
- The number of shares authorized and the par value of those shares
- The name and address of the registered agent
- The name and address of the incorporator

Beyond the information required by the state, the information included in the articles of incorporation is often kept to a minimum. Because the articles of incorporation are filed with the state, an additional state filing must be made and an additional state filing fee paid in order to amend them.

Bylaws

As previously mentioned, the bylaws outline the rules and procedures established for the internal governance of the corporation. Bylaws are not filed with the state, and therefore no state filing is required to amend them. Because the bylaws can be changed more easily than the articles of incorporation, more detailed information on the corporation is often included within the bylaws.

Bylaws are explained more thoroughly in Chapter 14, but as a brief outline, the bylaws typically include such information as:

- How to hold shareholders' meetings
- How to hold directors' meetings
- An outline of the rights and responsibilities of the shareholders, directors, and officers
- Provisions regarding general corporate business practices
- Provisions regarding making amendments to the bylaws

In many respects, the bylaws are an internal road map for the corporation. They should be reviewed often and amended as necessary so that they remain up-to-date with the needs and direction of the corporation.

As you are reading, please keep in mind that each state has different statutes for corporations. Since there thus are fifty state statutes, plus the statutes for the District of Columbia, this book would be incredibly long if every state's requirements were specifically addressed. The state information tables located at www.bizfilings.com/learning/detailedstateinfo.htm will address a number of these requirements. The text throughout this book will look at the more general picture.

CHAPTER 2

Comparing the Types
of Business Structure

There are a number of types of business entities from which you can choose when you are deciding on the structure of your business. Because of this, the decision as to what type of entity to form often proves to be a difficult one for business owners. Some structures are very different from one another, while others have a number of identical characteristics. As you evaluate whether or not to incorporate your business, you should be aware of the other possible entities and their advantages and disadvantages. This information is intended to help you decide what type of structure is best for your particular business.

> *Major topics covered:* This chapter addresses the different types of business structure—sole proprietorship, general partnership, limited partnership, C corporation, S corporation, and limited liability company (LLC)—and outlines the advantages and disadvantages of each. The chapter also includes a "quick-glance" table that compares these business structures, and a more in-depth comparison of the C corporation, S corporation, and LLC. Finally, this chapter includes information on the statutory close corporation, the nonprofit corporation, and the professional corporation.

As you review the characteristics of each type of entity, be sure to keep in mind both the present and future needs of your business. Chances are that when you're starting your business, it will be quite small, as will be the number of owners. Some questions you should ask yourself are: Do you want to keep the ownership of your business small and relatively controlled? Do you want to grow your business, and consequently the ownership of your company? Do you have personal assets that you want to protect and keep separate from the assets of the business? Do you want to seek funding from outside investors? Do you want to take your company public? Your current needs and future goals will affect your decision as to which type of entity is best for your business. Also, if you have specific questions regarding your particular business situation, it is always advisable to seek the advice of an attorney or accountant.

SOLE PROPRIETORSHIP

A sole proprietorship is a business that is owned and operated by an individual. Starting a sole proprietorship is quick, fairly uncomplicated, and relatively inexpensive. You do not need to file documents with the state to form this type of entity, as you do with corporations and limited liability companies (LLCs). If one person begins a business for profit, that person has formed a sole proprietorship.

If you plan to conduct business under a trade name rather than your legal name (e.g., Field's Landscaping rather than John Field), you will need to file a DBA or Doing Business As (also often called an assumed name or fictitious name) certificate with your local or state office. DBAs are typically issued at the county level, but there may be state requirements as well. The state and city in which you will operate your business may also require additional licenses (e.g., a sales tax license, a liquor license, etc.); these requirements vary by state. You should check with your local and/or state government office regarding the types of licenses required for your specific type of business. At the state level, there is often a state Department of Licensing or similar body, and at the county level, the county recorder's office or a similar body can provide information on the requirements for your business.

With a sole proprietorship, the owner and the business are legally considered to be the same. For example, the identifier used by the Internal Revenue Service (IRS) for a sole proprietorship is the owner's Social Security number. Also, there are no separate business taxes. Because of this lack of separation, sole proprietorships do not offer business owners the same limited liability as corporations and LLCs, leaving the owner of a sole proprietorship personally responsible for the debts and liabilities of the company.

Some advantages of a sole proprietorship are as follows:

- They can be created in relatively little time and with relatively little expense.
- There are relatively few regulatory requirements and necessary formalities.
- Most states do not impose a fee on them for the mere privilege of existing.
- There is no separate income tax filing for the company—income and losses are reported on the owner's individual tax return.

Some disadvantages of a sole proprietorship are as follows:

- The owner is personally responsible for the debts and liabilities of the company, meaning that the owner's personal assets may be used to satisfy business liabilities should the company face such events as lawsuits or bankruptcy.
- Raising capital for the business can be more difficult because of the inability to sell stock or the possible perception that the company is "a one-man shop."

GENERAL PARTNERSHIP

A general partnership is simply an association of two or more persons operating a business for profit. Like sole proprietorships, general partnerships are easy to establish. A partnership comes into existence when two or more persons agree to share the profits from and control of a business. No state filing is required, no meetings need to be held, no documents need to be signed, and no fees need to be paid in order to form a partnership, although the owners may need state and/or local licenses to operate. For example, if you and your neighbor agree to hold a yard sale together, you automatically have a partnership because you will be sharing in the control of and the profits from the yard sale.

As in sole proprietorships, in partnerships the owners and the business are legally viewed as the same. Thus, there is no limited liability with general partnerships. All of the partners can be held personally responsible for the business's debts and liabilities.

Because of their more informal nature, it is a good idea for partnerships to have detailed partnership agreements in place at the time the partnership is formed. Partnership agreements should clearly address the rights and responsibilities of each partner, and state what is to happen if those rights are violated or those responsibilities are not fulfilled. A partnership agreement should address such items as the amount of capital each partner will contribute, what will happen if more capital is needed, how profits and losses will be distributed, which partners are responsible for particular management tasks, what happens if a partner wants out of the partnership, and what happens if a partner dies. If no partnership agreement is in place, state laws will determine what happens in these situations, possibly providing a less than desirable result.

Some advantages of general partnerships are as follows:

- They allow multiple owners, unlike sole proprietorships.
- They can be created in relatively little time and with relatively little expense.
- There are relatively few regulatory requirements and necessary formalities.
- Most states do not impose a fee on them for the mere privilege of existing.
- Partnerships do not pay taxes at the entity level; instead the profits and losses of the partnership are reflected directly on the personal income tax returns of the partners.
- There is considerable flexibility in establishing the responsibilities (capital, management, etc.) of the partners.

Some disadvantages of general partnerships are as follows:

- Partners are personally responsible for the debts and liabilities of the partnership.
- Each partner is responsible for the business-related actions of all other partners.
- A partnership's life is limited.
- To transfer ownership in a partnership, the other partners must typically approve the transfer.

LIMITED PARTNERSHIP

A limited partnership (LP) is a partnership of two or more people in which there are two different partnership levels: general partners and limited partners.

Like the partners in a general partnership, the general partners in an LP are personally liable for the debts and liabilities of the business. The general partners are generally also involved in the management and daily operations of the business. The role of a limited partner, however, is that of an investor. A limited partner invests capital in the business but is not involved in the management or operations of the business. A limited partner is also not personally liable for the debts and liabilities of the company, beyond the possible loss of his or her investment.

Limited partnerships should also have detailed partnership agreements in place at the time the partnership is formed. As with general partnerships, having a formal partnership agreement is not a legal requirement, but it is a sound business decision.

Some advantages of LPs are as follows:

- They can be created with relatively little time and expense; however, a state filing is required.
- There are relatively few regulatory requirements and necessary formalities.
- LPs do not pay taxes at the entity level; instead, the profits and losses of the partnership are reflected directly on the personal income tax returns of the partners.
- The possibility of investments by limited partners helps the business raise capital more easily.

Some disadvantages of general partnerships are as follows:

- General partners are personally responsible for the debts and liabilities of the partnership.
- Each partner is responsible for the business-related actions of all other partners.
- Limited partners may be personally responsible for business debts and liabilities of the partnership if they are deemed to have participated in the management of the LP.
- Limited partnerships somewhat resemble corporations and LLCs in that a filing must be made with the state, and necessary filing fees paid, for them to come into existence.

CORPORATION

In order to form a corporation, business owners must file certain documents with the state. A corporation is a separate legal entity that is owned by its shareholders. The standard corporation (also called a C corporation) is allowed to have an unlimited number of shareholders, who are typically protected from the debts and liabilities of the corporation. A shareholder's personal liability is generally limited to the amount the shareholder invested in the company.

Corporations may experience double taxation, which is often considered the biggest disadvantage to organizing as a corporation. For income tax purposes, a corporation is considered a legal, taxable entity separate from its owners, unlike a sole proprietorship or a partnership. Therefore, corporations must pay taxes on their earnings. If corporate earnings are then distributed to shareholders in the form of dividends, the dividend income is taxed as regular income to the shareholders. Dividends are optional payments made by corporations to shareholders from the corporation's profits. The double taxation occurs because income is taxed (1) at the corporate level and (2) at the individual level. S corporations, LLCs, and limited liability partnerships (LLPs) are pass-through taxation entities that are not subject to the double tax.

Some advantages of a corporation are as follows:

- Shareholders generally are not personally responsible for the debts and liabilities of the corporation.
- Ownership in the corporation is easily transferable through the sale of stock.
- Additional capital can be raised easily through the sale of stock (shares) in the corporation.
- Corporations have an unlimited life, extending beyond the illness or death of their owners.
- Reasonable business expenses (such as salaries, certain insurance payments, building lease payments, etc.) are tax deductible.
- Corporations have the ability to retain earnings for future investment.

Some disadvantages of a corporation are as follows:

- There is the possibility of double taxation.
- Corporations are more expensive to form and operate than sole proprietorships or partnerships.
- More corporate formalities (i.e., annual paperwork) and more state rules and regulations apply than with sole proprietorships or partnerships. To learn more about your state's requirements, see the state tables at www.bizfilings.com/learning/detailedstate-info.htm

S CORPORATION

The S corporation, sometimes called a subchapter S corporation, is a standard corporation that has elected a special tax status with the IRS. This special tax treatment eliminates the possibility of double taxation that faces standard corporations. Although the S corporation must still complete a corporate tax return, it does not pay taxes directly. Instead, the income or loss of the corporation, as shown on the corporate tax return, is passed through the corporation to its shareholders. The shareholders report the income or loss generated by the S corporation on their individual tax returns.

Not all corporations are permitted to make the S corporation election. While some business owners may consider the restrictions on S corporations advantageous, they are often viewed as disadvantages of this type of business entity.

In order to qualify for S corporation status, the corporation must have fewer than 75 shareholders, and all shareholders must consent in writing to the S corporation election. In community property (meaning marital property) states, such as Wisconsin, the spouse of a shareholder must also consent in writing. These shareholders must be individuals, estates, or certain qualified trusts. Shareholders cannot be nonresident aliens. Also, an S corporation can have only one class of stock (disregarding voting rights). Generally, a corporation is considered to have only one class of stock if all outstanding shares of the corporation's stock confer identical rights to distribution of any profits and of the proceeds of liquidation should the company be dissolved.

Finally, a corporation must make a timely filing of Form 2553 with the IRS in order to elect S corporation status. The S corporation election and what you should do to make this election is discussed in more depth in Chapter 11.

Some advantages of the S corporation are as follows:

- Its special tax treatment avoids the possibility of double taxation faced by standard corporations.
- Like the shareholders of standard corporations, S corporation shareholders are not personally responsible for the debts and liabilities of the corporation.
- S corporations are permitted to use the cash method of accounting, which may be considered an advantage.
- Most of the other advantages of the standard corporation also apply to the S corporation.

Some disadvantages of the S corporation are as follows:

- In order to qualify for S corporation status, the corporation can have only one class of stock.
- Shareholders must number fewer than 75.
- Shareholders must be individuals, estates, or certain qualified trusts, and all must consent in writing to the S corporation election.
- Shareholders cannot be nonresident aliens.
- Losses are generally limited to shareholder basis.
- S corporations are generally required to have a calendar fiscal year.
- More corporate formalities (i.e., annual paperwork) and more state and federal rules and regulations apply than with sole proprietorships and partnerships.

LIMITED LIABILITY COMPANY

A limited liability company (LLC) is a distinct business entity that offers an alternative to partnerships and standard corporations by combining the corporate advantage of limited liability with pass-through taxation. The LLC is typically taxed like a partnership or an S corporation, in that the LLC's income is not taxed at the entity level, although LLCs can elect to be taxed like C corporations. Even when an LLC is taxed like a partnership, however, a separate tax return for the LLC must still be completed. The income or loss of the LLC, as shown on this return, is passed through the LLC and is reported on the owners' individual tax returns.

An LLC is owned by its members, and there are no restrictions on the number of members it can have. Members are analogous to partners in a partnership or shareholders in a corporation, depending on how the LLC is structured. When forming an LLC, you can choose to have it managed by the members (owners) or by nonmember managers. The choice will be specified in the articles of organization that you file with the state at the time the LLC is formed. If the LLC utilizes management by one or multiple nonmember multiple managers, the members will more closely resemble the shareholders of a corporation. In this situation, the members will not directly participate in the management of the LLC. If the members manage the LLC, they will more closely resemble the partners in a partnership, because they will have a direct say in the company's decision making.

A member's ownership in the LLC is represented by membership interest, just like a partner's interest in a partnership or a shareholder's interest in a corporation. Membership interest in an LLC is not as easy to transfer as stock in a corporation, because the other members must typically approve any transfer of ownership; however, the LLC's operating agreement can be written to allow for freely transferable membership interest. Whether freely transferable interest is included in the operating agreement usually depends upon the goals the members have for the LLC. If they wish to keep the ownership small and controlled, they most likely will not include such language. If attracting additional owners is desirable, then freely transferable interest would be beneficial.

There is also a business structure called the limited liability partnership (LLP). Some states specify that LLPs can be formed only to provide professional services, such as architectural or legal services. Like LLCs, LLPs offer limited liability to all the partners. This is in contrast to the LP, which offers limited liability only to the limited partners. If you're interested in possibly forming an LLP, you should check with the state in which you want to form your business to ensure this business structure is allowed for your particular type of business.

Some advantages of LLCs are as follows:

- Pass-through taxation, where earnings are treated like those in a partnership or S corporation, exists.
- Members are not held personally responsible for the debts and liabilities of the company.
- There are no restrictions on the number of owners (members) allowed.
- LLCs allow for flexibility in structuring the management of the company.
- The LLC does not require as much annual paperwork or have as many formalities as corporations and S corporations.

Some disadvantages of LLCs are as follows:

- There is more paperwork required than with a general partnership.
- Ownership is harder to transfer than with a corporation.
- The life of the LLC is often limited, meaning that some states require a dissolution date to be included in the articles of organization. This is a holdover from the old IRS rule allowing LLCs to be taxed as pass-through taxation entities only if they had two or less of the four corporate characteristics (limited liability, centralized management, unlimited life, and free transferability of interest). Assigning a dissolution date allowed the LLC to differ from

corporations in terms of unlimited life. The IRS changed its rules in 1998 to make all LLCs pass-through taxation entities, but many states still require a dissolution date to be included in the articles of organization.

- The LLC is a relatively new entity, and there is not as much case law to rely on for determining precedent.

ENTITY COMPARISON TABLE

Figure 2-1 compares the sole proprietorship, general partnership, limited partnership, corporation, S corporation, and LLC on a variety of points. This table is designed to be a quick reference. If you have questions regarding your specific business and which business structure may be best for it, we recommend that you contact an attorney or accountant.

A DEEPER COMPARISON OF THE C CORPORATION, S CORPORATION, AND LLC

When business owners decide that having limited liability is an important advantage, they often compare the C corporation, the S corporation, and the limited liability company. Because each of these three entities provides limited liability to the owners, the other characteristics of these entities are then more closely evaluated to determine which best fits the business owner's current and future goals. Because of this, we've provided a more in-depth look at these structures in comparison to one another.

C Corporation and S Corporation

As discussed earlier in this chapter, a standard or C corporation can make an election with the IRS to be taxed as a pass-through entity. This type of taxation is allowed for by subchapter S of the Internal Revenue Code. When a C corporation makes this election with the IRS, it is called an S corporation.

Similarities

- *Formation.* The formation documents filed with the state are the same for both entities.
- *Limited liability.* Both entities offer limited liability to the owners (shareholders), meaning that the owners generally are not personally responsible for the debts and liabilities of the business.

FIGURE 2-1

Entity Comparison Table

CHARACTERISTICS	SOLE PROPRIETORSHIP	GENERAL PARTNERSHIP	LIMITED PARTNERSHIP	LIMITED LIABILITY COMPANY	S CORPORATION	CORPORATION
FORMATION	No state permission required	Agreement of parties involved— no state permission required	File with state for permission	File with state for permission	File with state for permission	File with state for permission
DURATION	Dependent on sole proprietor	Life span is limited	Life span is limited	Typically limited to a fixed amount of time	Perpetual	Perpetual
LIABILITY	Sole proprietor has unlimited liability	Partners have unlimited liability	General partners have unlimited liability, limited partners have limited liability	Members not typically personally liable for the debts of the business	Shareholders not typically personally liable for the debts of the business	Shareholders not typically personally liable for the debts of the business
SIMPLICITY OF OPERATION	Relatively few legal requirements	Relatively few legal requirements	Some formal requirements, but less formal than corporations	Some formal requirements, but less formal than corporations	Formality of board of directors, officers, annual meetings, and annual reporting	Formality of board of directors, officers, annual meetings, and annual reporting
MANAGEMENT	Full control of management and operations	Typically each partner has an equal voice unless otherwise arranged	General partners typically responsible for the management	Members have operating agreement that outlines management	The corporation is managed by the board of directors, who are elected by the shareholders	The corporation is managed by the board of directors, who are elected by the shareholders
TAXATION	Sole proprietor has unlimited liability	Each partner pays tax on his/her share of the income and can deduct losses against other sources of income	No tax at the entity level — income/loss is passed through to the partners	If properly structured, no tax at entity level — income/loss is passed through to members of the LLC	No tax at the entity level — income/loss is passed through to the shareholders	Corporation is a taxable entity
PASS-THROUGH INCOME/LOSS	Yes	Yes	Yes	Yes	Yes	No, corporate losses cannot be deducted by shareholder
DOUBLE TAXATION	No	No	No	No	No	Yes
COST OF CREATION	None	None	Filing fee with the state	Filing fee with the state	Filing fee with the state	Filing fee with the state
RAISING CAPITAL	Difficult, unless owner contributes money	Contributions from partners or an addition of more partners	Possible to sell interest in the partnership	Possible to sell interest — subject to operating agreement restrictions	Sell shares of stock to raise capital	Sell shares of stock to raise capital
TRANSFERABILITY OF INTEREST	No	No	Possibly, but often subject to consent	Possibly, but often subject to consent	Yes, subject to consent	Shares of stock in a corporation are easily transferable

- *Formalities.* Both entities are required to comply with the same formalities, such as paying annual statement fees and/or state franchise taxes, holding shareholders' and directors' meetings, and keeping a set of corporate records.
- *Same entity.* It should be noted that both entities are corporations, although the S corporation has elected a different tax treatment.

Differences

- *Taxation.* C corporations are separately taxed entities. Profits are taxed at the corporate level and may be taxed again at the individual level if the corporation distributes them to shareholders in the form of dividends. This creates the double taxation. A corporation becomes an S corporation, or a pass-through taxation entity, by filing Form 2553 with the IRS. The profits and losses of the corporation are then reported on the owners' personal income tax returns.
- *Ownership restrictions.* S corporations have ownership restrictions that C corporations do not have. S corporations can have no more than 75 shareholders, all of whom must be U.S. residents, and other business entities (such as C corporations, LLCs, etc.) typically cannot be shareholders. Also, S corporations can only have one class of stock, whereas C corporations can have multiple classes of stock.

C Corporation and Limited Liability Company

While these two distinct entities provide business owners with a number of the same benefits, the differences between them can be viewed as either positive or negative, depending on the goals of the business. Since business situations are rarely exactly alike, it is advisable to speak with an attorney or accountant regarding the specifics of your situation.

Similarities

- *Formation.* Both are separate legal entities created by filing formation documents with the state.
- *Limited liability.* Both offer limited liability to the owners, meaning that the owners generally are not personally responsible for the debts and liabilities of the business.
- *Ownership.* Ownership (stock with corporations and membership interest with LLCs) can be divided into numerous classes.

Also, both entities have virtually no ownership restrictions. Owners can be non-U.S. citizens, corporations, LLCs, or certain trusts.

Differences

- *Taxation.* Corporations are separately taxed entities. Profits are taxed at the corporate level and may be taxed again at the individual level if the corporation distributes them to shareholders in the form of dividends, creating double taxation. Unless an LLC elects to be taxed as a C corporation, LLCs are pass-through taxation entities, where the profits and losses of the business are reported on the owners' personal income tax returns.
- *Formalities.* Corporations are legally required to comply with certain formalities, such as holding annual meetings of directors and shareholders, and must keep certain corporate records. LLCs are not required to comply with such formalities or to hold annual membership meetings; however, documenting major business decisions and holding regular meetings is advisable. Also, both must pay annual statement fees and/or franchise taxes to the state in which they are formed.
- *Transfer of ownership.* Stock (ownership) in a corporation is typically freely transferable, whereas membership interest in a LLC generally is not. Typically, the other members of the LLC must approve any transfer of interest.
- *Raising capital.* Corporations can typically raise capital more easily through the sale of stock. In many LLCs, all members must approve the addition of new members, which can hinder the LLC's ability to raise outside capital.
- *Management.* LLCs can choose to be managed by their members or by nonmember managers. When the members manage an LLC, it resembles a partnership. When nonmember managers manage it, the LLC more closely resembles a corporation. Officers, who in turn report to the corporation's board of directors, generally manage a corporation.

S Corporation and Limited Liability Company

Both the S corporation and the LLC are pass-through taxation entities, making them appealing to many business owners. We felt that it would be beneficial to compare and contrast these two structures as well.

Similarities

- *Formation.* Both are separate legal entities created by filing formation documents with the state.
- *Limited liability.* Both offer limited liability to their owners, meaning that the owners generally are not personally responsible for the debts and liabilities of the business.
- *Taxation.* Both are typically pass-through taxation entities, where the profits and losses of the business are reported on the owners' personal income tax returns.

Differences

- *Ownership restrictions.* S corporations have ownership restrictions that LLCs do not have. S corporations can have no more than 75 shareholders, all of whom must be U.S. residents, and other business entities (such as C corporations, LLCs, or most trusts) typically cannot be shareholders. Also, S corporations can only have one class of stock, whereas LLCs can have multiple levels of membership interest.
- *Transfer of ownership.* Stock (or ownership) in an S corporation is typically freely transferable, whereas membership interest in an LLC generally is not. Typically, the other members of the LLC must approve any transfer of interest.
- *Subsidiaries.* LLCs are allowed to have subsidiaries without restriction. S corporations are not allowed to own more than 80 percent of another corporation's shares.
- *Existence.* The S corporation's existence is perpetual. LLCs typically have a limited life span. Many states require the LLC to list a dissolution date in the formation documents. Also, events such as a member's death or withdrawal from ownership can cause the LLC to dissolve.
- *Formalities.* S corporations are legally required to comply with certain formalities, such as holding annual meetings of directors and shareholders, and they must keep certain corporate records. LLCs are not required to comply with such formalities or hold annual membership meetings; however, documenting major business decisions and holding regular meetings is advisable. Both entities must typically pay annual statement

and/or franchise tax fees to the state in which they are formed.

- *FICA taxes.* Currently, shareholders of S corporations are required to pay self-employment taxes (FICA taxes) only on money that is paid to them as compensation for services rendered, not on profits that pass through the S corporations as distributions to them. With LLCs, all income that a member of an LLC receives is currently subject to FICA taxes, as long as the member actively participates in the business. Because of the relative complexity of this characteristic of S corporations and LLCs, Figure 2-2 includes additional information on the IRS-proposed tax regulations for LLC self-employment taxes as of the writing of this book.

F I G U R E   2-2

FICA Taxes with LLCs and S Corporations

The basic rule is that all income that a member of an LLC receives is subject to self-employment taxes (FICA taxes). Shareholders of an S corporation are only required to pay FICA taxes on money paid to them as compensation for services, not on profits that pass through the S corporation as distributions to them.

The IRS-proposed tax regulations on LLC self-employment taxes say that LLC members must pay FICA taxes on the entire share of LLC pass-through profits, if any one of the following four conditions apply.

1. The member participates in the company's trade or business (work) for more than 500 hours during the LLC's tax year.

2. The member works in the LLC any amount of time, and the LLC renders professional services in the fields of health, law, engineering, architecture, accounting, actuarial science, or consulting.

3. The member has personal liability for debts of the LLC by reason of being a member.

4. The member has authority to execute contracts on behalf of the LLC. (Under the law of most states, all members of a member-managed LLC have this type of "agency" authority, but non-managing members in a manager-managed LLC do not.)

For specific questions regarding your particular situation, contact your accountant.

Thus, S corporations may be advantageous from a self-employment tax perspective. For more information, please contact your attorney or tax advisor.

OTHER ENTITIES

There are other types of corporations that are formed less often, but that you should be aware of—the statutory close corporation, the nonprofit corporation, and the professional corporation. In order to form your business as one of these entities, your company must fit a specific set of criteria. Note that some states have different or additional requirements for these structures.

Statutory Close Corporations

A statutory close corporation is a standard corporation with a small number of shareholders that is formed pursuant to a state's close corporation statutes. State statutes are typically geared toward large, publicly held companies. The needs of a small company are often different. A company with thousands of shareholders faces different issues from one with three or four shareholders. Not all states have close corporation statutes, so forming a close corporation may not be an option in your state. To determine whether your intended state of incorporation allows for close corporations, contact its secretary of state's office.

While there is no set definition of what allows a corporation to be classified as a close corporation, there are three primary principles that are often considered: a small number of shareholders, no market for the corporation's stock, and shareholders who are significantly involved in the management of the corporation. In states that recognize close corporations, the general close corporation statute specifies that any corporation with 50 or fewer shareholders may elect close corporation treatment. When there is no market for a corporation's stock, shares will not be readily bought and sold, as they are with public companies. When shareholders are significantly involved in the management of the company, they are typically acting as directors and possibly also officers of the corporation, as is the case with many small companies. If a corporation wishes to elect close corporation status in a state that allows this classification, it must make this declaration in the articles of incorporation.

Close corporations are different from closely held corporations; however, there are similarities between them. *Closely held* is a term that is synonymous with privately held, meaning that the stock of the corporation is not traded on a national exchange such as the New York Stock Exchange or NASDAQ. Statutory close corporations are almost always closely held corporations, but the reverse is not true. Closely held corporations do not need to make an election with the state to be deemed such. While closely held companies are often smaller companies, there is no set size guideline. For example, a closely held company may have one employee who is also a shareholder, or it may have a hundred employees with a small number of shareholders.

The state statues for close corporations allow these corporations exemptions from some standard corporate structures and rules. Shareholders are generally allowed to restrict the sale or transfer of the corporation's stock, and some state statutes automatically include certain restrictions on buying or selling of the stock unless the close corporation specifies that it does not wish to be subject to those restrictions. Because there is no market for the stock of close corporations, this is a method of protecting the ownership interest of the current shareholders. For example, Jeremy, Sherry, and Harry are shareholders of Sound's Piano Store Corporation, which elects close corporation status. As the only shareholders of this corporation, they wish to protect their ownership interest, and therefore they specify that all three shareholders must approve a sale or transfer of any shares of the corporation's stock.

Certain state statutes may also allow close corporations to eliminate the board of directors. Since shareholders are intimately involved in the day-to-day management of close corporations, there may be no need, or a reduced need, for directors. By eliminating the directors, one set of standard corporate formalities has also been eliminated, because no initial or annual meetings of directors can be held.

Realistically, the number of corporations electing close corporation status is fairly small. Part of the reason is that not all states allow this classification. Also, many states and courts now recognize that the needs of small companies are different from those of large corporations, and many states now have statutes that address these needs without requiring a corporation to elect close corporation treatment. A New York statute allows privately held corporations to give what would normally be the powers of the board of directors to an individual. For example, this person may be a shareholder who is also acting as the president of the company. As you can imagine, this statute does not apply to publicly traded companies, where the directors play a key role in the checks and balances for the corporation. In closely held companies, however, where shareholders are also typically directors and officers, the role of the directors may not always be so pronounced.

Whether a corporation decides to be recognized as a close corporation or to function as a closely held corporation is often a matter of personal choice for the owner(s). Because of the overlap between close corporations and closely held corporations, the benefits of electing close corporation status may not be that great. If you are interested in forming your business as a statutory close corporation, it is advisable to research your state's close corporation statutes to ensure that you are familiar with the various restrictions and requirements. Additionally, to determine if close corporation status would be beneficial to your business, it is best to seek the advice of an attorney.

Nonprofit Corporations

A nonprofit corporation (also called a not-for-profit corporation) is one that is formed pursuant to a different state law from a standard for-profit corporation. The most common type of nonprofit corporation, one that is formed pursuant to Section 501(c)(3) of the Internal Revenue Code, must be formed for some religious, charitable, educational, literary, or scientific purpose. While a standard business corporation is designed to benefit and generate a profit for its shareholders, nonprofits do not have the profit motive.

Like for-profit corporations, nonprofits also provide limited liability. This means that directors or trustees, officers, and members generally are not personally responsible for the debts and liabilities of the nonprofit corporation.

Nonprofit corporations are allowed to apply for tax-exempt status at both the federal and state levels, allowing the corporation to be exempt from the payment of federal and state income taxes. At the federal level, IRS Form 1023 must be filed in order to qualify for 501(c)(3) tax-exempt status. Contact your state's department of taxation to receive your state's required tax-exemption forms.

A 501(c)(3) nonprofit is eligible to receive both public and private grants. As of the time of this writing, individual donors can claim a federal income tax deduction of up to 50 percent of income for donations made to 501(c)(3) groups.

As noted previously, if you are forming a 501(c)(3) nonprofit corporation, your company must be organized for some specific religious, charitable, educational, literary, or scientific purpose. However, nonprofits may also be formed for other purposes specified in different sections of the IRS code. For example, a nonprofit social or recreational club would be formed pursuant to Section 501(c)(7), and a nonprofit childcare organization would be formed pursuant to Section 501(k) of the Internal Revenue Code.

There is a great deal of information regarding nonprofit corporations that could be included here, such as more elaboration on the business purposes that would allow you to form a nonprofit, the other sections of the IRS tax code involved, and the filing of the appropriate forms with the IRS. Since most people purchasing this book will be researching how to form a for-profit corporation, we felt that it would be best to include a link to the Business Filings web site for those who want more information on the formation of a nonprofit corporation. Please visit the nonprofit frequently asked questions in the "Learn about Incorporating" section at www.bizfilings.com/learning/index.html. You can also visit the IRS web site at www.irs.gov to learn more about the IRS requirements for nonprofits.

Professional Corporations

Professional corporations (PCs) and professional limited liability companies (PLLCs) are corporations and limited liability companies that are organized for the purpose of providing professional services. The services that constitute professional services are defined by state law and can differ from state to state. Typically those in professions requiring a license, such as doctors, lawyers, accountants, architects, or engineers, are required to form professional corporations and PLLCs.

The formation of a professional entity differs only slightly from the formation of a standard corporation or LLC. With professional entities, approval of the formation documents by the proper state licensing body is often required before the documents can be filed with the secretary of state. Further, the articles of incorporation (for a PC) or articles of organization (for a PLLC) typically must contain the signature of a licensed professional as incorporator, and that person's license number may be required. Also, the formalities are typically the same for professional entities as they are for the standard business entity.

There are a few distinct differences between PCs and standard corporations. Professional corporations are taxed like standard C corporations (unless they make the S corporation election with the IRS); however, some PCs do not have the advantage of graduated corporate federal income tax rates. As of the writing of this book, professional corporations that are "qualified personal service corporations" pay a flat federal income tax rate of 35 percent. Qualified personal service corporations provide services in the fields of health, law, engineering, architecture, accounting, actuarial science, or consulting. To determine whether your business would be classified as a qualified personal service corporation, it is highly recommended that you speak with your accountant or tax adviser.

With qualified personal service corporations, it is also required that all of the stock be owned by either employees performing that type of professional service, retired employees who had performed such services, the estate of someone who had performed such services, or someone who inherited the stock from a deceased employee who had performed such services (but such a person can own the stock only for a period of 2 years from the date of death).

This type of ownership restriction typically holds true for PLLCs as well. Typically, only licensed practitioners of the specific service a PLLC provides may have membership interest in that PLLC. For example, only licensed doctors who provide medical services may hold membership interest in a professional limited liability company providing medical services.

Close corporations, nonprofits, and professional corporations have a number of similarities to standard corporations, including the method by which they are formed with the state; however, they, particularly nonprofit and professional corporations, are organized for very different purposes. As with the other business structures outlined in this chapter, you may wish to consult an attorney or accountant before forming one of these business entities.

CHAPTER 3

Evaluating Incorporation

We're assuming that you purchased this book because you have an interest in forming your business as a corporation. Now that you have learned more about this entity and the various other types of business structures from which you can choose, you should know more about the advantages and disadvantages of forming a corporation. When they evaluate the option of incorporating a business, business owners most often focus on two primary factors: limited liability and corporate taxation. Whether these factors are positives or negatives will depend on your own situation, but this chapter will help you better understand the basics.

> *Major topics covered: This chapter outlines the advantages and disadvantages of incorporating your business, and also explains the basics of corporate taxation.*

ADVANTAGES OF INCORPORATING YOUR BUSINESS

There are a number of advantages to forming a corporation. Limited liability, which was briefly discussed in Chapter 1, is the primary reason most business owners decide to incorporate. This advantage and many others are discussed in more depth in this chapter.

Limited Liability

Since the corporate entity exists separately from its owners, the owners generally are not responsible for the debts and liabilities of the business. Many entrepreneurs make substantial financial commitments to get their businesses off the ground. By incorporating, business owners protect their personal assets if the business should have financial or legal troubles or if it should fail.

Shareholders' liability is generally limited to the amount they have invested in the corporation. For example, Dan invests $5000 in his brother's new corporation, even though he is not directly involved in or employed by his brother's business. In return for the investment, his brother gives him shares in the corporation. Unfortunately, the business takes on extensive debt and then fails. Even if Dan has a substantial personal net worth, the creditors generally cannot try to access his personal assets to pay the debts of the business in which he was a shareholder. The extent of Dan's liability is the $5000 he invested in his brother's business.

In this example, Dan is not directly involved with the corporation. His brother, Tony, on the other hand, may have greater exposure for a couple of reasons. It's highly likely that Tony, like most entrepreneurs, has dedicated numerous hours to his corporation. Now he is not only losing his monetary investment in the corporation, but also losing the time he invested and losing his job as well. For shareholders who also act as directors and officers of the corporation, there are often opportunity costs associated with the failure of a corporation that extend beyond the capital they contributed; however, Tony generally will not be personally liable for the debts of the corporation.

There are some situations in which a business owner may be held personally responsible for the debts and liabilities of the business. One of these is personal negligence. For example, if a dentist has incorporated his practice and a situation arises in which he is personally negligent and his practice is sued, the dentist's personal assets could be at risk to satisfy the debt and liability that his practice incurs as a result of the suit.

Another example is when the owner's limited liability has been compromised through a contract. For example, banks often require a personal guarantee by the corporation's owner or owners for any loans granted to new corporations. If the corporation cannot pay back the loan, the personal guarantee binds the owners to personally pay it back.

Note that the limited liability that the corporate entity provides to shareholders does not extend to criminal liability. If you, as a shareholder, engage in a criminal or fraudulent act, you can be held responsible for that act and face criminal charges. One example of this is the corporate accounting scandals from 2002. As we saw with companies such as WorldCom and Enron, officers (who were also shareholders) faced criminal charges for their roles in fraudulent corporate activities.

Tax-Deductible Payments

Certain payments that corporations make that are considered reasonable and necessary to the business are typically tax-deductible. Examples include salaries, office supplies, contributions to a 401(k) plan for employees, and certain insurance premiums. Reasonable and necessary business expenses will be discussed again in the basics of corporate taxation portion of this chapter; however, the IRS tax forms you complete will include information on which expenses are and which are not deductible.

Unlimited Life

As mentioned earlier, a corporation's life is not dependent upon the survival of its owners. If a shareholder dies, the corporation will continue to exist and could continue to do business. Conversely, because there is no separation between the business and the business owner in a sole proprietorship or partnership, the business no longer exists if a business owner dies.

Transferability of Interest

Not only does a corporation have unlimited life, but if a shareholder dies or wishes to sell his or her interest in the company, that interest can be freely sold or transferred to another shareholder. Shareholders in a corporation do not need to get the permission of other shareholders to transfer their ownership interest. In the case of a sole proprietorship, however, because there is no separation between the owner and the business, the owner cannot transfer his or her ownership without completely selling the business. With partnerships and often with limited liability companies (LLCs), owners must obtain the permission of the other owner(s) prior to selling or transferring their interest in the business. With corporations, ownership interest can be freely transferred to new or existing shareholders.

Centralized Management

Corporations have a representative form of "government" in which the shareholders elect a board of directors that has responsibility for all major business decisions. The board of directors then appoints officers to manage the day-to-day operations of the corporation.

Ease of Raising Capital

As long as a corporation has authorized and unissued shares outstanding, stock can be sold to raise additional capital for the corporation. Conversely, with a sole proprietorship, other than obtaining loans, the only way for the owner to raise outside capital would be to add a partner and share the responsibilities of the business with that partner. Additionally, corporations can often raise capital more easily because people are often more willing to invest in something in which their liability exposure is limited.

Increased Credibility

Many entrepreneurs, particularly independent professionals, may find entering into new relationships difficult if they operate as sole proprietorships or partnerships. Some large corporations and vendors will work only with companies that are incorporated or formed as limited liability companies. For example, Ken starts his own technology consulting company focusing on computer network security consulting. A company such as IBM or Sun might be able to use his services but may not be willing to hire Ken Smith, the consultant. They might, however, contract with Secure Consulting Incorporated, the corporation of which Ken Smith is the employee-owner, for its services. As an entrepreneur, incorporating your business may give you more credibility in your relationships with customers, vendors, and partners.

DISADVANTAGES OF INCORPORATING YOUR BUSINESS

There are a number of positives to incorporating your business; however, there are aspects of incorporation that may be considered disadvantages. Whether an owner considers these aspects to be disadvantages often varies depending on the owner's personal preference or particular business situation. Many entrepreneurs consider the primary disadvantage of corporations to be double taxation. We've also outlined other aspects that may be considered by some to be disadvantages of the corporate structure.

Double Taxation

As Chapter 2 outlined, C corporations may face double taxation. This occurs because profits are taxed at the corporate level and again at the individual level if they are distributed to shareholders in the form of dividends. This chapter's section on the basics of corporate taxation illustrates double taxation in a fictitious corporation example.

State Requirements

States have requirements that corporations must meet at the time of formation as well as ongoing requirements that can result in expenditures of both time and money. To form a corporation, the articles of incorporation must be filed with the state in which you want to form your business, and the necessary filing fees must be paid to that state. Most states also have annual corporate requirements, such as annual statements and/or franchise taxes.

Increased Formalities

Corporations face both external and internal formalities. External corporate formalities include staying in good standing with the state by filing any annual statements required and paying all annual fees and corporate taxes. Internal formalities include holding and documenting meetings of shareholders and directors, and keeping accurate records of items such as stock transfers, meeting minutes, and financial transactions. The importance of complying with both the external and internal corporate formalities cannot be overstated. Corporate formalities and the potential consequences of noncompliance are addressed more fully in Chapter 18.

Doing Business in Other States

Since corporations are created by a state filing, they are typically viewed as state-specific entities. Doing business in states other than your state of incorporation may necessitate qualifying with those other states to conduct business there. Foreign qualification is discussed in more depth in Chapter 10.

THE BASICS OF CORPORATE TAXATION

One of the primary concerns that crosses business owners' minds when they are evaluating whether to incorporate a business is taxation. There are a number of business entities from which you can choose when you form your business. Among those with limited liability, the

primary choices are a corporation or a limited liability company (LLC).
If you choose a corporation, you can then choose a C corporation or
a subchapter S corporation, each of which has a different taxation
structure.

With standard or C corporations, the corporation incurs a tax at the
corporate level. If corporate profits are distributed to shareholders in the
form of dividends, they are taxed again at the individual level as ordinary income to the shareholders. This situation creates double taxation,
which owners of small businesses often consider to be the primary disadvantage of forming a standard C corporation.

The possibility of double taxation can be eliminated if the corporation elects with the Internal Revenue Service (IRS) to be taxed as a subchapter S corporation. With an S corporation, no tax is paid at the
corporate or entity level. Instead, the profits and losses of the corporation
are passed through to the shareholders and reported on their individual
tax returns.

The corporation's annual revenue, often called annual sales, is the
primary starting point when looking at taxation. From that revenue
amount, corporations can deduct reasonable business expenses, or those
that are ordinary and necessary for carrying on business. Examples of
reasonable business expenses include salaries, office lease payments,
advertising expenses, costs of office supplies, and certain general operating expenses. Subtracting these deductible business expenses from revenue produces the corporation's taxable income, which is the amount on
which the corporation is taxed. This is where the differences in taxation
begin.

Figure 3-1 shows an example of taxation for fictitious C and S corporations. The left side shows the taxation of a C corporation and illustrates the double taxation. In this example, the corporation has $500,000
in sales and $300,000 in allowable deductions (salary, rent, office supplies,
etc.), creating a taxable income of $200,000. Assuming a 35 percent cor-
porate tax rate, this corporation pays $70,000 in taxes at the corporate
level, leaving a net income of $130,000. The corporation then decides to
distribute the entire net income amount to shareholders in the form of a
dividend. Because the distribution is made as a dividend, the shareholders must pay an income tax on this distribution at the individual level,
thereby creating double taxation. Assuming a 35 percent individual tax
rate, the shareholders pay $45,500 in taxes. With a total of $115,500 paid
in taxes, the cash received by shareholders is $84,500.

Both the S corporation and the limited liability company are called
"pass-through" taxation entities because the profits or losses are passed

through the corporation to its shareholders. With pass-through taxation entities, the business's income is not taxed at the corporate level. Instead, taxation of the business's profits, or reporting of its losses, occurs at the individual level.

The right side of Figure 3-1 shows an example of pass-through taxation for a fictitious S corporation. In this example, the S corporation has the same sales, deductions, and taxable income as our fictitious C corporation. Since S corporations do not pay taxes at the corporate level, the full $200,000 of taxable income is considered to be net income. As with our C corporation example, the full amount of the net income is distributed to shareholders. (Note that whether the S corporation's net income is distributed to shareholders or left in the company, it will be taxed at the individual level.) Assuming a 35 percent individual tax rate, $70,000 is paid in taxes, creating a cash-received amount of $130,000. In this example, the shareholders of the S corporation receive $45,500 more in cash than the shareholders of the C corporation.

This example is meant only to illustrate the concept of double taxation. Many C corporations do not pay dividends to shareholders. They may decide to leave the profits in the business and use them to fund

F I G U R E   3-1

Corporate Taxation Example

C Corporation Taxation		S Corporation Taxation	
$500,000	sales	$500,000	sales
(300,000)	allowable deductions	(300,000)	allowable deductions
$200,000	taxable income	$200,000	taxable income
(70,000)	corporate income tax	(0)	corporate income tax
$130,000	net income	$200,000	net income
$130,000	distributed as dividends	$200,000	distributed as dividends
(45,500)	individual income taxes	(70,000)	individual income taxes
$84,500	cash received	$130,000	cash received
$115,500	total taxes paid	$70,000	total taxes paid
$84,500	total cash left	$130,000	total cash left
$200,000	taxable income amount	$200,000	taxable income amount

future growth. That is also true for S corporations. An S corporation does not always distribute the full amount of its net income to its shareholders. Since the shareholders incur tax on the S corporation's net income even when that net income is left in the company, the differences between the amount of taxes paid by C corporations and their shareholders and by the shareholders of S corporations may not be so extreme. Because of the complexities of taxation, it is advisable to speak with an attorney or accountant to determine which structure would be best for your business.

Even though S corporations do not pay taxes at the corporate level, they are still required to file a federal corporate tax return. The corporate income tax forms, Form 1120 for C corporations and Form 1120S for S corporations, are quite similar. The major difference is in the handling of the taxation, with the C corporation paying taxes at the entity level and the S corporation passing its profits or losses through to the individual tax returns of its shareholders.

There are a few points to keep in mind when thinking about corporate taxation. First, the reasonable business expenses mentioned earlier are different from capital expenditures. Capital expenditures are those that add to the value or useful life of property, and they are generally deducted by means of depreciation, amortization, or depletion. Office furniture, computer equipment, computer software, and manufacturing equipment are examples of capital expenditures. It is important to keep capital expenditures separate from reasonable business expenses, as the costs of capital expenditures are deducted for tax purposes over a time period prescribed by the IRS, rather than being expensed as incurred.

Also, salary expenses must be reasonable. Salary expenses are listed separately when deducting business expenses from the corporation's revenue; therefore, this number is easily seen on the corporation's tax return. Salary expenditures that seem unreasonable to the IRS may result in an audit of the corporation. If the IRS deems the salaries to be unreasonable, it may view the amounts paid as a dividend rather than a salary. This is called a "deemed dividend payment." In this case, these payments are no longer tax-deductible to the corporation, increasing the corporation's taxable income. Moreover, the corporation would most likely owe additional and/or back taxes.

In deciding on your salary payment, the basic rule is that your salary should be comparable to what you would receive if you performed the same duties for another company. For example, if you work 100 hours a year providing consulting services for your corporation, setting your salary at $200,000 a year ($2000 per hour) would probably be considered too high. The IRS would be likely to view part of this salary as a deemed dividend payment. In this example, if the IRS deemed a reasonable salary for consulting for 100 hours a year to be $40,000, the remaining $160,000 would be considered a dividend. The corporation would then lose the salary deduction and would be responsible for paying taxes on the $160,000 that is now considered a dividend payment.

For questions regarding corporate taxation, including the current corporate tax rates, it's advisable to speak with an accountant. You can also visit the IRS web site at www.irs.gov. The IRS web site allows you to download current and prior-year tax forms, review specific publications on topics of interest to you, and find answers to frequently asked questions on a wide range of topics. There are also many groups that offer tax assistance to small business owners. These include VITA (Volunteer Income Tax Assistance), SCORE (Service Corps of Retired Executives), your local Small Business Development Centers (which are often associated with universities or located in major cities), and the federal Small Business Administration. Most of these organizations have national web sites you can go to for additional information, or you can consult your local phone book.

CHAPTER 4

Who Will Incorporate Your Business?

We realize that starting your own business can be stressful. You face many questions, and you must make a number of decisions. Do you need employees? How will you find customers and bring in revenue? What type of business entity best fits the needs of your company?

When you decide to incorporate, you then face making a decision as to who will incorporate your business. There are three primary ways in which to incorporate—to file your own paperwork with the state, to use an incorporation service provider, or to use an attorney. This chapter analyzes all three options.

> *Major topics covered: This chapter outlines the options entrepreneurs have for incorporating their businesses, including doing it themselves, using an incorporation service provider, or using an attorney, while looking at the cost and convenience factors for each.*

The costs associated with incorporating are sometimes a concern for entrepreneurs, who often start their businesses with little capital. In reality, incorporating a business is quite affordable, especially when you consider the limited liability that this step offers to the owners of corporations and limited liability companies (LLCs). Regardless of who incorporates your business, you must pay the state's filing fees. These are fees imposed by each state on anyone forming a corporation or LLC within that state; they are often less than $300. With incorporation service providers and attorneys, you can expect to pay a service fee in addition to the state filing fees, although the convenience factor typically rises with these options.

FILING YOUR OWN PAPERWORK WITH THE STATE

One option that is available to you is to prepare your own documents and file them with the appropriate state agency in the state in which you want to incorporate your business. This is typically the most affordable option, but it is often not the easiest. There are more steps involved, from researching the state's requirements to interacting with the appropriate state body regarding your filing. Therefore, the affordability of this option may be overshadowed by the extra steps involved.

In most states, the secretary of state's office is responsible for business incorporations. Each state requires that you prepare articles of incorporation (or a certificate of incorporation) for your business. The articles of incorporation document will be covered in more depth in Chapter 8, but, simply stated, it is the document explaining the who, what, when, where, and why of your business, as far as the state is concerned.

Each state has different requirements regarding the format of the articles of incorporation and, to a certain extent, the information they contain. For example, some states require that the documents be submitted within the state's template, which can be downloaded from the state's web site, while others offer more flexibility. As an example of differences in the information to be included, certain states require the directors of the corporation to be listed in the articles of incorporation, whereas other states do not have this requirement.

Beyond the paperwork, the states often have different requirements for the corporate entity itself. Most states require that corporations have one or more directors. Certain states require the directors to be at least 18 years of age. Some states impose franchise and/or state income taxes on corporations, and others do not. The Business Filings web site includes information on certain specific corporation requirements, such as corporate name endings, directors, and taxation information, for each state.

If you are considering filing your own documents when you incorporate your business, you should research your state's requirements beforehand. This will save you time and possibly money in the long run. You should note that states will reject your filing if the information included in your articles of incorporation is incorrect or incomplete. Also, if you plan to file your own documents, be sure to perform a company name availability search with the state in which you are forming your corporation prior to filing your documents. A name availability search ensures that the company name you wish to use is available for use in that state; this is discussed further in Chapter 7.

Preparing and filing the necessary incorporation documents is only one of many steps that corporations must undertake. Corporations are required to obtain an employer identification number (EIN) from the Internal Revenue Service (IRS), which is used for taxation purposes. Corporations are also required to comply with a number of corporate formalities, such as holding an organizational meeting and annual meetings of directors and shareholders. If you incorporate your own business, you will also be responsible for carrying out these business steps. Incorporation service providers and attorneys often offer assistance with these steps, and you typically can utilize their offerings even if you did not use their services to incorporate your business.

Cost

As previously noted, preparing and filing your own documents is the most affordable option. You will be required to pay the state's filing fees when you submit your articles of incorporation to the state. State filing fees range from $40 to $500, depending on the state and the type of entity you wish to form (i.e., a corporation, a limited liability company, or a non-profit corporation); however, authorizing a higher number of shares could cause the standard state filing fees to increase. This will be addressed later in the book. In addition to the state filing fees, you may incur charges such as postage or shipping charges for sending your documents to the state, but you will not incur any additional service or legal fees.

Convenience

It is hard to estimate how much time you will need to properly research the state requirements and then to prepare and file your documents. Since many entrepreneurs are pressed for time, the convenience factor often prevails when they are deciding which method of incorporation to use. Many states now offer online filing for the incorporation documents, increasing the level of convenience associated with incorporating your business yourself; however, when convenience is the top priority, entrepreneurs often opt to use an incorporation service provider, an attorney, or possibly an accountant.

USING AN INCORPORATION SERVICE PROVIDER

Incorporation service providers are companies that help businesses with their incorporation documents. They generally also offer additional business formation–related products and services. These companies gather the necessary information about your business, then prepare the documents and file them with the state. Incorporation service providers are not legal service companies and do not provide legal advice.

This option became much more prevalent once business owners began turning to the Internet for quick and easy access to information, as well as for more affordable services. There are a number of incorporation service providers advertising their services on the Internet today. Many of these companies provide incorporation services in all states and Washington, D.C., while others focus solely on a certain state or cluster of states.

We'll use Business Filings Incorporated (www.bizfilings.com) as our example of an incorporation service provider. To incorporate a business using Business Filings, business owners can complete an online order form or place an order via the telephone. Ordering takes approximately 10 minutes, and payment is either by credit card or by check sent through the mail. Using the information you provide when you order, Business Filings prepares the required documentation and files it with the state. Business Filings collects information on the order form, such as two name choices for your company, the number of shares you intend to authorize and their par value, and information on the directors and officers. Chapter 12 includes two case studies on incorporating a business that run through all facets of the incorporation process, from the concept stage through completion. In that chapter, Figure 12-1 is a slightly abbreviated version of the Business Filings order form that displays the information typically required by an incorporation service provider.

Since incorporation is not necessarily an easy process to understand, many entrepreneurs research the incorporation process and different business entities, as you are doing now. If you plan to use an incorporation service provider, look for one with comprehensive incorporation information listed on its web site. These companies want to help you understand the process and the advantages and disadvantages of incorporating.

In addition to completing the documents required for company formation, many incorporation service providers offer a broad suite of products and services that are complementary to the incorporation process. These products and services often include corporate kits, preparation of the S corporation election form, and preparation of the form to obtain a federal employer identification number. For many business owners, having these additional steps and IRS filings completed at the time of incorporation is a real benefit. As previously mentioned, all corporations (and other businesses that have employees) must obtain an employer identification number (also called a federal tax identification number) from the IRS for tax purposes. Having an incorporation service provider prepare the form to secure the EIN when you are incorporating helps you to consolidate the steps required when starting a business.

As mentioned previously, incorporation service providers are not law firms and do not provide legal advice. If you have a question that is very specific to your business that leads you to wonder whether you should form a corporation or a limited liability company (LLC), an incorporation service provider will not be able to help you answer this question. The provider can tell you the characteristics of corporations and LLCs and outline the pros and cons of each, but it cannot advise you on which type of entity to form. For help in answering specific questions, the incorporation service provider will recommend that you speak to an attorney or an accountant.

For general questions, incorporation service providers may be very helpful. Let's return briefly to our example of Business Filings. While Business Filings cannot answer questions that are specific to your particular business situation, its customer service representatives can help you answer many broader questions. You can rely on them for answers regarding, among other things, the incorporation requirements of specific states, the calculations states use for imposing franchise taxes on corporations, and whether having a specific number of shares of stock for your corporation will affect your state filing fees.

Cost

Using an incorporation service provider is a relatively inexpensive option. As mentioned earlier, you can expect to pay a service fee in addition to the state's filing fees. Service fees can vary widely, but for a basic filing, you should expect a service fee in the range of $75 to $175 in addition to the state filing fees. One thing to note is that providers often have lower fees for incorporating in Delaware than for incorporating in other states. An advertised low price may apply only to Delaware filings, and incorporating in Delaware is not always the best option for small businesses. This will be discussed further in the next chapter.

If you are evaluating several incorporation service providers, you should be aware that different companies' service fees may include different services. On a basic level, the service fee should include a preliminary name availability search with the state of incorporation (this is done to ensure that the business name you want is available in that state) and the preparation and filing of the documents. Once you reach the ordering process, some companies charge extra for shipping, thereby increasing their true service fee. If price is the primary factor in your decision, be sure that you are comparing apples to apples when you look at different incorporation service providers.

Most providers allow for ancillary products and services to be added to their basic formation offering. Others offer a package or several packages that include a number of products and services. With incorporation service providers, you can spend as much or as little as you want, depending on what fits the incorporation needs of your business.

Convenience

Convenience is an advantage of using an incorporation service provider, as the amount of time business owners have to spend on the process of incorporating is minimal, compared with the time required to do it themselves. With some providers, ordering can take as little as little as 10 minutes. Also, since most incorporation service providers have online order forms, you can research the information on their web sites and then submit your order at a time that is convenient for you. Waiting until business hours to submit your order is not necessary. Once you submit your order, the incorporation service provider does all the work, allowing you to concentrate on other aspects of your business.

The requirements imposed on corporations do not end with the filing of the formation documents, and there are a number of other steps that must be taken after the paperwork is filed, such as IRS filings, holding your organizational meeting, and adopting bylaws. Incorporation service providers can also assist you with these steps and provide an increased comfort level that your corporation is starting out on the right foot.

USING AN ATTORNEY

Using an attorney has traditionally been the primary means of incorporating a business. The advent of the Internet has led to the more widespread adoption of alternative incorporation options; however, attorneys remain a valuable resource for entrepreneurs who are starting a business. One of the primary ways in which attorneys provide assistance is by giving advice. As we've mentioned before, for questions regarding your specific business situation, it is best to seek the advice of an attorney.

In addition, attorneys can provide customized documentation for the business, which most incorporation service providers do not offer. Attorneys often assist businesses with the preparation of items for use around the time of incorporation, such as the creation of customized bylaws, and during the life of the corporation, such as contracts for use with vendors and partners. In the case of the bylaws, an extensive document that defines the rules for the internal governance of the corporation, an attorney can help to customize them to fit your particular type of business and the future goals you've outlined for your company. Attorneys can also provide assistance with preparing contracts for you to use if you intend to seek outside funding for your corporation, and by reviewing contracts your corporation receives from partners and vendors.

The one area of the incorporation process in which attorneys do not provide as much value is the actual preparation and filing of the incorporation documentation. This is not to discount their role—attorneys can provide higher levels of customization of the information included in the articles of incorporation. For example, if one of the future goals of your corporation is to bring in a number of outside investors, an attorney can word the information on stock in your incorporation paperwork to allow for multiple classes of stock. You can also do this if you are filing your own paperwork; however, you should thoroughly research the state's statutes and also understand how this could affect the annual franchise taxes imposed on your corporation by the state.

Another thing to consider is that many attorneys do not actually prepare and file the incorporation paperwork on behalf of their clients. There are a number of companies, which could be considered incorporation service providers, that work specifically with law firms on preparing and filing incorporation paperwork. This could also lead to an increase in the costs you incur by having an attorney prepare and file your paperwork.

Like attorneys, accountants may also be helpful, especially if you're seeking tax advice. As an example, if you are having a difficult time deciding whether a C corporation is definitely the right structure for your business, either an attorney or an accountant can provide guidance. Both attorneys and accountants will seek to learn more about your present needs and your future goals, and will take that information into account when they recommend a business structure for your company. Many businesses change their legal form during the lifetime of the business— for example, from sole proprietorship to corporation, or from S corporation to C corporation. Attorneys and accountants can help you choose the right path given your future plans. When it comes to preparing and filing the actual incorporation paperwork, however, accountants may not offer this service, and may instead refer you to another party.

If you feel that using an attorney is the right choice for incorporating your business, or if you wish to utilize an attorney's services to obtain legal advice or customized documentation, you should evaluate attorneys to ensure that the one you choose is the right match for your needs. It is also advisable to obtain a cost estimate up front, and to understand what is included in that cost. If you do not currently work with an attorney, but wish to do so, you can find one through referrals from family, friends, or other business owners. You can also search online. Web sites such as www.lawyers.com are geared toward helping both business users and personal users find attorneys in their geographic area with the specialization that they seek.

Cost

The cost of using an attorney is higher than that of the other options previously noted, and it tends to vary geographically. If you use an attorney to file your incorporation documentation, you should expect to pay attorney's fees, which are often charged by the hour, in addition to the state filing fees. The complexity of your particular situation may also affect the fees. For example, if you plan to seek funding from outside investors, the customization required in your documents may necessitate additional preparation time, which will probably lead to additional cost. If you choose to use an attorney for legal advice, such as advice regarding the type of entity you should form, or for assistance with customization of post-incorporation documents, but not to prepare and file your incorporation paperwork, be sure to obtain price quotes for this service.

Convenience

Convenience is an advantage of using an attorney for your incorporation needs. As with an incorporation service provider, your time requirements will be minimal, compared to those for preparing and filing your own documents. Attorneys also offer the added value and convenience of providing legal advice and providing documentation that is customized specifically for your business and its particular situation.

The right method of incorporating a business often depends upon the owner's personal preference. There are a number of resources available to small business owners today that can assist you with this important business step. Many of the state statutes and requirements are now accessible online, making preparing and filing your own paperwork easier. Incorporation service providers offer an affordable means of incorporating and also typically provide a broad suite of formation-related offerings. While an attorney may not be the most logical choice for preparing and filing your paperwork, the value attorneys provide cannot be discounted.

While these three options have been discussed separately here, there can be overlap between them. For example, you could use an incorporation service provider to prepare and file your documents and an attorney to customize your post-incorporation documents. You could prepare and file your own formation paperwork and use an incorporation service provider to obtain a corporate kit. You could also seek the advice of an attorney regarding the proper business entity for your business, use an incorporation service provider for your incorporation documents, and file your own paperwork with the IRS to obtain your employer identification number. Each of the incorporation options discussed in this chapter offers value to entrepreneurs. The ultimate decision on which is best for your particular situation rests with you.

CHAPTER 5

Where Should You Incorporate Your Business?

When you are preparing to incorporate your business, another important decision you must make is where to incorporate. You are not required to incorporate in the state in which your business is physically located. You can incorporate in any state, and certain states work hard to attract corporations. You have probably heard about Delaware's popularity, but it may not be the right choice for you. Business owners incorporate for different reasons and have different goals for their businesses. Keeping these reasons and goals in mind, there are a number of factors that you should consider when you make this important decision.

> ***Major topics covered:*** *This chapter outlines factors that you should consider when deciding where to incorporate and includes information on the advantages and disadvantages of incorporating in Delaware, Nevada, or your home state.*

You should realize that states benefit from corporations. Corporations provide states with revenue, in the form of both the filing fees charged to incorporate in that state and the tax revenue received from corporations on an annual basis. Delaware has been particularly successful in attracting corporations. Being a tiny state with a small population, Delaware recognized over 100 years ago that it would need to find a way to boost state revenue. It created a favorable climate for corporations and heavily marketed its advantages. Today, over 50 percent of the Fortune 500 companies are incorporated in Delaware.

Other states have tried to replicate Delaware's revenue success story by creating conditions that will entice corporations to incorporate in that state, instead of in Delaware or in the corporation's home state. Nevada is a prime example; therefore, the advantages and disadvantages of both Delaware and Nevada are outlined in this chapter. It could be, however, that incorporating your business in your home state, which is the state in which your company is physically located, is the best option. That is often the case with very small businesses.

Before making a decision about where to incorporate, you should understand (generally speaking) how incorporating in certain states can affect your fees, both at the time of incorporation and on an annual basis. Understanding where your company will primarily do business and the role your company's capitalization structure plays in this process are also important. By evaluating both your current needs and your future goals in terms of where you will transact business and your capitalization, you can better evaluate the advantages and potential disadvantages of incorporating your business in one state rather than another.

ITEMS TO CONSIDER

As you begin to evaluate your options for where to incorporate your business, you should ask yourself a number of questions. Some of these may not have even crossed your mind yet. While we don't want to scare you with these questions, the answers are factors determining why one state may be more advantageous to your business than another.

Where do you plan to conduct most of your business—in the state in which you are located, in a number of states, or maybe internationally? When you form your corporation, do you plan to seek outside investors to provide additional capital (funding) for your business? If you currently have employees, do you wish to offer stock options to them after incorporating? Your answers to some of these questions may be definitive, or you may have one answer for your current situation and a follow-up answer that fits with your future goals.

Because your capitalization structure and where you are transacting business can affect both the fees incurred at the time of incorporation and the annual fees imposed by the state that your corporation will incur thereafter, it is important that you be realistic about the current status of your business. At the same time, you do not want to ignore your future goals. After all, even today's largest companies started small. Keep in mind that you can change your state of incorporation as your situation changes, as will be discussed later in this chapter.

Transacting Business

For many small corporations, the primary factor determining where to incorporate is where the company plans to transact business. For the sake of this chapter, we will say that transacting business means that your corporation has a physical presence with employees, takes orders, and maintains a bank account in a particular state. Now ask yourself, will your company primarily transact business in its home state? Will it conduct business nationally, or possibly internationally? If you are currently focused on a small geographic area, do you envision expanding into new areas during the life of your business?

For a small company, where it transacts business tends to have the most influence on the costs incurred during the incorporation process and the annual costs thereafter. The primary reason for this is the concept of foreign qualification. When your business is incorporated in one state, but transacts business in another state or a group of other states, it may be required to foreign-qualify in order to transact business in those other states. Foreign-qualifying in another state is a method of informing that state that a foreign corporation is operating within its borders. It allows that state to regulate and collect taxes from that business, and it provides the corporation with access to that state's legal system. Additional information on transacting business and foreign-qualifying in other states is included in Chapter 10.

For example, Jeff is starting Jeff's Hamburger Haven, a fictitious fast-food operation in Nebraska. Jeff plans to incorporate his business before starting operations. His mother will be providing some additional capital to help Jeff get his business started, and Jeff and his mother will be the only two shareholders. Jeff currently plans to sell his hamburgers only in Nebraska; however, he hopes to open a number of restaurants in the future. Incorporating in Nebraska is probably the best choice for Jeff. His corporation will have a simple capitalization structure, and he will be transacting business primarily in Nebraska.

If next year Jeff decides to open a Hamburger Haven in Kansas, he will need to foreign-qualify his corporation to transact business in Kansas. As we previously mentioned, corporations provide revenue to the states. If your corporation will be transacting business in a state in which it is not incorporated, that state would also like to receive revenue from your corporation, and it has a number of ways in which to do so. To qualify to do business in another state, your corporation will need to file a certificate of authority and pay the state filing fees for this filing. In addition, states have annual requirements, such as annual statement and franchise tax and/or state income tax requirements, for foreign corporations, which is the term for corporations not incorporated in that state. Once your corporation becomes foreign-qualified, it is subject to these requirements.

Since entrepreneurs are typically very cost-conscious, and because starting a business and running it are not inexpensive, many entrepreneurs approach the decision on where to incorporate by looking for the cheapest place. This is not necessarily a wise approach, primarily because of the need to foreign-qualify if you transact business in a state or states other than the state in which you incorporated.

To expand upon the concepts of transacting business and foreign-qualifying and how these can affect your costs, let's use the example of Gloria and a fictitious antique store. Gloria owns a small antiques store located in Texas, but she's considering incorporating in Delaware. She conducts all of her business in Texas, and she does not foresee transacting business in other states. The state filing fee to form a corporation in Texas is currently $300. The state filing fee to form a corporation in Delaware is currently $74. At first glance, you may ask why Gloria wouldn't incorporate her business in Delaware.

If Gloria incorporates in Delaware, she must also foreign-qualify her business in Texas, since her antiques store transacts all of its business in Texas. The state filing fee to obtain a certificate of authority in Texas is currently $750. If Gloria incorporates her business in Delaware, then foreign-qualifies in Texas, her filing fees will total over $800, versus around $300 to simply incorporate in Texas. So the initial impression that incorporating in Delaware is cheaper is not accurate in this case.

Furthermore, Delaware has no state corporate income tax for corporations that do not transact business in Delaware, as well as relatively low franchise tax rates. But since Gloria needs to foreign-qualify in Texas, her antiques store would be subject to taxes in both the state of incorporation, Delaware, and the state of foreign qualification, Texas. So, not only would she pay more in formation fees to incorporate in Delaware and foreign-qualify in Texas, she would also pay more in annual taxes. Again, this is meant as an example only, and it is an example that involves a very small, local business with a simple capitalization structure. Note that while corporations transacting business in other states are required by state statutes to foreign-qualify in those states, the definition of what constitutes transacting business varies by state. While at first glance owning a small business and facing the need to foreign-qualify may seem like a disadvantage, there are advantages to foreign-qualifying; these are discussed in Chapter 10, on doing business in other states.

As you evaluate your incorporation location choices, where your corporation will be transacting business, both today and in terms of your future goals, needs to be kept in mind. If you plan to open stores in a number of states or nationally, incorporating in a state like Delaware may be the better option. While you will need to foreign-qualify in each of the other states in which you transact business, you would still incur those costs if you were incorporated in your home state. In cases like this, additional factors come into the decision, like the corporate laws or taxation structure of the state. If you are going to have multiple stores throughout the country, Delaware's corporation law and Court of Chancery may prove to be quite advantageous.

The state laws governing corporations and the state tax structures vary greatly. While this may not be a primary factor in your decision, having a basic knowledge of the requirements for the states you are considering can be beneficial. You can typically access information regarding a state's corporate law provisions on its web site. Most states also include taxation information on their sites. Because tax laws change so frequently, visiting the state's web site is recommended. This information is typically kept up-to-date.

Researching a state's statutes is not always an easy task. Most states include information on their corporate law within their secretary of state's web site, often in a subsection specifically for corporations. An example of a centralized location for finding all states' statues is the State Law section of the web site www.megalaw.com. One thing to note is that state statutes often employ legal terminology, and while you can find them on the Internet, understanding them is a completely different matter.

Capitalization Structure

In very basic terms, a corporation's capitalization structure relates to how it gets the necessary capital to start and continue its operations. A major component of a corporation's capitalization is its stock. It is common for corporations to provide stock to those who contribute capital to the business, whether that capital is in the form of money or equipment (property).

If you are funding your business entirely on your own, you will probably have only one shareholder, and therefore you will have a small, simple capitalization structure. If you would like to seek substantial funding from a number of outside investors and/or provide your employees with stock options in your corporation, you may choose to have a larger and more complex capitalization structure.

We should clarify what we mean exactly by "seeking substantial outside funding." The word *substantial* has different meanings for different people. In terms of this book, we'll say that seeking investments of $5000 each from your friend, your two sisters, and your dad is not seeking substantial outside funding. Seeking $50,000 from your cousin, $100,000 from an investment firm, and $150,000 from a company with which you are seeking to do business would be considered seeking substantial outside funding.

As you know, when you incorporate, you must pay a filing fee to the state, and each state's fees differ. Some can be considered pretty expensive, and others quite inexpensive. Most states also impose annual fees on the businesses incorporated in that state. These fees may be annual statement fees, franchise taxes, state income taxes, or a combination of all or two of those three. A number of states link the initial filing fees and the annual franchise taxes to the number of shares of stock the corporation authorizes. Therefore, having a large number of shares of stock could lead to a substantial increase in your state filing fees and annual taxes.

For example, if you incorporate in the state of Ohio and authorize 2000 shares, the current state filing fee is $150. If you increase the number of authorized shares to 50,000, the cost increases to a current amount of $1350. However, not all states tie their state filing fees to the number of shares a corporation authorizes. To see if the states you are considering do so, you can check the state pages located at www.bizfilings.com/learning/detailedstateinfo.htm or contact the secretary of state's office.

While Delaware is a state that ties its initial state filing fees and annual franchise taxes to the number of shares authorized, it has created a formula that makes its fees substantially lower than those of some other states. For companies with millions of shares, this formula can help them save a considerable amount of money in annual state franchise taxes. Does Delaware provide the same benefit for companies that have a small number of authorized shares? The answer is often no.

We cannot tell you how many shares to authorize or what capitalization structure is best for your business. You need to get advice on those matters from an attorney. However, we can provide general information on common situations. Typically, smaller corporations do not authorize a large number of shares of stock. They often authorize 1500 or 2000 shares. Conversely, companies that are seeking to attract substantial outside funding often authorize hundreds of thousands or millions of shares. Keep in mind that you can change the number of authorized shares for your corporation at a later date, should the needs of your corporation change. Amending your articles of incorporation to change the number of authorized shares and the par value will be discussed later in this book.

EVALUATING YOUR OPTIONS

The following is general information regarding incorporating in Delaware, in Nevada, and in your home state. Every state has different fees, requirements, corporate law systems, and taxation structures, which are not covered in depth in this chapter. For questions regarding your particular business situation, it is best to contact an attorney.

Delaware

As we mentioned at the beginning of this chapter, Delaware has been quite successful in marketing itself as *the* place to incorporate a business. Though this claim is not without merit, Delaware's offerings may not be so advantageous to small businesses, particularly those that transact business primarily in their home state and/or plan to have only a few shareholders and a low number of authorized shares of stock.

Many public companies are incorporated in Delaware; in fact, over half of the companies listed on the New York Stock Exchange are Delaware corporations. Corporations are attracted to Delaware for a number of reasons, the primary ones being Delaware corporation law, the low cost of incorporation, and the relatively low annual tax rates that Delaware offers to corporations with complex capitalization structures.

Delaware's corporation law is among the most flexible in the country, primarily because the corporation's shareholders and organizers are given wide latitude to establish whatever corporate governance rules they want. For example, Delaware specifies that for a corporation to be acquired, the acquisition must be approved by half of the corporation's shareholders, unless the corporation's bylaws state differently. Most other states do not allow a corporation's bylaws to take precedence. To public companies, the flexible law and the years of precedent often prove quite advantageous.

Delaware's formation fees are among the lowest in the country, and its taxation system is quite advantageous to companies with a large number of shares of stock. Also, the primary method used by Delaware for calculating the annual franchise taxes (taxes imposed on corporations for the privilege of being incorporated in that state) takes the number of shares of stock into consideration. You may be asking yourself why this would be advantageous to corporations with millions of shares of stock. However, the formula used for calculating the Delaware franchise tax is favorable to these corporations, and the tax often ends up being lower than the taxes that would be imposed on these corporations by their home states. Delaware wants to bring in tax revenue, but it also realizes that it can make more revenue by attracting and keeping a larger number of corporations.

For example, Public Company XYZ has 50 million authorized shares of stock. It might incur $20,000 in annual taxes if it incorporated in its home state, but if it incorporates in Delaware, its annual taxes may be only $10,000. These numbers are meant as examples only. Because of the relative complexity of the Delaware calculations, providing an actual example would be quite difficult; however, you can see the formula that Delaware currently utilizes on the Delaware page at www.bizfilings.com/learning/detailedstateinfo.htm, and it is discussed in the section of Chapter 18 on franchise taxes.

You can see the taxation advantages for large companies, but what about smaller corporations? For small corporations, the franchise taxes are also quite low, but they may not provide such a substantial cost savings. For example, for a corporation with 2000 shares of stock authorized, the annual franchise tax amount is currently $30. The franchise tax imposed on a corporation with the same number of authorized shares in another state might be only $100 or so.

Additionally, the Court of Chancery, which is unique to Delaware, is considered to be advantageous to corporations, particularly those that may face internal corporate disputes, such as shareholder lawsuits. These internal corporate disputes are more common in public companies and in privately held companies with outside investors. The Court of Chancery is a separate court system focusing solely on businesses and corporations, meaning that no other cases are tried there. It does not use juries; instead, cases are tried by judges appointed for their knowledge of corporate law. With Delaware's long history as a popular incorporation state, the court has many years of precedent on which to base its decisions.

If you believe that your company will one day seek to raise substantial amounts of capital from outside investors, or if you wish to eventually take your company public, incorporating in Delaware may be a favorable decision. Corporations that plan to seek outside funding from a number of investors typically create a capitalization structure with a higher number of authorized shares and multiple classes of stock. As previously mentioned, the annual taxes imposed by Delaware on these corporations may prove to be substantially less than those that the corporation would incur if it were to incorporate in its home state.

Advantages

- Delaware has flexible corporation law, giving corporations wide latitude in establishing internal corporate governance rules.
- The taxation structure is often favorable for companies with complex capitalization structures or with a large number of shares of stock.
- The cost to incorporate in Delaware is one of the lowest in the country.
- The Court of Chancery focuses solely on business and corporate matters, and utilizes judges instead of juries.
- There is no state corporate income tax for corporations that are incorporated in Delaware but do not transact business in the state.
- One person can hold all the officer positions of the corporation—president, secretary, and treasurer—and serve as the sole director. Delaware does not require these names to be listed in the articles of incorporation.
- Shareholders, directors, and officers of the corporation need not be residents of Delaware.
- Shares of stock owned by persons outside of Delaware are not subject to Delaware taxes.

Disadvantages

- For companies transacting business solely or primarily in their home state, the need to foreign-qualify in that state can lessen or negate the Delaware advantages of lower formation cost and no state corporate income taxes.
- The Court of Chancery is not as much of an advantage for smaller companies, since small companies rarely incur shareholder lawsuits.

Considerations

- Consider your future plans for your company. If you plan to seek substantial funding from a number of outside investors or if you desire to take your company public, you may strongly consider incorporating in Delaware.
- Be sure to evaluate whether you will be transacting business primarily in your home state or a single other state. If so, you may be required to foreign-qualify to do business in that state.

Nevada

While a number of states have changed their corporate law and corporate statutes to more closely resemble Delaware's, Nevada stands above the rest in its promotion of itself as an alternative to Delaware. While California, Texas, and Florida are popular states for incorporation mostly because of the number of business owners located within those states who choose to incorporate in their home state, Nevada has become a popular non–home state alternative.

Nevada's biggest advantage is that it has no corporate income tax, annual franchise tax, or personal income tax. After reading that states seek to gain tax revenue from corporations, you may be asking how Nevada can do this. The answer is that Nevada is not a completely fee-free state. Nevada currently requires that an initial statement of officers and directors be filed within 60 days of incorporation, and it imposes a fee for this filing. Thereafter, Nevada requires an annual statement and an associated fee. Also, the state filing fees imposed for formation of a new business and foreign qualification are higher than those in many other states.

Another advantage the state of Nevada touts is that shareholder information is not a matter of public record, which allows for anonymity of ownership. However, the corporation's directors must be listed in the articles of incorporation, and both directors and officers of the corporation must be listed in the annual statement. This requirement somewhat negates the benefit of anonymity of ownership for corporations where shareholders also act as directors and officers, because both the articles of incorporation and the annual statement are matters of public record. Another point to note is that shareholder information for privately held companies is not a matter of public record in most states. Therefore, the anonymity benefit of Nevada may not be as great for these companies.

Also, Nevada does not have an information-sharing agreement with the IRS, which increases the privacy of corporate information that Nevada maintains. Other states may share the information on state tax returns with the IRS. Because Nevada does not have a state income tax, this type of information-sharing agreement does not apply.

Additionally, Nevada allows "bearer shares" for added privacy for shareholders. With bearer shares, whoever holds the stock owns it, like a check made out to bearer. This provides added privacy because the corporation's stock transfer ledger will list the owner of those shares as bearer, instead of listing a specific person's name.

Advantages

- Nevada has no corporate income tax, annual franchise tax, or personal income tax.
- Nevada allows anonymity of ownership by not making shareholder information a matter of public record.
- Nevada allows bearer shares, providing additional shareholder privacy.
- Shareholders, directors, and officers need not be residents of Nevada.

Disadvantages

- The tax advantages of Nevada may be lessened or negated if the business must also foreign-qualify in its home state.
- Your formation costs could be higher if you incorporate in Nevada and also need to foreign-qualify in another state.
- Directors must be listed in the articles of incorporation, and directors and officers must be named in the annual statement, lessening the anonymity benefits.

Considerations

- Be sure to evaluate whether you will be transacting business primarily in your home state or a single other state. If so, you may be required to foreign-qualify in order to do business in that state.
- You should weigh the advantages of Nevada against those of incorporating in your home state, especially since many states are continuing to amend their corporate law and statutes to make them more corporation-friendly.

Your Home State

The state in which your business physically resides is called your home state. For companies with a number of offices in multiple states, the home state is the state in which the corporation's headquarters is physically located.

We wanted to address Delaware and Nevada before addressing your home state because many entrepreneurs know about the large number of businesses incorporated in Delaware and automatically think that Delaware is the state in which they should incorporate. Whether or not Delaware is the right choice for your business is a decision you will have to make, or a consideration that you should discuss with an attorney. However, we wanted you to have an understanding of Delaware's advantages before we outlined the advantages of incorporating in your home state.

For many entrepreneurs, incorporating in their home state proves to be the best option. When starting operations, many small businesses transact business primarily in their home states, unless they are starting an Internet-based business or a business primarily involving phone or catalog sales (which may be exempt from foreign-qualifying). Typically, for small companies transacting business primarily in their own state, local incorporation is the most affordable option. The cost of incorporating outside your home state and foreign-qualifying to do business in your home state typically ends up being higher than the cost of incorporating in your home state. Our previous example of Gloria and her antiques store illustrated this. With local incorporation, you have only one formation filing fee and annual state taxes from only one state.

Remember, you can change your state of incorporation at a later date, should the need arise. For example, if Greg incorporates Computer Software Company in his home state of Utah, but after a couple of years of operation determines that he would like to seek $5 million in funding from a number of outside investors, he may decide that being incorporated in Delaware would be more advantageous. In this case, Greg would incorporate his business in Delaware, then merge his Utah business into the Delaware corporation. The appropriate merger paperwork would have to be filed with the state of Utah, and the appropriate state fees paid.

Advantages

- With only one state filing, one set of taxes, and one annual statement, incorporating in your home state is often the least expensive option.

- For the same reasons, incorporating in your home state is typically easier.

Disadvantages

- For closely held corporations that are transacting business only in their home state, there are no real disadvantages to home state incorporation.
- Certain states have relatively high corporate taxes. The taxation structure for your home state could be considered a disadvantage, but if you incorporate elsewhere and must also qualify to do business in your home state, you must pay your home state's taxes anyway.

Considerations

- Will your business have a simple capitalization structure, meaning a lower number of shares and relatively few owners? If so, your home state may be the best place for you to incorporate.
- Will you be transacting business primarily in your home state? If so, and you incorporate elsewhere, you may have to foreign-qualify to do business in your home state, creating extra costs and annual requirements.

In summary, the primary point to remember is that the unique aspects of your particular business situation will generally determine where you should incorporate your business. Figure 5-1 includes questions that may help you in your evaluation of this important decision. Please note that this is intended to provide general information and items to consider. Each business owner's situation varies, and therefore for specific advice regarding your company or where to incorporate, you should contact an attorney.

F I G U R E   5-1

Where to Incorporate Worksheet

1. Where will your company mostly be transacting business?
   - ❑ A. Locally/in your home state
   - ❑ B. In two or less states
   - ❑ C. In three or more states
   - ❑ D. Internationally

   If you answered A or B, go to question 3. If you answered C or D, go to question 4.

2. Do you plan to seek funding from outside investors and/or go public?
   ❑ Yes   ❑ No   ❑ Uncertain

   If you answered yes, go to Scenario C. If you answered no or uncertain, go to question 4.

3. Do you plan to expand the area in which you transact business later
   in the life of your business?
   ❑ Yes   ❑ No   ❑ Uncertain

   If you answered yes or uncertain, go to question 4. If you answered no, go to Scenario A.

4. Are the costs of incorporating and annual requirements a primary
   concern to you?
   ❑ Yes   ❑ No   ❑ Uncertain

   If you answered yes, go to Scenario A. If you answered no or uncertain, go to Scenario B.

Scenario A –
Since you will be transacting business within your home state, a small number of
states, or possibly in a larger number of states, but your corporation will have a
simple capitalization structure, you may wish to consider incorporating in your home
state. If you incorporate in a state such as Delaware or Nevada, you may need to
foreign qualify your business in your home state and any other states in which
your corporation is transacting business, possibly resulting in higher formation and
annual costs. Also, the laws and courts of Delaware or Nevada may not be as
advantageous to you, with your business transacting in one or only a few states.

Scenario B –
If you are transacting business in a larger number of states or internationally, you
may wish to consider incorporating your business in Delaware or Nevada, which
have more flexible corporate laws. Your business may need to foreign-qualify in a
number of states, and as that number grows, the laws and courts of Delaware or
Nevada may be more advantageous to you.

Scenario C –
If you are considering seeking funding from outside investors or going public, you
may wish to consider incorporating in Delaware. Delaware can be advantageous to
companies with a large number of authorized shares and more complex
capitalization structures.

*This information is meant as general information only. For questions or advice on your
particular situation, please contact an attorney.*

CHAPTER 6

Pre-Incorporation Checklist

Incorporating is not a step that business owners typically rush into. Most business owners research the process and the different types of business structures beforehand, just as you are doing now. They talk with other business owners, friends, and family, and they often consult with an attorney or accountant regarding their particular situation. Now that you've been through some or all of these steps, and before you start the incorporation process, you'll want to ensure that you've determined answers to each of the items in this chapter's checklist.

> **Major topics covered:** *This chapter includes a checklist of the items you should consider and/or undertake prior to beginning the incorporation process.*

Each item included in the checklist in Figure 6-1 is discussed in more detail after the table, and each section includes a short to-do list.

BUSINESS STRUCTURE

Chapter 2 outlined the different types of business structure: sole proprietorship, general partnership, limited partnership, C corporation, S corporation, and limited liability company (LLC). It also addressed additional types of corporations for which some companies may qualify: statutory close corporation, nonprofit corporation, and professional corporation. At this point, it is important that you determine which structure best fits your business.

F I G U R E   6-1

Pre-Incorporation Checklist

☐ **DETERMINE YOUR BUSINESS STRUCTURE**
- *Status and goals* - Determine the current plans and future goals of your business by asking yourself a number of questions, including:
  - Do you have personal assets you want to protect from the debts and liabilities of your business?
  - Do you wish to keep the ownership of your company relatively small?
  - Do you plan to seek funding for your business from outside investors, and subsequently grow the ownership of your corporation?
  - Do you hope to take your business public?

- *Business entity type* - Decide whether your business will be a standard C corporation, S corporation, limited liability company (LLC), limited partnership, general partnership, or sole proprietorship. Keep in mind the following:
  - The C corporation, S corporation, and LLC provide limited liability protection to their owners.
  - With general partnerships and sole proprietorships, the owner(s) is legally considered to be the same as the business, and the owners personal assets can therefore be used to satisfy business debts and liabilities.

☐ **DETERMINE YOUR INCORPORATION METHOD**
- *Prepare and file your own paperwork* - While this is the most affordable option, you should know your state's requirements, and be prepared to secure all other formation-related items on your own.
- *Use an incorporation service provider* - Incorporation service providers not only prepare and file your incorporation documents, but also typically offer a broad suite of formation related products and services, such as obtainment of the employer identification number, assistance with the S corporation election documents, corporate kits, corporate forms, and more.
- *Use an attorney* - Attorneys provide great value to entrepreneurs in their ability to provide legal advice and customized documents specifically for your business, such as bylaws, shareholder agreements, contracts for seeking outside funding, and reviewing contracts your business receives from partners and vendors. Remember, attorneys may not provide as much value in the preparation and filing of your incorporation documents.

☐ **DETERMINE YOUR STATE OF INCORPORATION**
In order to decide which state of incorporation best fits your particular business, you should evaluate where your company will be transacting business and whether your corporation will have a simple or more complex capitalization structure.
- *Your home state* - If you are transacting business primarily in your home state and will have a simple capitalization structure, you may wish to incorporate in your home state. Keep in mind that if you incorporate outside your home state, but transact business there, you may need to foreign-qualify your business in your home state.
- *Delaware or Nevada* - If you plan to seek funding from outside investors thereby making a more complex capitalization structure and/or transact business in a larger number of states or internationally, you may wish to incorporate in Delaware. Nevada also offers advantages to companies transacting business in a number of states.

☐ **MOVE FORWARD!**
Now that you've determined the three factors above, you're ready to take the final preparation steps and also to learn about the incorporation process.

Since you are reading this book, the chances are high that you are seriously considering incorporating. Maybe you've been operating your business as a sole proprietorship or partnership for quite some time, and evolving business conditions have you considering incorporation. It could also be that you're just starting a business, and you believe that incorporating your business will provide the most benefits. Whatever your current situation, you need to take into account the future goals of your business.

It is not uncommon for business owners to change business structures at some point in time; however, if you carefully consider the current needs and future goals of your business, this may not be necessary. Other business owners are often an excellent source of information regarding this process. You can talk to other entrepreneurs about their choice of business entity. Why did they choose that particular business entity? What are the primary advantages and disadvantages they've experienced with their particular business structure? When seeking feedback from other business owners, keep in mind that even if someone's situation is similar to yours, the path that owner chose for his or her business may not be the best for your business.

If you determine that it is best for your business to operate as a sole proprietorship or partnership at this time, you do not need to continue reading this book; however, completing it will help you to better understand the incorporation process. If you decide to form an LLC, you will find that this book offers some information that is applicable to LLCs, although the majority of the information is specific to corporations.

To Do

- Evaluate the current needs and future goals of your company. Ask yourself questions such as, Do you have personal assets that you want to protect? Do you want to keep the ownership of your corporation small and relatively controlled? Do you hope to seek funding from outside investors for your company and subsequently grow the ownership? Do you want to take your company public?
- Decide which business entity provides the most advantages for your business. Is limited liability important to you? If so, the entities that provide limited liability to owners are the corporation (in its various forms) and the limited liability company.
- Consult with an attorney for legal advice if you remain uncertain about the best business structure for your particular situation.

INCORPORATION METHOD

As Chapter 4 outlined, you have three primary options for preparing your incorporation documents and filing them with the state: do it yourself, use an incorporation service provider, or use an attorney. Doing it yourself is typically the most affordable option, but it will most likely require more of your time. You should research the state statutes and requirements prior to submitting your paperwork. There are also a number of business steps to undertake around the time of incorporation that incorporation service providers and attorneys can assist you with. If you prepare and file your own documents, you can still enlist their services for these other steps, or you can seek to manage them on your own.

Using an incorporation service provider for the preparation and filing of your formation documents is an affordable option that makes it convenient for you to research the process and the provider's offerings and then place your order online, at a time that is convenient for you. In addition to handling your incorporation paperwork, these providers also typically offer a broad suite of services related to the formation process that you can utilize.

Attorneys provide value to entrepreneurs through their ability to provide legal advice and to offer direction in certain business decisions, such as the type of business entity to form and where to incorporate. They also provide value by preparing customized documents for business owners. Using an attorney for the actual preparation and filing of your incorporation documents, however, is not always the best choice, particularly with the other options available today.

To Do

- If you choose to prepare and file your own incorporation documents, be sure to do the necessary research.
- If you use an incorporation service provider, you will also be able to utilize a number of offerings related to the formation process. In addition to preparing and filing incorporation documents, these providers often offer corporate kits and forms, assistance in obtaining your employer identification number, and assistance in completing the S corporation document.
- Attorneys provide value to entrepreneurs through the advice and document customization that they can provide, but not nec-

essarily in the step of actually preparing and filing the formation documents. If you choose to use an attorney for this step, be sure to get a fee estimate and know what is included in that fee.

STATE OF INCORPORATION

As Chapter 5 outlined, the decision concerning where to incorporate is important. This decision can greatly affect your cost of incorporation, as well as annual costs such as annual statement fees and taxes.

As previously mentioned, it is important that you take the future goals of your business into account. Determine whether you plan to transact business only locally, or whether you plan to conduct all of your business online. Situations like these can have an effect on your choice of a state of incorporation.

Researching the incorporation requirements for each state you are considering will help you to estimate not only incorporation costs, but also the costs your corporation will incur for annual statement fees and franchise taxes. These rates and methods of calculation vary greatly by state, and may be a determining factor in your decision.

To Do

- Determine whether you will be transacting business primarily in your home state, giving thought to your future goals for business expansion.
- If you believe that incorporating outside your home state, possibly in Delaware or Nevada, is advantageous, you should research whether your company may need to foreign-qualify to do business in your home state or another state.
- If you intend to seek funding from outside investors, you may want to consider Delaware as your state of incorporation.
- Consult with an attorney for legal advice if you remain uncertain about the best state in which to incorporate your business.

MOVING FORWARD

Now that you've determined each of these aspects, it's time to think ahead to the incorporation process. There are additional details that you should consider prior to filing your incorporation documents, such as naming your business, determining the directors for your corporation, and deciding how many shares of stock your corporation will be authorized to issue. Part Two of this book addresses these as well as other aspects of incorporation and items of which you should be aware as you move forward with the incorporation process.

Part Two covers the following topics:

- Naming your company
- Information required in the incorporation paperwork
- Costs and time frames for incorporating your business
- Doing business in other states
- Other filings that may be necessary or that you may want to consider
- Incorporation case studies

Moving Forward–
Incorporating
Your Business

CHAPTER 7

Naming Your Corporation

Choosing the name for your corporation is not a step to take lightly. This is both an exciting and an anxiety-provoking step, as a name can make or break a company. Business owners often rush into naming their companies without completely evaluating the potential effect of the names they are considering. There are a number of questions that you should ask yourself, and items that you should consider, as you evaluate corporate names.

> *Major topics covered: This chapter outlines items to consider as you are choosing a company name, state requirements for corporate name endings, ways to check the availability of the names you are considering, and methods for protecting your chosen name.*

When you start a new business, you should give as much thought to your company name as you do or did to your business idea. If you already have a business that you've been operating as a sole proprietorship or partnership, and you're now considering incorporating, you should still give careful thought to your company name.

There are a number of steps involved in naming a business, starting with choosing potential names. While a name may come to some business owners overnight, for others this can be a fairly painstaking process. Once you have selected a name or made a list of potential names, there are a number of steps you should undertake to ensure that the name(s) is available for your use. You should check each potential name by verifying the availability of an associated domain name, ensuring that another company does not have trademark rights to it and that it is available for use in your intended state of incorporation. It is common to encounter problems with availability during at least one of these steps; therefore, it is important that you undertake all of these steps prior to filing your incorporation paperwork. Having all of these elements come together prior to incorporating can save you a number of potential headaches down the road.

CHOOSING YOUR CORPORATE NAME

When you begin the process of naming your business, you should have a thorough knowledge of your business and your target audience. Compile a list of possible names, and then ensure that these names convey the appropriate image. Test these names on your family, friends, or potential customers. Once you've narrowed your list of names to a few, check the availability of these names. The following sections provide a path for you to follow as you work through the important step of naming your business.

Knowing Your Business

As you consider possible names for your company, it is important that you know your business and your target audience. While this statement may seem elementary or even downright insulting, its importance cannot be overstated. For example, you may know that your intended business is travel-related services, but have you further defined your business and what benefits you provide in the market? Do your services fit a specific need or appeal to a certain group of people? The more questions you continue to ask yourself, such as what, why, and to whom, the more detailed your business description will be.

Also, be sure that you know your target audience well. While this is again a somewhat elementary concept, the more you can define your target audience, the easier it will be for you to appeal to potential customers. For example, let's say you're just starting a travel-related business, and you want to target college students. You know your offering, but how do you compete in the current market of online travel sites and travel agencies? As you think more about your target audience, you think about their characteristics. Many college students like to travel, and travel cheaply. College students are often looking to do more with less, and luxury and comfort may not be their primary criteria when they evaluate travel options. The more you know about what appeals to this group, the better chance you have of selecting a name that catches their attention.

Now that you've better defined your target audience, ask why your particular services should appeal to them. Do you focus on a specific area of the world or a specific type of travel, or does your company offer all types of travel worldwide? In our travel-related service example, let's say you focus specifically on Europe. While you can satisfy most travel needs, your specialty is air/rail packages for seeing a number of countries during one trip. Let's also say that your packages give travelers substantial flexibility. They can change the parameters of the package after their trip has started. Since college students often have more time and flexibility than business travelers or families vacationing in the area, the added flexibility is considered a real benefit, and you may wish to reflect this in your company's name and/or image.

While you are evaluating your business, don't forget your competitors. What are the names of your competitors' businesses? You'll want to ensure that you don't choose a name that is too similar to theirs. The last thing you want is a name that can be easily confused with a competitor's. While this might result in some business meant for that company coming to you, it could also result in business meant for you going to your competitor.

As well as knowing your competitors' names, you should also research their offerings. What differentiates your business or offerings from theirs? What do you offer that would make college students more apt to purchase from you rather than from an online travel site or travel agent? Let's say that most of your competitors offer a breadth of services, instead of focusing on packages, cruises, or a particular area of the world. If one of these competitors also focuses on the college market but does not focus specifically on Europe, you've determined one primary differentiator. Maybe the second major differentiator is the flexibility we mentioned. No other company offers the ability to change travel plans, penalty-free, once a trip has begun.

To continue with our example, we'll say that your evaluation of your business has provided you with the knowledge that your target audience is college students. You know that they often have the ability and desire to take long trips, but that they want to do as much as possible for as little cost as possible. You've also determined that the flexibility your packages offer is a primary differentiator from your competition. With those ideas in mind, you should now compile a list of possible company names.

Compiling a List of Potential Names

As noted at the beginning of this chapter, a name can make or break a company. Something to keep in mind is that while the process of naming has always been somewhat complex, it is even more so today with the Internet having such a large role in business. The reality of business today is that many customers search the Web for products and services prior to buying them, even if they do not plan to buy online. When you evaluate company names, it is advisable that you also give thought to the use of those names online. As you compile a list of potential names, be sure to also note potential domain names.

Once you've compiled a list of names, here are some questions you should use to pare it down:

- Does the name help you to stand out?
- Does the name convey the right image?
- Is the name either too broad or too limiting?
- Is the name simple to spell and to understand?
- Does the name convey your expertise, value, and/or uniqueness?
- Does your name have longevity (or is it trying to capitalize on a current trend)?

Let's return to our example of the travel company. As the owner, you've now developed a list of names—EuroFlex, Europe with Flexibility, Europe Savers, Europe for Less, FlexiSavers, College Today and Europe Tomorrow, and 18-22 Travel. For each of these names, you've also made a list of possible domain names—for example, www.euroflex.com, www.europe-for-less.com, www.flexisavers.com and www.18-22travel.com.

For each of these names, you should now ask yourself the questions just noted. Does the name help you to stand out? Most of these names will help to set you apart from your competition. Does the name convey the right image? Most of the names portray your benefits and/or offerings. Is the name either too broad or too limiting? The answer to that question is often a matter of personal opinion. Many experts say that you should not choose a geographically limiting name. In this example, however, if you plan to focus only on Europe, this may not be a negative. If you eventually plan to offer packages to other parts of the world, the choices without Europe in the name may be preferable.

The name 18-22 Travel may be both too limiting and difficult for people to understand. The numbers 18 and 22 were chosen because these are the ages of many college students. While this is your target audience, this name may discourage other people who also want to see as much of Europe as possible and do not want to spend a lot of money in the process. It could also be that many people will not understand what the 18 and 22 symbolize. They may think that those numbers are your business address (you often see this with restaurants). When you make people guess what your business name means, either it will stick in their head because it's clever, or you'll lose potential customers because they don't know exactly what you do.

Other than 18-22 Travel, most of the names in the list are simple to spell and understand; however, the longer names could pose a problem when looking at potential domain names. The longer or more complex your domain name, the harder you make it for customers to find you online. With the name College Today and Europe Tomorrow, you probably would not want to choose a domain name such as www.collegetodayeuropetomorrow.com or even www.college-today-europe-tomorrow.com. You increase the chance that customers will misspell your domain name and not find your web site. You also create problems for yourself, like fitting such a long domain name on your business cards and marketing materials. You may wish to shorten the domain name to www.europetomorrow.com. The question then arises whether this domain name accurately conveys your business image.

For the question of whether the name conveys your expertise, value, or uniqueness, each of the names in this list touches on at least one of these aspects. Does the name have longevity? While traveling cheaply and wanting flexibility in travel plans are not exactly passing trends, their importance may grow and fade. Considering your target audience of college students, the likelihood is pretty good that cheap, flexible travel will be just as important to them 15 years from now as it is today.

Now that you've evaluated each of your potential names more thoroughly, it's best to narrow your list. This will give you a more manageable list, both for testing potential names and for checking the availability of these names.

Testing Your Potential Names

There is no set rule for the number of names you should test prior to determining the name of your corporation. It could be that you've had the name of your business picked out for years, ever since you first thought of the concept and began working toward opening your own business. It could also be that you've always known you wanted to start your own business, but it was a struggle to find the business that was the best fit for your talents. In any case, it is still advisable to test the name or names you've picked. It's much better to learn that your business name is a dud before you incorporate, create business signs and marketing materials, and enter into a number of contracts. This could save you many headaches and possibly a lot of money in the long run.

Once you have compiled your list of names, give the list to your friends, family, and coworkers. Ask them to give you their initial impressions. Also provide them with your list of possible domain names. Do they think it would be easy to locate your web site using any of these domain names? Providing the list both to people who know about your business or business idea and to those who have no previous knowledge of it can give you valuable feedback, since these groups will probably take different approaches in evaluating your name choices.

Talking to other entrepreneurs can also be helpful during this stage. This group can sympathize with how difficult selecting a proper business name can be. They also may have valuable feedback about naming approaches they tried that did or did not work.

Testing your names on a group from your target audience is also advisable. There is no group better able to tell you if your names appeal to your market than a group of potential customers. To return to our travel company example, an option would be to spend an afternoon on a college campus polling college students on your list of names.

If one name becomes the clear favorite, the decision has been made easy for you. If your testing does not provide a clear favorite, however, you'll need to make the determination yourself. Obviously, you should eliminate any names that elicited negative feedback from your test groups. When it's time to make your final name determination, you'll want to pick a name that you can be excited about. Since this is your business, and you will be spending a lot of time and probably a lot of money to get it off the ground, you'll want to have a name that excites you. After all, if you're not excited about your business, why should your customers be excited about doing business with you?

CORPORATE NAME ENDINGS

While the question of your corporate name ending is not vital during the name evaluation and testing process, it should be addressed and understood, as you will be required to have a name ending that signifies your corporate status when you file your incorporation paperwork.

Most states require companies to include an identifier in their name that signifies that they have been incorporated or formed as limited liability companies (LLCs), thereby distinguishing them from unincorporated businesses. Samples of corporate identifiers include the words *Corporation, Incorporated, Company,* and *Limited* and the abbreviations *Corp., Inc., Co.,* and *Ltd.* The standard identifiers for professional corporations are the words *Professional Corporation* or the abbreviation *P.C.* Identifiers often used for nonprofit corporations include *Association, Foundation,* and *Fund.* Note that you cannot use the identifier *LLC* or *Limited Liability Company* if you are forming a corporation. Those name endings may be used only for an LLC.

Each state has different requirements regarding the types of identifiers allowed and also regarding what words may not be included in company names. For example, Texas does not allow the use of the word *Lottery* in a corporate name, and Oregon does not allow the use of the word *Cooperative.* Also, certain states require regulatory board approvals for companies that wish to use certain industry-specific words in their names, such as the word *Bank* or *Insurance.* For example, in California, if your intended name uses the word *Bank, Trust,* or *Trustee,* it needs the superintendent of banks' approval. In Nevada, including any word relating to insurance in your company name would necessitate the approval of the insurance commissioner.

Most states also require that your company name not suggest that your company performs or offers something other than what is outlined in the business-purpose portion of your articles of incorporation. For example, if you state as your business purpose that your company is in the restaurant business, you would not be allowed to have the name GreenTree Landscaping.

The state information tables located at www.bizfilings.com/learning/detailedstateinfo.htm outline which corporate name endings are allowed by each state and also address each state's name restrictions.

ENSURING NAME AVAILABILITY

As you narrow down your list of names, begin researching their availability. There are three primary ways of checking the availability of your company name choices: check the availability of potential domain names, perform a preliminary trademark search, and perform a preliminary name availability search with your intended state of incorporation.

It is advisable to perform all three of these searches, because generally there are gaps in the information provided by each. While you may not want to undertake all of these searches for a large number of names, you also probably don't want to complete all the steps previously outlined in this chapter, select a name you love, and then learn that the name is not available or has been trademarked by another company.

Domain Name Availability

Whether or not you plan to have an online presence, it is advisable to check domain name availability. This is one of the quickest methods of seeing whether the names you've listed might be available. If the possible domain names that you compiled for a prospective company name are not available, the chances are that the company name, or a name substantially similar to it, is already in use.

You can check domain name availability for free on the web sites of companies such as VeriSign's Network Solutions (www.networksolutions.com) or Register.com (www.register.com), two of the larger domain name registrars. If the names you want are not available, you can also check domain auction web sites for domain names in your particular industry that are for sale.

As you may know, domain names come with a variety of extensions, such as .com, .net, .org, .biz, and .info. These are called top-level domains, or TLDs. There are also country-specific extensions, such as .us, .ca (Canada), and .de (Germany). The most popular extension is .com, and therefore the availability of .com domain names may not be as great. While you may wish to have a .com name for your domain name, it may be that this extension is not available for your particular name, but that the name with a .net, .biz, .org, or .info extension is. You can register the domain name you want with one of these other extensions. Let's return to our travel company. If the owners choose EuroFlex as their intended company name, and www.euroflex.com is not available but www.euroflex.biz is, they could register the .biz domain name for their business.

If the .com version of a particular domain name is taken, you should consider two things before registering that domain with an alternative extension: Will customers have difficulty finding your web site? And does the company that registered the .com version have trademark rights to your desired corporate name? For example, if the company that registered the .com name offers products similar to yours, you may lose customers to this company. If customers try to type in your domain name, but mistakenly end up at this other site, they may decide to purchase from the other company. If a company has trademark rights to that corporate name, you could potentially be infringing on its trademark rights by beginning to use the name. Therefore, if either or both of these considerations are true, it is advisable to search for a different domain name.

It should also be noted that just because a particular domain name that you want is registered does not necessarily mean that it is currently in use. It could be that a person bought it, but never started the business for which he or she planned to use it. There are also a number of people and companies that purchase large quantities of domain names and then try to sell them to interested parties. If the domain name that is of interest to you is not available, but no web site resides at the URL, you can locate the information on the owner of that domain. Both Network Solutions and Register.com have "whois" searches on their web sites. The whois search will provide you with the name and contact information for the person or company that owns the domain name that is of interest to you.

Trademark Searches

It is also advisable to perform a trademark search on the name(s) you are considering. There are different types of trademark searches that provide different levels of information. One type of general search is a free trademark search that basically tells you whether there are pending or approved federal trademark registrations on your desired name. You can undertake a free trademark search on the web site of the U.S. Patent and Trademark Office (USPTO), which is located at www.uspto.gov.

Note that this free search is not all-encompassing. In addition to federal trademarks, there are also state and common-law trademark designations, and these data are often stored in different databases or are not aggregated at all. Therefore, performing a free search and locating no relevant results does not guarantee that your desired name is not already in use by another company. Information regarding common-law trademarks is particularly difficult to aggregate. Merely using a mark (whether it be a company name, a product/service name, or a logo) in commerce, even without undertaking a trademark registration, establishes common-law rights to that mark. Basically, this means that if there is an existing company that uses your desired business name, and if that company challenges your trademark filing, it may have rights to the name superior to those of your company. Because the free trademark searches fail to investigate common-law data, undertaking a comprehensive trademark search is advisable.

A full or comprehensive trademark search is one that checks your name against existing and expired federal, state, and common-law trademarks, and often checks it against existing domain names as well. When you undertake this type of search, you will typically receive an extensive report (often around 100 pages) that looks at phonetic and other variations of your desired name, helping to uncover potential trademark conflicts and prevent potential infringement issues. Because of the depth of the information uncovered, this type of search is advisable not only for your corporate name, but also as you select product/service names and your logo. Comprehensive trademark searches vary in cost with the complexity of your desired mark, but generally range from $300 to $500. Three primary providers of comprehensive trademark reports are CCH CORSEARCH (www.corsearch.com), NameProtect, Inc. (www.nameprotect.com), and Thomson & Thomson (www.thomson-thomson.com).

While you probably will not want to order a comprehensive search for each name you are evaluating, you should consider taking this step once you have settled on a name and before you incorporate. Since free trademark searches often do not provide complete information, making a decision on your name based solely on the results of such a search could cause problems later. Conducting domain name searches on variations of your desired name and undertaking a name availability search with the intended state of incorporation will also shed light on whether your desired name may already be in use; however, a comprehensive trademark search will provide the most complete picture.

Preliminary State Name Availability Searches

The states typically have preliminary name availability searches that allow you to learn whether your desired business name is already being used by another corporation, LLC, foreign-qualified corporation, or foreign-qualified LLC in that state. If your desired name, or a name that is substantially similar, is already in use, the state will not allow you to incorporate using this name.

Keep in mind that corporate names are state-specific. Incorporating your business secures your right to use that business name only in the state of incorporation. Because of this, the same name, or a name that is substantially similar, could be in use in another state. For example, even if a preliminary name check in Florida shows that the name Pet Bakery Incorporated is available, it is entirely possible that there is a bakery using this same name operating in Indiana. This is another good reason for also undertaking a trademark search to see if another company already has trademark rights for your intended name.

As noted previously, the state name availability searches utilize a database of names of corporations (including nonprofits and professional corporations), LLCs, foreign-qualified corporations, and foreign-qualified LLCs. If a company operating as a sole proprietorship or partnership within that state is using your desired business name, the state name check will not provide that information.

Note that if you're using an incorporation service provider or an attorney for filing your incorporation documents, these providers will perform a preliminary name availability search with the state prior to submitting your paperwork. The cost of performing this search is typically included in the service fee. You can also undertake this process yourself by contacting the state directly.

If you complete a preliminary name availability search and your desired name is shown to be available, but you are not yet ready to incorporate, you can often reserve the name with the state. The states charge a small fee for name reservations, typically between $10 and $50, and impose a time limit on how long the reservation will last. Reservations generally last between 30 and 90 days, depending on the state. Name reservations guarantee that another company cannot incorporate using that name, or a deceptively similar name, prior to either the incorporation of your business using your reserved name or the expiration of the reservation (whichever comes first). Since many business owners incorporate relatively quickly after performing their research, name reservation is not that common a tool; however, it should be noted as an option available to you.

PROTECTING YOUR CORPORATE NAME

Filing for a federal trademark is the best way to protect your usage of a name. As noted previously, incorporating your business prevents another company from incorporating in the same state using the same name or a name that is considered deceptively similar. It does not prohibit other companies from incorporating in other states using the same name, however. In addition to filing for a federal trademark, you can also establish trademark rights based on legitimate use of the mark; however, usage of the mark must be quite obvious and well documented.

According to the USPTO web site, registering a mark provides the following advantages:

- Constructive notice to the public of the registrant's claim of ownership of the mark
- A legal presumption of the registrant's ownership of the mark and the registrant's exclusive right to use the mark nationwide on or in connection with the goods and/or services listed in the registration
- The ability to bring an action concerning the mark in federal court
- The use of the U.S. registration as a basis for obtaining registration in foreign countries
- The ability to file the U.S. registration with the U.S. Customs Service to prevent importation of infringing foreign goods

There are a number of ways in which you can trademark your name. As with incorporating your business, you can file the trademark paperwork yourself, you can enlist the help of an online or standard trademark service provider, or you can use an attorney. If you file your own trademark documents, you should expect to pay only the fee charged by the USPTO. Trademark service providers will charge a service fee in addition to the USPTO fee, and attorneys typically charge their hourly rate for the time spent on your paperwork plus the USPTO fee. The complexity of the trademark registration will be a factor determining the fees you incur when you use a trademark service provider or an attorney. You can expect to pay anywhere from a couple of hundred dollars to a couple of thousand dollars, depending on your choice of provider and the complexity of your mark. For current fees charged by the USPTO for trademark registrations, it is best to visit the USPTO web site at www.uspto.gov.

CORPORATE DBAS

One item that deserves mention in this chapter, even though the issue often does not arise until after incorporation, is the fact that a corporation can register for a DBA (doing business as) name if it will be transacting business under a name other than its legal name. DBAs are also often called assumed names or fictitious names. We first introduced DBAs in Chapter 2 in talking about sole proprietorships. Many sole proprietors file for DBAs instead of doing business under their legal names (e.g., Field's Landscaping instead of John Field). This same principle applies to corporations. We'll return to our travel example from earlier in this chapter, and say that EuroFlex Incorporated was the chosen name. Later in the life of the business, the corporation expands its offerings and begins to sell luggage. While there is some overlap between travel and luggage, the owners do not feel that the name EuroFlex would be appropriate for selling luggage. They decide to file a DBA to transact business under the name Luggage Online. DBA filings are typically made at the county level; however, some states require corporations to file DBAs with the state. For more information regarding DBA requirements, it is best to contact your county clerk or secretary of state.

In summary, there are a number of steps you should undertake when you name your corporation. It is not as easy as simply selecting a name and starting to use it. If you did that, you could infringe on another company's trademark, and possibly face legal action. One of the questions many entrepreneurs have relates to the order in which to undertake these steps. There isn't a right answer to this question, but a logical order is:

1. Derive a list of names you like, test those names, and narrow the list to one or a few.
2. Check the availability of domain names.
3. Search for current or pending trademarks on your desired name and domain name (at a minimum, undertake the free trademark search on the USPTO's web site, but strongly consider undertaking a comprehensive trademark search).
4. Perform a state name availability search to ensure that the name is available in your intended state of incorporation.
5. Once you have selected a name, if these steps do not show any conflicts, register for a federal trademark on your name. This will establish your rights to use this name nationwide and help to prevent another company from using or trying to register your name.

If all goes well, these steps will show your desired name to be available. If it is not, you will need to evaluate your options and make a determination on how best to proceed.

CHAPTER 8

What Information Is Required?

The document that is filed with the state to incorporate a business is called the articles of incorporation, or in some states the certificate of incorporation. There are a few exceptions to this—for example, in Massachusetts it is called the articles of organization, and in Tennessee it is called a charter. This is the most important document for a corporation because without it, the corporation does not exist. This chapter not only explains what information is required in the articles of incorporation, but also provides you with a better understanding of what these requirements mean to you and your business.

> *Major topics covered:* This chapter outlines the information required in the articles of incorporation, explains optional items of information, addresses the registered agent requirement, and includes examples of articles of incorporation.

As previously mentioned, the states have different statutes governing the formation and existence of corporations, and the annual requirements placed on corporations also often vary from state to state. Statutes are laws enacted by a legislature, and, as you can imagine, many politicians are not experts in corporate law; therefore, there can be wide variations in what the different states require. The Revised Model Business Corporation Act (RMBCA), which was brought into existence by the American Bar Association, seeks to bring a degree of uniformity to corporate statutes. While there is still a long way to go, the RMBCA has helped to simplify the information required in many states' articles of incorporation and the requirements imposed on corporations transacting business in other states. This chapter addresses the information the states typically require to be included in the articles of incorporation, and also outlines information that is either optional or required in a lesser number of states. You can also visit the Business Filings web site for additional information on some of the formation and annual requirements imposed on corporations by your intended state of incorporation.

ARTICLES OF INCORPORATION

While the concept of articles of incorporation is universal among the states, each state's corporation law or code dictates what information is required in the incorporation paperwork. Certain information is standard across most, if not all, states. The next section outlines and describes that information. The subsequent section outlines optional information that some states may include in this document. Note that the states can change their requirements at any time. For the most up-to-date requirements, it is advisable to check the corporation information on your state's web site.

Required Information

The following information is generally required by all states:

- Company name
- Business purpose
- Stock information
- Name and address of the registered agent
- Name and signature of the incorporator

Company Name

The previous chapter discussed the importance of your corporate name and provided tips on choosing it and protecting it. Your corporate name is a required piece of information in your articles of incorporation. Because of this, it is advisable to perform a preliminary name availability search with the state prior to filing your incorporation paperwork. This helps to ensure that the proposed name for your company is not currently being used by another corporation, limited liability company (LLC), limited partnership, foreign-qualified corporation, or foreign-qualified LLC in that state. If a preliminary name check has not been completed before you file your articles of incorporation, you run the risk of having your filing rejected by the state.

Remember that the name you include in your articles of incorporation must include a corporate name ending. Name endings were also discussed in the previous chapter, and details on each state's requirements are included at www.bizfilings.com/learning/detailed-statepages.htm.

Business Purpose

The business purpose clause included in the articles of incorporation outlines what your business does or will do. Most states allow, or even require, the use of what is called a general-purpose clause. The general-purpose clause basically states that the corporation is being formed in order to engage in "any lawful business" for which a corporation may be organized under that state's corporation law or code.

For states in which the general-purpose clause is optional, the primary benefit to using this clause is that if you do so, your business is not limited in what activities it can undertake. Furthermore, if a corporation uses a general-purpose clause, businesses of different types can be operated out of that one corporation. For example, if a company's business purpose states that it will provide real estate services, that is the only type of business service that the corporation can offer. If the corporation used a general-purpose clause, it could offer real estate services, sell books, and sell other products or services and still be within the scope of the business purpose outlined in its articles of incorporation. Examples of this general-purpose language are included in the sample articles of incorporation at the end of the chapter.

Certain states require you to list your specific business purpose. Examples of descriptive business-purpose clauses would be, "The purpose of the corporation is to sell products and services," and "The purpose of the corporation is to provide landscaping services." Massachusetts is one example of a state that currently requires the use of a specific business-purpose clause. A sample articles of organization document for Massachusetts is included at the end of this chapter as Figure 8-4.

If you are forming a professional corporation in any state, your business-purpose statement should be very specific. Since business owners engaged in professions that require a license (such as doctors, chiropractors, dentists, lawyers, accountants, and architects) are typically required to form a professional corporation (PC) or professional LLC (PLLC), the states require more specific language for these business-purpose clauses. An example of a business-purpose clause for a professional corporation would be, "The purpose of this corporation is to provide medical services to the pediatric population."

Similarly, for nonprofit corporations, the business-purpose clause must be quite descriptive and must comply with the Internal Revenue Code so that the nonprofit can be granted tax-exempt status. The Internal Revenue Code includes a number of classifications of nonprofit corporations, with the most common classification being a 501(c)(3) nonprofit corporation. To qualify for 501(c)(3) federal tax-exempt status, the nonprofit corporation must be organized and operating for some religious, charitable, educational, literary, or scientific purpose. When applying for tax-exempt status with the IRS, you must submit a copy of your articles of incorporation along with the required IRS form.

In the case of 501(c)(3) nonprofits, the purpose clause may be required to state: "This corporation is organized exclusively for charitable, religious, educational, and scientific purposes, including, for such purposes, the making of distributions to organizations that qualify as exempt organizations under section 501(c)(3) of the Internal Revenue Code, or the corresponding section of any future federal tax code" and then be followed by the specific purpose of the nonprofit.

If you are incorporating a nonprofit that has any other operational premise, it is best to check with your attorney or accountant, or use the IRS web site at www.irs.gov, to determine the appropriate IRS classification for your type of nonprofit.

Stock Information

Ownership interest in a corporation is represented by shares of stock. While many people think of stock in connection with publicly traded companies, all corporations have shares of stock. Corporations can have as little as one share of stock or as many as millions of shares.

The number of owners a corporation will have typically determines the number of shares to authorize. If a corporation will have numerous owners, it will probably want to authorize a higher number of shares. There is no limit to the number of shares a corporation may authorize. However, the number of shares can have an effect on the state filing and annual fees; this is addressed later in the chapter.

The articles of incorporation define the maximum number of shares of stock that the corporation is authorized to issue. If the corporation will issue different classes of stock or preferred stock, which are concepts discussed in Chapter 16, this is also stated in the articles of incorporation. You will need to determine this information prior to filing your incorporation paperwork, as it must be included in the articles of incorporation.

When deciding on the number of shares of stock for your corporation, you should also determine the stock's par value, as the par value of your authorized shares is also given in the articles of incorporation. Par value is the stated minimum value of a share of stock, and it has little significance for the actual value of the stock. Historically, par value played a greater role in determining the actual value of stock than it does today. Today, the primary thing to keep in mind when you determine par value is that your shares cannot be sold for less than this amount; however, shares can be and often are sold for more than the par value. Setting a high par value on your shares could lead to an inability to sell the stock. For example, if you set your par value at $15 and you are seeking outside investors as you are starting your business, potential investors may not want to pay so high a price per share, especially for the shares of a new company. They may therefore decide not to invest in your company. Also, in some states, having a higher par value can cause your annual franchise taxes to increase. Common par values used in the articles of incorporation are $1, $0.01, and no par.

The actual value of your stock is determined by its fair market value, which is simply what someone is willing to pay for the stock. With public companies, the fair market value is the price per share as reflected on the national stock exchange that trades that company's shares. For example, if Microsoft's shares trade at $20, that would be considered the fair market value. As anyone who owns shares of a public company's stock knows, the market value of these shares can change daily (or by the minute). With privately held companies, the determination of fair market value is more subjective, and is often based on the current overall performance of the corporation. Another method of valuing stock is "book value," which is an accounting formula in which the corporation's assets less its liabilities are divided by the number of shares of stock.

As stated earlier, there is no limit on the number of shares a corporation can authorize; however, the main negative of authorizing a large number of shares is that it may cause the initial state filing fees and the annual statement fee or franchise taxes to increase. A number of states link their corporate filing fees and annual fees to the number of authorized shares and the amount of the par value, meaning that the higher these values, the higher the fees charged. As we discussed in Chapter 5, on where to incorporate your business, Delaware is one of these states, but the formula used may make the fees charged by Delaware more advantageous to corporations with a large number of authorized shares.

You should be realistic in determining both the number of shares you wish to authorize and the par value of these shares. For example, if you plan to wait 2 or 3 years before seeking capital from outside investors, you may not want to authorize a large number of shares at the time of incorporation. If you are incorporating in a state that ties franchise taxes to the number of shares and par value, you may pay higher than necessary taxes in your first years of existence if you authorize a large number of shares. You can amend the number of shares and par value given in your articles of incorporation just before you seek outside funding.

Note that in order to change the stock information given in your articles of incorporation, you need to file a certificate of amendment with the state and pay the state's fee for this filing. States recognize that business owners may need to change the information in their articles of incorporation, and therefore they charge only a nominal fee for amendments. Also, to see whether your intended state of incorporation ties state fees to the number of shares of stock and par value, check the pages at www.bizfilings.com/learning/detailedstateinfo.htm.

A corporation is not required to issue all of the authorized shares of stock. The directors of the corporation may issue any amount of stock that they see fit, up to the maximum amount authorized in the articles of incorporation. The amount issued depends upon the company's particular situation. For example, Adam, his brother Bob, and their sister Nancy form ABN Contractors, Inc. They are the sole directors and shareholders of the company, and they wish to maintain this ownership structure. Let's say that they authorized 1200 shares of stock. They may choose to issue all 1200 authorized shares to themselves, since they do not intend to bring additional shareholders into the company.

As another example, Sarah is starting Highflight Adventures Corporation, and she plans to seek investors for her business. Sarah's articles of incorporation authorize 1 million shares. At the time of incorporation, she is the only director and shareholder. Sarah can issue any number of the 1 million authorized shares to herself, but given her desire to seek investors, she will leave a portion of the shares for issuing to new investors throughout the life of her business.

It is important to consider the long-range goals of your company, particularly the long-range goals for the ownership of your business, as you are evaluating the number of authorized shares to include in your articles of incorporation. Is having a small or a larger number of shareholders desirable? In either case, keep in mind that you can increase the number of shares at a later time, if necessary. Just remember that not only must you file an amendment with the state and pay the state's filing fee to make this change, but an increase in shares may also lead to an increase in your annual fees.

Name and Address of Registered Agent

Most states require corporations and LLCs to have a registered agent within the state of incorporation. The registered agent is responsible for receiving important documents, such as service of process (also called notice of litigation) documents, annual statements, and franchise tax documents, on behalf of the corporation. The registered agent's address is often different from the company's legal address (which is the address of the company's physical location). This, along with the responsibilities of a registered agent and the requirements for acting as such, is discussed in more depth later in this chapter. We wanted to highlight here, however, that all but a couple of states require the registered agent's name and address in the articles of incorporation.

Name and Signature of the Incorporator

The incorporator is the person(s) filing the company's incorporation documents with the state. Most states require the name of the incorporator to be listed on the articles of incorporation, and require this person to sign the document prior to filing it with the state. Some states also require the address of the incorporator. Many states do not have specific requirements on who can act as an incorporator; however, most states require the incorporator to be at least 18 years of age.

Optional Information

While the information discussed in the previous section is almost universally required in a company's articles of incorporation, this section outlines information that either is required by only a small number of states or is optional in all states:

- Legal address of the company
- Director information
- Officer information
- Preemptive rights
- Cumulative voting rights
- Indemnification clause
- Close corporation election

The states recognize that some corporate information may change more frequently, such as the company's physical address and information on directors and officers. When this information or information that may not be universal for all corporations (such as stock voting rights) is not required in the articles of incorporation, corporations are not required to update it with the state as it changes. Once information on matters such as preemptive rights, cumulative voting rights, and indemnification language is included in your articles of incorporation, however, most states require you to file a certificate of amendment and pay a state filing fee to amend it.

States can obtain certain information about your corporation even when it is not required in the incorporation documents. For example, in the annual statements that most states require, corporations must often provide the legal address of the company, directors' names and addresses, and the names and addresses of the officers. If any of this information changes, it is updated with the state by changing it in the next annual statement.

Note that the information included in a corporation's articles of incorporation is a matter of public record. Information that is a matter of public record is discussed later in this chapter, but in summary this means that the information is accessible by the general public. If there is information outlined in this section that you prefer not be public knowledge, you may wish to exclude it from your articles of incorporation.

Legal Address of the Company

The legal address of the company is the address at which the company physically resides. Typically the states require the legal address to be a physical address rather than a post office box. If your company has more than one location, its legal address is usually the primary or headquarters address.

Relatively few states require you to include your company's legal address in the articles of incorporation, because most states send correspondence for your corporation to the registered agent. Therefore, having the legal address of your business listed in your articles of incorporation is not considered a necessity.

Director Information

As Chapter 1 briefly outlined, the directors oversee and direct the affairs of the corporation. They are responsible for the major corporate decisions, but they generally are not responsible for the day-to-day operation of the business. While their involvement may be minimal during the incorporation process, their responsibilities increase once the business has been incorporated. The role of directors is outlined in more depth in

Chapter 15, but this section includes items to consider as you are preparing to incorporate.

Only a few states require the names and addresses of directors to be listed in the articles of incorporation. The detailed state information pages on Business Filings' web site note whether this is required or optional information for each state. Regardless of whether states require director information to be included in the articles of incorporation, they routinely require the names and addresses of directors to be included in the annual statements. In most states, the information included in the annual statements is also a matter of public record. Therefore, not including the optional director information in your articles of incorporation may not keep this information confidential.

One of the formalities a corporation is required to observe is holding an initial meeting of the corporation's directors, at which the directors issue stock, adopt the bylaws, and appoint officers. The logistics of this meeting will be discussed in Chapter 13; however, the actions of the directors during the initial meeting basically complete the process of forming the corporation. This meeting cannot be held unless the directors of the corporation have been named. If the directors are listed in the articles of incorporation, you can hold this meeting immediately upon incorporating. If the directors are not listed in the articles of incorporation, a "statement by incorporator" is needed prior to holding this meeting. This document is prepared by the incorporator; it names the directors of the corporation and basically passes the corporation to the director(s) upon incorporation. It is an internal document that is not filed with the state, but it should be kept with the corporate records.

Another potential advantage of listing the directors in the articles of incorporation is that it may make it easier to open a bank account. Typically, with small businesses, one of the corporation's directors opens the bank account, and the bank employee will be able to match that person's name with the director's name in the articles of incorporation.

The maximum number of directors a corporation can have is often included in the corporation's bylaws. Some states have statutes regulating the minimum number of directors required. In most states, the minimum number of directors is one. Some states, however, require a corporation to have at least three directors, but if the number of shareholders is less than three, the number of directors can equal the number of shareholders.

The state-specific tables on Business Filings' web site outline additional information on directors, including the minimum number of directors required, whether the state requires that directors reside in that state, and if there is a minimum age requirement for directors.

Another point to note about director information that is included in the articles of incorporation is that some corporations choose to include a clause specifying that the directors of the corporation will have staggered terms. For example, if your corporation plans to have six directors, you may wish to have two up for reelection each year, instead of having all six be reelected in the same year. Larger corporations and/or those with a larger number of directors commonly specify this information in the articles of incorporation; however, since many entrepreneurs start their corporations with only one or a few directors, noting the staggering of terms in the articles of incorporation is not very common.

Officer Information

Most states do not require the inclusion of officer information in the articles of incorporation, since officers are typically appointed during the initial meeting of the directors; however, Massachusetts is one example of a state that does ask for this information in the incorporation documents. A corporation's officers usually consist of a president, vice president, secretary, and treasurer, and most states allow one person to occupy all officer positions. Officer information is typically provided to the state in the corporation's annual report, and can be updated in subsequent annual reports.

Preemptive Rights

A preemptive right is the right of a shareholder to buy the same proportion of any new issue of stock as the shareholder currently owns. If the shareholder elects not to exercise this right, the shares can be sold to other existing or new shareholders.

For example, 123EZ Corporation has issued a total of 30 shares to its only shareholders, Anna, Bill, and Chris, each of whom owns 10 shares. 123EZ Corporation wants to issue 300 additional shares of stock. Anna, Bill, and Chris would each have the right to buy 100 shares, or one-third of the new issue, which is the proportion that each of them currently owns. If they decide not to buy these additional shares, the shares may be sold to third-party investors.

The main reason preemptive rights are used is to protect minority shareholders from having their ownership diluted. Dilution of ownership typically occurs when new shares are issued to other parties, thus lessening the ownership percentage of the current owners of the corporation. For example, if a corporation has issued a total of 99 shares of stock in equal amounts to Paul, Judy, and Sue, each of them owns 33 percent of the corporation. If the corporation later decides to issue another 33 shares to a new owner, Victor, the ownership percentage of the initial owners has been diluted. They will each own only 25 percent of the corporation after the new shares have been issued. The main negative of preemptive rights is that they can impede the ability of a corporation to raise new capital. This impediment is caused by the requirement that new shares must first be offered to existing shareholders before they can be offered for general sale.

In some states, preemptive rights exist automatically unless they are excluded in the articles of incorporation. In other states, if you want preemptive rights, you must include a clause to this effect in the articles of incorporation. You should research your state's statutes on preemptive rights, and you may wish to include a clause in your articles of incorporation specifying whether you do or do not want preemptive rights, in order to ensure that you receive the rights you want.

Finally, preemptive rights only apply to shares that are newly issued by the corporation. They do not affect sales by existing shareholders.

Cumulative Voting Rights

Cumulative voting is a way to protect minority shareholders' rights. It applies only to the election of directors, and it is designed to ensure that minority shareholders have representation on a corporation's board of directors.

Without cumulative voting, each director is elected separately by majority vote; therefore, the majority shareholders have the power to elect all of the directors. This method of electing directors is called straight voting.

With cumulative voting, shareholders multiply the number of shares they hold by the number of directors up for election to get the number of votes they have; they are able to distribute these votes however they want. With this method of voting, a minority shareholder is far more likely to obtain representation on the board of directors.

For example, Circle Corporation has two shareholders, Fred and Marilyn. Fred owns 70 shares, and Marilyn owns 30 shares. Three directors will be elected to the board of Circle Corporation. With straight voting for these directors, Fred would be able to elect each director by majority vote. With cumulative voting, Fred would have a total of 210 votes and Marilyn would have a total of 90 votes. No matter how Fred divides his 210 votes, he does not have the votes to win all three director positions. For example, if he casts 91 votes each for Director One and Director Two, he has used up 182 votes and has only 28 votes to cast for

Director Three. Marilyn can then cast all of her 90 votes for Director Three, and so Director Three will be elected to the board by the minority shareholder, Marilyn.

Like preemptive rights, in some states cumulative voting automatically applies unless the articles of incorporation preclude it. In most states, however, cumulative voting rights must be included in a clause in the articles of incorporation if you want your corporation to have this provision.

Indemnification Clause

Another piece of optional information for your articles of incorporation is the indemnification clause. This clause indemnifies the directors against being held personally responsible or liable for breach of their duty of due care to the corporation, provided that they acted in good faith and reasonably believed that their actions were in the best interest of the corporation. This type of clause indemnifies the directors only in terms of monetary damages and does not cover directors in the event of criminal or knowingly fraudulent conduct.

The main advantage of including an indemnification clause is that it helps attract directors who are not also owners of the company. A director who is charged with a breach of duty to the corporation can face substantial damages, and so without an indemnification clause, people probably would not be as willing to serve as directors of the corporation.

An example of a more detailed indemnification clause is the one for Delaware. It reads,

> No director of the corporation shall be personally liable to the corporation or its stockholders for monetary damages for breach of fiduciary duty as a director; provided, however, that the foregoing clause shall not apply to any liability of a director (i) for any breach of the director's duty of loyalty to the corporation or its stockholders, (ii) for acts or omissions not in good faith or which involve intentional misconduct or a knowing violation of law, (iii) under Section 174 of the General Corporation Law of the State of Delaware, or (iv) for any transaction from which the director derived an improper personal benefit. This Article shall not eliminate or limit the liability of a director for any act or omission occurring prior to the time this Article became effective.

An example of a more standard indemnification clause is California's. It reads,

> The liability of the directors of the corporation for monetary damages shall be eliminated to the fullest extent permissible under California law.

Close Corporation Election

As Chapter 2 outlined, a statutory close corporation is a standard corporation with a small number of shareholders that is formed pursuant to a state's close corporation statutes. Close corporations are typically those with fewer than 50 shareholders, no market for the corporation's stock, and shareholders who are significantly involved in the day-to-day management of the corporation. Not all states have close corporation statutes, and not all companies that fit these specifications elect close corporation status. If you are incorporating in a state that recognizes close corporations, and you wish to have your business treated as such, your articles of incorporation must declare the corporation's intent to be recognized under that state's close corporation statutes.

THE REGISTERED AGENT

Most states require corporations and LLCs to have a registered agent, sometimes called a registered office, within the state of incorporation. As mentioned previously, the registered agent is responsible for receiving important legal and tax documents, including service of process (also called notice of litigation) documents, franchise tax forms, and annual report forms.

The registered agent may be an individual or a company located at a street address in the state in which the company is incorporated. The states do not accept a post office box as the address for the registered agent. Most states do not allow a corporation to act as its own registered agent; however, a director or officer of a corporation can act as that corporation's registered agent in her or his individual capacity. For example, John Brown is incorporating Brown's Candy Corporation in his home state. Brown's Candy Corporation cannot be its own registered agent, but John Brown, using the address of Brown's Candy Corporation, can be the registered agent.

If another company is acting as registered agent for your business, that company must be registered as a corporation with the state. We'll use John Brown for our example again. Let's say he does not want to act as the registered agent for Brown's Candy Corporation. His friend Jane Smith operates a partnership with her sister. Mr. Brown would like to use Ms. Smith as the registered agent for Brown's Candy Corporation, but Ms. Smith's company is not eligible to be a registered agent because her business is not incorporated with the state. Ms. Smith herself could act as the registered agent, but her partnership cannot.

When corporations are not incorporated in their home state, they need a registered agent in the state of incorporation. Delaware is an example of a state where this frequently happens. Most businesses incorporated in Delaware do not have a physical presence in the state, and therefore must use a registered agent service provider. Most incorporation service providers and attorneys also offer registered agent services for an annual fee. If you are filing your own paperwork, you can still enlist the services of an incorporation service provider for registered agent services, and the secretary of state's office will often have a list of registered agent service providers in that state.

There are a number of advantages to using a registered agent service provider, but the benefits often differ for large and small companies. For large and/or public corporations, the primary benefit comes from having service of process and state documents sent to the registered agent. The registered agent typically has delivery instructions to ensure that these documents reach the correct contact(s) within the corporation. For example, Big Company Incorporated has 2000 employees at its corporate headquarters. If the address of its corporate headquarters is listed as the address of the registered agent for the corporation, documents would probably be delivered to the mailroom, which might complicate the process of getting these important documents to the right person. If the secretary of the corporation is listed as the registered agent for Big Company Incorporated, these documents may make it to him or her, but they may not be set apart from the normal mail, and thus they could become lost in the pile of papers most of us have on our desks.

If Big Company Incorporated uses a registered agent service provider, that provider may have instructions to express ship any service of process documents received for the corporation to Employee A, and to express ship all annual statements and state franchise tax documents to Employee B. This ensures that the documents reach the proper contact within the corporation and that they are set apart from standard mail. For companies served with a large number of lawsuits, this is indeed an advantage. The last thing a corporation wants is to have service of process documents be buried on someone's desk.

For small companies, one of the primary advantages of using a registered agent service provider is maintaining a consistent address with the state. If you act as the registered agent for your corporation, you are responsible for notifying the state if you change your address, meaning that you must file an amendment and pay the necessary state fee for this filing. Chances are that if you are moving your business, the furthest thing from your mind is ensuring that you change your address with the secretary of state. If the state does not have the correct address for your corporation's registered agent, this could cause a delay in the delivery of these important documents to you, or, worse, you may never receive them at all.

Another potential disadvantage to acting as the registered agent for your own corporation is that legal documents may be served on you in front of your customers, possibly causing an embarrassing situation. For example, Joe acts as the registered agent for his corporation, Joe's Hair Design, and lists his business address as the registered agent's address. Joe's Hair Design is sued, and while Joe is cutting a customer's hair, the sheriff walks in to serve him the notice of litigation. Having the sheriff show up at your business may not produce the most positive of impressions.

A second potential disadvantage to acting as your corporation's registered agent is that the information on the registered agent is a matter of public record. This concept is discussed in more depth in the next section, but basically it means that anyone has access to your name and address. This is more of a disadvantage in states that do not require the legal address of the corporation to be listed in the articles of incorporation, or if you are operating a business out of your home. Using your business address as the registered agent's address eliminates any anonymity afforded to you or your corporation by not including the legal address of your corporation in the articles of incorporation.

As previously mentioned, most incorporation service providers and attorneys offer registered agent services. You should inquire as to what is included in their offering, and also how the fees are structured. As an example, Business Filings Incorporated, an online incorporation service provider, offers registered agent services in all states. Registered agent customers can access their accounts at any time through Business Filings' Online Corporate Status Center. Business Filings forwards any service of process documents and all correspondence received for the company from the secretary of state to the customer. Any legal notices are recorded in the customer's information record and scanned into the Online Corporate Status Center, giving the customer online access to these documents, and are also sent to the customer via overnight delivery. Business Filings charges an annual fee for this service; this is currently $125.

INFORMATION AS A MATTER OF PUBLIC RECORD

As mentioned earlier in this chapter, the information included in the articles of incorporation is a matter of public record. This means that any member of the public can access it. However, how this information is accessible varies by state.

The information you provide is, of course, kept in the state's database. The state must maintain a record for your corporation for annual statement and taxation purposes. Some states post the list of new business filings on their web site. Some states have publication requirements, which stipulate that new business filing information must be published in the local newspaper for the area in which the corporation is located. Both of these are ways in which your information becomes readily accessible.

The practice of mining the information on new business filings and using it for direct marketing purposes is becoming more prevalent. There are companies that specialize in creating these lists, then selling the names to companies for direct mail purposes. Since the information is on public record, there is currently no way to prohibit this practice. Also, this is not specific to new business filings; almost every filing at the state or county level is on public record.

SUMMARY

Since this chapter included a lot of information and introduced a number of new terms, we want to provide a summary that briefly outlines the information that is typically required in your articles of incorporation, and also information that is required only in some states or is optional in all states.

Required information includes:

- *Company name*. You will need to list the full name of your corporation, including a corporate identifier, such as *Incorporated, Corporation, Company, Inc., Corp.,* or *Co.* Currently acceptable corporate name endings for your intended state of incorporation are listed at www.bizfilings.com/learning/detailedstateinfo.htm.
- *Business purpose*. Some states may accept or require the use of a general-purpose business clause, whereas others require corporations to include language outlining the specific type(s) of business the corporation will engage in.
- *Stock information*. For your corporation, you need to list the number of shares of stock authorized and the par value for those shares. Par value is the minimum value of the shares; they cannot

be sold for less than this amount. Keep in mind that some states link their initial state filing fees to the corporation's number of authorized shares. So, be realistic in determining the number of shares your corporation needs to authorize at this point in time.

- *Name and address of the registered agent.* Virtually all states require corporations to have a registered agent (registered office) in the state of incorporation. The registered agent must have a physical address (not a P.O. box) in that state, and is responsible for receiving important legal and state documents on behalf of the corporation.

- *Name and signature of the incorporator.* The states also require the incorporator—the person who files the documents on behalf of the corporation—to be named in the articles of incorporation and to sign this document, thus certifying that the information therein is accurate.

Information that is required in a lesser number of states or is optional in all states includes:

- *Legal address.* Because many states send all corporate correspondence to the registered agent, only certain states require that the corporation's legal address be included in the articles of incorporation. Other states obtain this information from the corporation's annual statement.

- *Director information.* Some states require that the names and addresses of the corporation's directors be included in the articles of incorporation. Other states obtain this information from the corporation's annual statement. Additionally, some corporations choose to include information on staggered terms for directors, particularly if the corporation will have a large number of directors.

- *Officer information.* Few states require officers' names and addresses to be included in the articles of incorporation. Most states obtain this information from the corporation's annual statement.

- *Preemptive rights.* Preemptive rights allow shareholders to buy the same proportion of any new issue of shares as the shareholder currently owns, in order to keep their ownership percentage the same. In some states, preemptive rights exist automatically unless they are excluded in the articles of incorporation. In other states, if you want preemptive rights, you must include a clause to that effect in the articles of incorporation.

- *Cumulative voting rights.* This is a method of voting for directors that allows shareholders to multiply the number of shares they own by the number of directors up for election to get the number of votes they have; they then can distribute these votes as they wish. The idea behind cumulative voting is to protect the voice of minority shareholders. In some states, cumulative voting automatically applies unless the articles of incorporation preclude it; however, in most states, a clause specifying cumulative voting rights must be included in the articles of incorporation if you want your corporation to have this provision.

- *Indemnification clause.* This clause indemnifies the directors against being held personally responsible or liable for breach of their duty of due care to the corporation, provided that they acted in good faith and reasonably believed that their actions were in the best interest of the corporation. This type of clause indemnifies directors only in terms of monetary damages; it does not indemnify them in the case of criminal or fraudulent acts.

- *Close corporation election.* If you plan to incorporate in a state with close corporation statutes, and you wish to have your corporation recognized under those statutes, this must be declared in your articles of incorporation.

ARTICLES OF INCORPORATION EXAMPLES

Figure 8-1 is an example of the Delaware certificate of incorporation document. The company is named in the title as well as in the first section. The second section is for the registered agent (called the registered office in Delaware) information. The third section is the business-purpose clause. This example includes a general-purpose clause. In the fourth section, you would provide the number of authorized shares of stock and also the par value of those shares.

Figure 8-1 also includes the optional indemnity clause in the fifth section. The sixth section gives the information on the incorporator—the person filing the document. While Delaware does not require information about directors to be listed on the certificate of incorporation, this example includes this optional information for one director in the seventh section. Section 8 includes the optional cumulative voting rights language. Finally, the incorporator must sign the certificate of incorporation prior to filing it with the State of Delaware.

Figure 8-2 is an example of the California articles of incorporation document. California's standard template is quite basic, requiring only four sections—the corporate name, the California general-purpose business clause, the number of authorized shares (par value is not required), and the name and address of the registered agent. This example includes a fifth section that gives the indemnification clause and a sixth section that details the optional preemptive rights information. As with the Delaware document, the incorporator must sign the articles of incorporation prior to submitting them to the California secretary of state. With California's articles of incorporation, the language used in the business-purpose section must be the exact language provided by the State of California, as it is in this example.

F I G U R E   8-1

Delaware Certificate of Incorporation Example

CERTIFICATE OF INCORPORATION OF:

_____

FIRST: The name of the corporation is: _____.

SECOND: The address of the registered office of the corporation in the State of Delaware is located at:

_____.

Located in the County of _____.

The name of the registered agent at that address is:

_____.

THIRD: The purpose of the corporation is to engage in any lawful act or activity for which corporations may be organized under the Delaware General Corporation Law.

FOURTH: The total number of shares of stock which the corporation is authorized to issue is _____ shares of common stock having a par value of _____.

FIFTH: No director of the corporation shall be personally liable to the corporation or its stockholders for monetary damages for breach of fiduciary duty as a director; provided, however, that the foregoing clause shall not apply to any liability of a director: (i) for any breach of the director's duty of loyalty to the corporation or its stockholders, (ii) for acts or omissions not in good faith or which involve intentional misconduct or a knowing violation of law, (iii) under Section 174 of the General Corporation Law of the State of Delaware, or (iv) for any transaction from which the director derived an improper personal benefit. This Article shall not eliminate or limit the liability of a director for any act or omission occurring prior to the time this Article became effective.

SIXTH: The name and address of the incorporator is:

_____.

SEVENTH: The name and address of the initial director of the corporation is:

_____.

EIGHTH: At all elections of directors, each shareholder shall be entitled to as many votes as shall equal the number of votes which the shareholder would be entitled to cast for the election of directors with respect to the shareholder's shares of stock multiplied by the number of directors to be elected by the shareholder. The shareholder may cast all of such votes for a single director or may distribute them among the number to be voted for, or for any or two or more of them as the shareholder sees fit.

I, the undersigned, being the incorporator, for the purpose of forming a corporation under the laws of the State of Delaware do make, file, and record this Certificate of Incorporation and do certify that the facts herein are true.

_____

Incorporator

F I G U R E 8-2

California Articles of Incorporation Example

Article I

The name of the corporation is: _____.

Article II

The purpose of the corporation is to engage in any lawful act or activity for which a corporation may be organized under the General Corporation Law of California other than the banking business, the trust company business, or the practice of a profession permitted to be incorporated by the California Corporations Code.

Article III

This corporation is authorized to issue only one class of shares of stock; and the total number of shares which this corporation is authorized to issue is _____.

Article IV

The name in the State of California of this corporation's initial agent for service of process is:

_____.

Article V

The liability of the directors of the corporation for monetary damages shall be eliminated to the fullest extent permissible under California law.

Article VI

Shareholders are granted preemptive rights to subscribe to any or all issues of shares or securities.

_____
Incorporator

Figure 8-3 is an example of the Florida articles of incorporation document. Many of the items included are the same as or substantially similar to those in Figures 8-1 and 8-2; however, the Florida articles of incorporation require the principal office address for the corporation to be listed. Another difference in the Florida articles of incorporation is that Florida requires the registered agent to sign the articles of incorporation, thus stating that he or she agrees to act in that capacity. Furthermore, Florida also requires that the name of the person completing the articles of

F I G U R E 8-3

Florida Articles of Incorporation Example

ARTICLE I   NAME
The name of the corporation shall be: _____.

ARTICLE II   PRINCIPAL OFFICE
The principal place of business and mailing address of this corporation shall be:
_____.

ARTICLE III   PURPOSE
The purpose for which the corporation is organized is: _____
_____.

ARTICLE IV   SHARES
The number of shares of stock that this corporation is authorized to have
outstanding at any one time is _____. The par value of each
share of stock is _____.

ARTICLE V   DIRECTORS

The names and addresses of the initial directors of the corporation are:

_____.

ARTICLE VI   REGISTERED AGENT
The name and Florida street address of the registered agent is:
_____

Located in the County of _____

ARTICLE VII   INCORPORATOR
The name and street address of the incorporator to these Articles of
Incorporation is: _____.

****
I hereby accept the appointment as registered agent and agree
to act in this capacity.

Signature: _____   Date _____
          Registered Agent

Signature: _____   Date _____
          Incorporator

The document was prepared by: _____

incorporation to be included, primarily to provide the state with a contact person should there be any questions about the information included.

Figure 8-4 is an example of the Massachusetts articles of organization. This document is quite long, and therefore the figure is quite long; however, we felt it was important to include it as an example of one of the strictest formats. The articles of incorporation for most states are only one page in length. As you see, the Massachusetts document is four pages long. When you submit your articles of organization to Massachusetts, you must

FIGURE 8-4

Massachusetts Articles of Organization Example

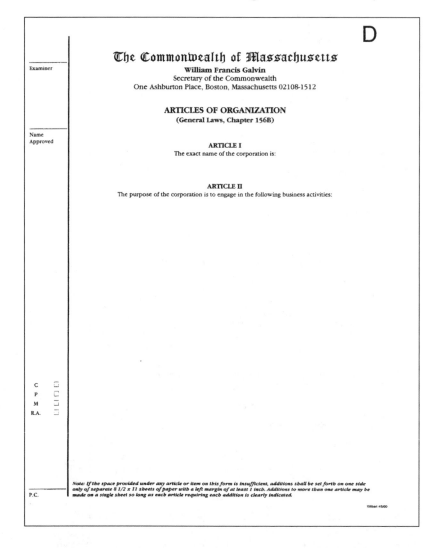

use Massachusetts's template, which can be downloaded from the web site of the Massachusetts secretary of state (in this case called the secretary of the commonwealth). You cannot submit them in any other format. Note that including the exact format of Massachusetts's template caused this figure to be smaller than the other figures. Resizing an $8\frac{1}{2} \times 11$-inch document to fit the specifications of this book made the wording small; however, since Massachusetts has one of the most detailed documents and

FIGURE 8-4

(Continued)

ARTICLE III

State the total number of shares and par value, if any, of each class of stock which the corporation is authorized to issue.

WITHOUT PAR VALUE		WITH PAR VALUE		
TYPE	NUMBER OF SHARES	TYPE	NUMBER OF SHARES	PAR VALUE
Common:		Common:		
Preferred:		Preferred:		

ARTICLE IV

If more than one class of stock is authorized, state a distinguishing designation for each class. Prior to the issuance of any shares of a class, if shares of another class are outstanding, the corporation must provide a description of the preferences, voting powers, qualifications, and special or relative rights or privileges of that class and of each other class of which shares are outstanding and of each series then established within any class.

ARTICLE V

The restrictions, if any, imposed by the Articles of Organization upon the transfer of shares of stock of any class are:

ARTICLE VI

**Other lawful provisions, if any, for the conduct and regulation of the business and affairs of the corporation, for its voluntary dissolution, or for limiting, defining, or regulating the powers of the corporation, or of its directors or stockholders, or of any class of stockholders:

**If there are no provisions state "None".
Note: The preceding six (6) articles are considered to be permanent and may ONLY be changed by filing appropriate Articles of Amendment.

is the most formal in appearance, we felt that it was important to include it in this chapter.

The initial information required is similar to that required by other states. The Massachusetts articles of organization include more information on the corporation's stock than those of most states. Article III allows

F I G U R E 8-4

(Continued)

ARTICLE VII

The effective date of organization of the corporation shall be the date approved and filed by the Secretary of the Commonwealth. If a *later* effective date is desired, specify such date which shall not be more than *thirty days* after the date of filing.

ARTICLE VIII

The information contained in Article VIII is not a permanent part of the Articles of Organization.

a. The street address (*post office boxes are not acceptable*) of the principal office of the corporation *in Massachusetts* is:

b. The name, residential address and post office address of each director and officer of the corporation is as follows:

	NAME	**RESIDENTIAL ADDRESS**	**POST OFFICE ADDRESS**
President:			
Treasurer:			
Clerk:			
Directors:			

c. The fiscal year (i.e., tax year) of the corporation shall end on the last day of the month of:

d. The name and business address of the resident agent, if any, of the corporation is:

ARTICLE IX

By-laws of the corporation have been duly adopted and the president, treasurer, clerk and directors whose names are set forth above, have been duly elected.

IN WITNESS WHEREOF AND UNDER THE PAINS AND PENALTIES OF PERJURY, I/we, whose signature(s) appear below as incorporator(s) and whose name(s) and business or residential address(es) *are clearly typed or printed* beneath each signature do hereby associate with the intention of forming this corporation under the provisions of General Laws, Chapter 156B and do hereby sign these Articles of Organization as incorporator(s) this _____ day of _____ .

_____

_____

_____

_____

Note: If an existing corporation is acting as incorporator, type in the exact name of the corporation, the state or other jurisdiction where it was incorporated, the name of the person signing on behalf of said corporation and the title he/she holds or other authority by which such action is taken.

---

for the distinction between common and preferred shares of stock, which is defined further in Chapter 16, and Article IV allows for descriptions of these designations. Article V allows the corporation to define and impose restrictions on the transfer of shares. This article allows for information on preemptive rights and/or allows language to be included that restricts

F I G U R E 8-4

(Continued)

THE COMMONWEALTH OF MASSACHUSETTS

ARTICLES OF ORGANIZATION
(General Laws, Chapter 156B)

I hereby certify that, upon examination of these Articles of Organization, duly submitted to me, it appears that the provisions of the General
Laws relative to the organization of corporations have been complied
with, and I hereby approve said articles; and the filing fee in the amount
of $ _____ having been paid, said articles are deemed to have been
filed with me this _____ day of _____ 20 _____.

Effective date: _____

WILLIAM FRANCIS GALVIN
Secretary of the Commonwealth

FILING FEE: One tenth of one percent of the total authorized capital
stock, but not less than $200.00. For the purpose of filing, shares of
stock with a par value less than $1.00, or no par stock, shall be deemed
to have a par value of $1.00 per share.

TO BE FILLED IN BY CORPORATION
Photocopy of document to be sent to:

_____

_____

_____

Telephone: _____

the transfer of shares between owners (which is not overly common with
corporations). Article VI allows for the inclusion of items such as indemnification language or a dissolution date (which is also not common with
corporations). Massachusetts permits a delay in the effective date of the
organization, which is basically the corporation's birthday, to be specified
within Article VII. If you need your corporation to be officially formed as

of a certain date, you can do so in Massachusetts, as long as the effective date is not more than 30 days from the date your articles of organization are approved and filed by the secretary of the commonwealth.

As noted earlier in this chapter, Massachusetts is the only state that requires officer information to be included in the articles. Article VIII includes information on the address of the corporation's principal office, the names and addresses of officers and directors, the date of the ending of the corporation's fiscal year, and the name and address of the registered agent. As you can see, the form states that the information included in Article VIII is not a permanent part of the articles of organization. This information can change often, and it need not be corrected with the secretary of the commonwealth's office at the time of the change. Changes can be noted when you file your annual statement.

Massachusetts is somewhat of an anomaly in that it asks for information in its articles of organization that generally is not determined until a corporation holds its organizational meeting of directors, such as the names of officers and whether the bylaws have been adopted. Article IX states that the bylaws of the corporation have been adopted and that the officers noted in Article VIII have been elected. Massachusetts is not looking for any form of a reply within this article. The wording is there simply to state that these tasks have been done.

These examples are meant to demonstrate the differences in the types and amounts of information states require in order to approve the formation of a corporation. If you are planning to incorporate your own business, you can typically access a state's articles of incorporation template on the secretary of state's web site. If you use an incorporation service provider or an attorney for your business formation needs, that provider will use forms similar to the examples provided herein.

CHAPTER 9

Costs and Time Frames

There is a common misconception that incorporating a business is something that can be done in a matter of hours, or at most a matter of a few days. Having your business incorporated in that short a time frame may significantly increase the cost, and the turnaround you desire may not be available in all states. There are significant differences in the states' standard costs and processing times. This chapter will help you get an accurate idea of how much incorporating your business may cost and how long it may take.

> *Major topics covered: This chapter contains information regarding costs and standard and expedited completion time frames for incorporating your business.*

BASIC COST STRUCTURE

As we've previously mentioned, the states impose filing fees for the formation of all types of corporations, and also for limited liability companies (LLCs) and limited partnerships. These fees must be paid at the time you submit your incorporation documents to the state. They cover all facets of the state review process, and also the return of the documents to you upon approval (or rejection, if that should happen).

When your incorporation documents are sent to the state, they are reviewed to ensure that all of the necessary information is included and correct, and also that the name you've provided meets the state's requirements. The preliminary name availability search we recommended in

Chapter 7 will tell you only whether or not your proposed name is being used by another corporation, LLC, foreign corporation, or foreign LLC in that state. However, the preliminary name availability search will not tell you if your proposed name meets state specifications. The final authority on whether or not your company may use the name you've proposed rests with the state body responsible for business formations, typically the secretary of state's office.

It is possible that your specific company will face additional fees at the time of formation, depending upon your location and business purpose. Items not included in state filing fees include:

- *Certified copies.* In some states, you must pay extra if you would like a certified copy of your articles of incorporation. A certified copy may be required to open a bank account.
- *Publication fees.* Some states have publication requirements, meaning that your company will be required to publish notice of its incorporation in a local newspaper for a certain amount of time. More information on publication requirements is included later in the chapter.
- *Expediting fees.* Most states charge additional fees to expedite the processing of your documents. Expediting fees are explained in more detail later in the chapter.
- *County filing fees.* In addition to the state filing required to incorporate your business, a few states require a county filing in order to formalize your state filing—some in the county in which your business is located, and others in the county in which your registered agent's address is. To inquire whether your state has a county filing requirement, it is best to contact your secretary of state's office.

It is also important to know that most states impose annual statement fees and/or franchise tax fees on corporations throughout the life of the corporation. These annual requirements are addressed in Chapter 18.

State Fee Ranges

Filing fees vary widely by state and by type of business entity. In many cases, the cost of forming a corporation is different from the cost of forming an LLC or a nonprofit corporation. Currently, the state in which forming a standard C corporation is least expensive is Maryland, where the state filing fee is $40. The state in which forming a standard C corporation is most expensive is currently Texas, where the state filing fee is $300. Conversely, the state in which forming a limited liability company is most expensive is currently Massachusetts, where the state fee is $500.

As a point of reference on the difference in price for forming different types of business entities, the state filing fee to form an LLC in Texas is $200, and the fee to form a nonprofit there is $25. States can change the filing fees at any time. As with any pricing change, if a change is going to be made, the price will most likely be increased, not decreased.

Publication Fees

As mentioned earlier, certain states have publication requirements for newly formed corporations and/or LLCs in that state. To satisfy this requirement, your company must publish notice of its incorporation in a local newspaper for a specified amount of time. Historically, a number of states required publication in order to notify the general public that these businesses had been formed as corporations. At that time, the number of incorporated businesses was not as great as it is today, and most states have since repealed this requirement. Arizona, Georgia, and Pennsylvania are some states that still have publication requirements for corporations. Certain states have these requirements only for corporations or only for LLCs. Arizona is an example of a state that currently has publication requirements for both types of entity.

Typically, publication fees range from $40 to $200, but in certain counties they can be much more expensive. The particular newspaper or newspapers that can be used largely drive the publication fee. For example, for businesses located in Arizona's Yuma County, the publication fee can be up to $300.

Each state's publication requirements vary. In some places you can select the newspaper in which to publish the necessary information, and in others the newspaper is assigned to you. Often, your notice must run in the newspaper for the city or county in which your business is physically located. Other states require the notice to be run in the paper for the city or county where your registered agent's address is located. There are also differences in the length of time the information must run. If you are planning to incorporate in one of the states that require publication, and you plan to file your own paperwork, it is advisable that you research that state's publication requirements prior to filing your documents. This will help you not only to estimate the cost of fulfilling this requirement, but also to better understand what exactly that state demands.

If you use an incorporation service provider or an attorney to file your incorporation paperwork in a state with a publication requirement, the provider may include the publication fee in the pricing for that state, and in such a case the provider will fulfill the requirement for your business as part of its service. If you plan to use one of these providers for assistance in incorporating your business, it is advisable that, before you engage a provider, you ask whether your intended state of incorporation has a publication requirement, and if so whether the provider's fee covers the requirement for your specific county.

AVERAGE PROCESSING TIMES

The typical processing time for incorporating your business currently runs between 4 and 6 weeks. This standard filing time often comes as a surprise to business owners. There are a number of factors that can affect filing times and can push this time frame out further. One factor is whether you mail your documents to the state. You must allow delivery time for your documents to reach the state, and also for them to be returned to you from the state. Some states allow for fax filing or online filing, which can speed up standard processing.

Other factors, such as state budget situations, government furloughs, world events, and events like labor strikes at airlines or major package carriers, can also affect the processing time for your filing. In addition, the beginning of a calendar year is often a popular time for forming corporations, and states may become backlogged at this time.

California is an example of a state that typically has a long turnaround time. Generally, the processing time for standard filings is 5 to 6 weeks. In states that allow for fax or online filing, the standard processing time can be reduced dramatically, but this is not an absolute rule. If you need to have your business incorporated in a certain time frame, it is advisable for you to expedite your filing with the state.

EXPEDITING A FILING

The states realize that business owners cannot always wait 4 to 6 weeks to have their businesses incorporated. They also recognize that expediting the filing process is a way to gain additional revenue from that process. Most states have expedited filing options in order to lessen the processing time. For the convenience of having the processing time shortened, the states typically impose additional fees.

The expediting fees vary by state, as do the expedited turnaround times. Typically, expediting fees range from $10 to $100, and the average completion time is 1 to 10 days. In addition, a number of states have varying levels of expediting. For example, Delaware currently offers three levels of expedited service. There is a 24-hour service, which has a current price range of $20 to $100. With this service, your filing will be completed within 24 hours of receipt (holidays and weekends excluded). The second level of expediting is a same-day service, which has a current price range of $40 to $200. With this service, the state will complete your filing on the same day it is received, as long as it is received by 2:00 P.M. Eastern time. The final level of expediting offered by Delaware is called "Priority One" service, which has a current fee of $500. With this service, the state will complete your filing within 2 hours of its receipt, as long as the filing is received by 6:00 P.M. Eastern time. These fees for expedited service are charged in addition to Delaware's current state filing fee, which is $74 for standard C corporations with a small number of authorized shares of stock and low or no par value. (Delaware ties both its initial state filing fees and its annual franchise taxes to the number of authorized shares a corporation has.)

Note that the time frames quoted by Delaware are state processing times. It is possible that it will take longer to get possession of the completed, approved incorporation documents. For example, if you use the Priority One service, it is possible that you will not receive the state-approved documents until the next day. Unless you can pick them up directly from the secretary of state's office, you will need to provide your own express shipping number for the state to use in overnight shipping your documents to you.

In certain states, California being one, you can expedite a filing only via "over-the-counter" service. That means that the filing must be hand-delivered to the secretary of state's office in order to expedite the processing time. California has five secretary of state locations (Sacramento, Fresno, Los Angeles, San Diego, and San Francisco) to help facilitate this requirement.

If you are using an incorporation service provider or an attorney, keep in mind that the expedited processing times noted here are the state's processing times. When you use a provider, it will take additional time for the provider to create your documents, send them (whether by fax, online, or overnight shipping) to the state, have them returned from the state, record them, and then ship them to you.

CHAPTER 10

Doing Business in Other States

The concepts of doing business in states outside your state of incorporation and the possible need for foreign-qualifying your business in those states were briefly touched upon in previous chapters. A corporation is considered a "foreign" corporation in all states except its state of incorporation. States have requirements for foreign-qualified corporations and limited liability companies (LLCs) similar to those for domestic entities. This chapter will discuss in detail the concept and process of foreign-qualifying, and what it means to your business.

> *Major topics covered:* This chapter contains information on transacting business in other states, the foreign qualification process, and the consequences of not foreign-qualifying, and evaluates foreign-qualifying versus incorporating in multiple states.

FOREIGN-QUALIFYING TO TRANSACT BUSINESS IN OTHER STATES

Corporations may be required to foreign-qualify in states other than their state of incorporation if they are transacting business in those other states. The definition of "transacting business" depends upon the state and the situation. In general, states consider a number of factors when determining whether a foreign corporation is transacting business within their borders. Some criteria evaluated include:

- Whether the corporation has a physical presence in the state
- Whether the corporation has employees in the state

- Whether the corporation accepts orders in the state
- Whether the corporation has a bank account in the state

This is not a complete list, and different states may have different criteria. Also, simply doing business by mail order or over the Internet typically does not constitute transacting business; however, the determination of whether a company is transacting business is made on a case-by-case basis. Therefore, it is advisable to discuss your particular situation with an attorney for a legal opinion on this matter.

We'll provide examples of a company that probably would need to foreign-qualify and one that probably would not need to do so. Fictitious Greenbush Telecom Inc. is a telecommunications company providing services in four southern states. Greenbush is incorporated and maintains its headquarters in Georgia. It also offers its services in Florida, Alabama, and Tennessee by employing contractors in these states. The company has offices and employees in these other states, and it offers services to and accepts orders from residents of these states. Most likely, Greenbush Telecom would be required to foreign-qualify to transact business in Florida, Alabama, and Tennessee.

Fictitious FlowerBulbsOnline.com is incorporated in Washington and sells its products only online. Customers of this corporation may be located anywhere in the United States or the world. Since the company is physically located in Washington, the order fulfillment happens there as well. The company's employees are located there, and its only contact with other states is by Internet or phone. This company most likely would not need to foreign-qualify in other states.

As we previously mentioned, corporations are a revenue generator for the states. If state A realizes that your corporation is transacting business within its borders, it would like revenue from your corporation, even though your corporation is incorporated in another state. When you foreign-qualify your business in another state, your corporation becomes subject to that state's requirements, such as annual report and state tax requirements, providing the state with annual revenue. As we mentioned in Chapter 5, incorporating your business in a less expensive state (in terms of either the filing fees or the annual fees) is not always the least expensive or best option, particularly for closely held corporations that transact business in only one state. In Chapter 5, we used Delaware as an example, since business owners often hear of Delaware's popularity and think that that is where they should incorporate their businesses. For owners of small businesses that are primarily transacting business in their home states and that have a simple capitalization structure, incorporating in a "less expensive" state often results in higher formation fees and annual fees if the business must foreign-qualify in its home state.

To further illustrate this point, we'll use an example with Nevada and California. Nevada is a tax-free state in terms of state taxes. Conversely, California imposes a minimum franchise tax of $800 per year on domestic and foreign corporations after their first tax year. We'll say that Sam, the owner of Ocean Retail, has a small shop on a beach in California where he sells beach-related materials to tourists. Ocean Retail conducts all of its business in California. Sam is evaluating where to incorporate, and he is considering Nevada because it does not impose franchise or income taxes on corporations.

Because Sam conducts all of his business in California, he probably will have to foreign-qualify Ocean Retail there. Sam will thus incur state filing fees for the incorporation in Nevada plus foreign qualification fees in California, and he will be subject to the annual franchise tax in California after his corporation's first tax year. The fact that Nevada is a tax-free state is not a real benefit to Sam, since he must still pay the California franchise tax. Since California's foreign qualification fees are very close in price to its formation fees for corporations, there is not a substantial cost savings there either. Realistically, the formation fees paid to Nevada result in additional, and possibly unnecessary, costs, since Sam must still incur the franchise taxes he was hoping to avoid.

While incorporating in Nevada is not a benefit to our fictitious Sam, since he was primarily interested in avoiding the California state franchise tax, it can prove quite beneficial to businesses that are located there and/or that transact business there. Being in a state with no corporate income or franchise taxes can save corporations a substantial amount of money each year, but again, each company's situation is different.

THE FOREIGN QUALIFICATION PROCESS

In order to become a foreign-qualified corporation in another state, you must register in that state for a certificate of authority, which is a document that grants a foreign corporation permission to transact business in that state. Applying for a certificate of authority is similar to filing articles of incorporation. A name check must be performed in the qualifying state to ensure that the name of your company is not already in use in that state by another corporation, LLC, foreign corporation, or foreign LLC. State filing fees for the certificate of authority must also be paid. If your current corporate name is not available in the state of qualification, your corporation will be required to use an assumed name in that state.

As with the articles of incorporation, the information each state requires in the certificate of authority differs. Common information includes:

- Corporate name
- Date and state of incorporation
- Name and address of a registered agent in the state of qualification
- Names and addresses of officers
- Number of authorized shares and a listing of the different classifications of stock
- Signature of a corporate officer (often the president)

While this information is commonly included in the certificate of authority, additional information is also requested by some states:

- Names and addresses of directors
- Duration of the corporation (which is almost always perpetual)
- Number of issued shares of stock
- Financial information, including information on assets
- Specific business-purpose clause outlining the type(s) of business the corporation will undertake

Before permitting you to foreign-qualify, most states require a certificate of good standing from your state of incorporation. The certificate of good standing is a document that states that your company has met all the necessary requirements for corporations imposed by your state of incorporation. Failing to file your annual statements or failing to pay or being delinquent in paying your annual statement fees and franchise taxes could cause your company to be in bad standing with the state. If your corporation is not in good standing with its state of incorporation, it will not be granted a certificate of authority in another state. States that do not require a certificate of good standing typically require a certified copy of your articles of incorporation to be included when you file for a certificate of authority.

Costs and Time Frames

Like formation filing fees, state filing fees for foreign-qualifying vary greatly by state and depend upon whether you are qualifying a corporation, an LLC, or a nonprofit. Currently, the least expensive state is Maryland, with a fee of $50 for corporation qualification. The most expensive state is Texas, with a current corporation qualification fee of $750.

You will also need to pay a fee to obtain a certificate of good standing from your state of incorporation. These fees range from $5 to $50. You should allow approximately 2 to 4 weeks to obtain the certificate of good standing; however, most states allow this process to be expedited. Expediting fees for a certificate of good standing range from $5 to $40, and this amount is paid in addition to the standard state fee.

Once you have the certificate of good standing and you send your paperwork to the state or states in which you are foreign-qualifying, you should allow about 4 to 6 weeks for the return of your completed and approved documents. You can also expedite this filing. Expediting the certificate of authority filing typically improves the time frame to 2 to 4 weeks and increases the cost by between $25 and $100.

Virtually all states require foreign-qualified corporations to have a registered agent in the state of qualification. Like the registered agent in the state of incorporation, the registered agent for a foreign corporation must be located at a physical address (not a P.O. box) in the state of qualification and is responsible for receiving important legal and state documents on behalf of the foreign corporation. If your corporation will need to foreign-qualify in a number of states, utilizing a registered agent service provider may be advantageous. For example, suppose you open sales offices in three additional states and must foreign-qualify in these states. You decide to list the office manager for the sales office in each state as the registered agent for your corporation in that state. Do you fully trust that person to ensure that service of process documents and annual statement and franchise tax documents received at the sales office are forwarded to you in a timely manner? In some cases, the answer may be yes, but if the person fails to do this, the results can be damaging to your business. Remember, corporations can get into bad standing with the state for not filing annual statements and paying franchise taxes on time. Additionally, you would not want to miss the opportunity to respond to a service of process if your corporation is being sued in that particular state. Registered agent service providers typically charge an annual fee for their services, but this fee is often worth the peace of mind associated with knowing that a company specializing in this type of service is handling your documents.

Many incorporation service providers and attorneys can facilitate the foreign qualification process for you, and can also provide registered agent services for foreign-qualified businesses. Typically, their foreign-qualification fee will include the preliminary state name availability search, the obtaining of the certificate of good standing from your state of incorporation, and the preparation and filing of the documents necessary to obtain your certificate of authority. As noted previously, the fee charged for registered agent services is typically an annual fee.

CONSEQUENCES OF NOT FOREIGN-QUALIFYING

One of the questions you may be asking is, "What if I don't foreign-qualify with the state in which I am transacting business?" You've read that there are additional costs to this process, since you must file for a certificate of authority with the state and you then are subject to that state's annual statement fees and franchise taxes. Maybe this seems like an unnecessary burden; however, state laws require corporations that are transacting business within their borders to foreign-qualify.

What could happen to your business if you don't foreign-qualify? You lose access to that state's court system until you foreign-qualify. If an employee or customer within a state in which you are transacting business were to sue your corporation, you would not be able to defend the lawsuit in that state's courts because your corporation is not recognized as a business there. Typically, if this happened, your corporation would be given time to undertake the qualification process in order to allow you to defend such a lawsuit.

The second consequence of not foreign-qualifying your business is that if this is later discovered, your corporation will typically be subject to fines and penalties, as well as being liable for the back taxes for the period in which your corporation transacted business in the state without being foreign-qualified. If your company is going to be transacting business in any states outside your state of incorporation, you need to foreign-qualify it in those states. Because what is considered transacting business can be a gray area, you should seek the advice of an attorney if you have questions as to whether your corporation is or will be considered to be transacting business in a particular state.

FOREIGN-QUALIFYING VERSUS INCORPORATING IN MULTIPLE STATES

There is an alternative to foreign-qualifying: You can incorporate your business in the other states in which you intend to transact business. The primary difference is that with foreign qualification, you are notifying the states that a foreign corporation is doing business within their borders. You have a single corporation that is operating and registering in multiple states. If you incorporate your business in multiple states, your corporation becomes a domestic corporation in each of these states, thereby creating separate entities.

The increase in corporate formalities is the biggest disadvantage of forming separate domestic corporations. Corporate formalities and ongoing compliance will be discussed in Chapter 18, but we'll outline a few examples here.

When you create a separate corporation in each state, each of these corporations will have its own stock and its own directors and officers. Each corporation will be required to have its own bylaws and to hold its own meetings of directors and shareholders. Since corporations must record the adoption of and changes to the bylaws, stock purchases and transfers, and resolutions and minutes from directors' and shareholders' meetings, the record keeping associated with corporations greatly increases when you operate multiple domestic corporations.

When you foreign-qualify, there is only one corporation. Regardless of the number of states in which this corporation foreign-qualifies, it will require only one set of directors, officers, and stock. Bylaws will need to be adopted only once, and the holding of and record keeping for annual directors' and shareholders' meetings happen only once.

The advantage of forming a new corporation in each state is the separation of liabilities. For example, if a corporation in one state is forced into bankruptcy, the assets of the corporations in the other states typically would not be used to pay the debts of the bankrupt corporation. If you have foreign-qualified your business in each state, only one corporation exists, so there is no separation of liabilities.

As always, if you have questions regarding your specific business situation, such as whether you should foreign-qualify or incorporate in other states, you should contact an attorney for a legal opinion on the matter.

Other Filings and Items to Consider

There are a number of items complementary to the incorporation process that can be pursued at the time of incorporation or shortly thereafter. Certain Internal Revenue Service (IRS) filings, such as the S corporation election and the obtaining of your employer identification number, are among these items. While not every business may need the items outlined in this chapter, it is beneficial for you to know about them.

> *Major topics covered: This chapter contains information on obtaining the employer identification number (EIN) for your corporation, making the S corporation election with the IRS, purchasing a corporate kit to assist with the formalities required immediately upon formation, obtaining local business licenses, and making certain necessary state tax filings.*

If you choose to use an incorporation service provider or an attorney for your incorporation needs, they may offer some of these services; therefore, we felt it would be beneficial to address them at this point in the book. Furthermore, if you plan to prepare and file your own incorporation paperwork, you will know what steps you need to take in order to obtain each of these items on your own.

IRS ITEMS

There are two IRS-related items that entrepreneurs either consider or often must acquire—the employer identification number and the S corporation election. While the employer identification number is a necessity for businesses that will have employees, the S corporation election is optional.

Employer Identification Number (EIN)

The employer identification number (EIN), often called the federal tax identification number, is a nine-digit number that is assigned to all partnerships, corporations, limited liability companies, estates, trusts, and other entities for tax filing and reporting purposes. The EIN is basically a Social Security number for businesses. It is the identity of that business, as far as the IRS is concerned. Just as a baby needs a Social Security number right after he or she is born, a corporation needs an EIN right after it is created. Also, banks typically require businesses to have an EIN in order to open a business bank account.

If you have been operating your business as a sole proprietorship or general partnership, you will need to apply for a new EIN upon incorporation. The IRS uses the sole proprietor's Social Security number as the identification number for all sole proprietorships. Because a sole proprietor's Social Security number is the sole proprietorship's EIN, this EIN can be used for any number of businesses that the sole proprietor operates. In contrast, an owner of multiple separate corporations requires an EIN for each.

You should wait until you have received your approved incorporation documents from the state before applying for your EIN, since the EIN form requests information from your articles of incorporation. To return to our baby example, you would not apply for your baby's Social Security number before he or she is born. If you think you are having a boy, and apply for a Social Security number for little Ian, but you end up having a girl, you will need to reapply for the Social Security number for little Katie. It is the same for corporations. If you submit your incorporation documentation with the name Dynamic Corporation, apply for your EIN using that name, and then learn from the state that that name is not available, you will have to reapply for your EIN under your new name. It is best to wait until the state has returned your approved articles of incorporation and the formation of your corporation is official before you apply for the EIN.

To apply for an EIN, you must complete IRS Form SS-4, which is shown in Figure 11-1. The information you provide on this form establishes your business tax account with the IRS. The EIN for your corporation will be included on documents such as the W-2s you provide to your employees for tax purposes, and also on any tax payments your corporation makes to the government.

You can download Form SS-4 and the accompanying instructions from the IRS web site at www.irs.gov. There are three ways of applying for an EIN: telephone, fax, or mail. Included on the instruction sheet are the address and the phone and fax numbers for the IRS service center responsible for the state in which your corporation's principal office is located. This is the contact information you should use when applying for your EIN.

Obtaining your EIN by phone is the quickest method. In order to apply and obtain your EIN by phone, you should complete Form SS-4 and have that information ready when you call. The IRS representative will ask for the information included on this form, and will then provide your EIN over the phone. You may be asked to fax or mail a copy of your SS-4 to the service center that processed your phone call. Note that when you apply by phone, the person making the call must be authorized to sign Form SS-4 or be an authorized designee, such as an incorporation service provider, an attorney, or an accountant. Not every regional IRS office permits telephone application for an EIN. The instruction sheet for the SS-4 gives phone numbers for the locations that allow this practice.

When you apply for your EIN by fax, you should receive your number, also by fax, from the IRS within about 4 business days. When you apply by mail, you should receive your EIN by mail in approximately 4 to 5 weeks. Keep in mind that processing times can change. Events such as budget constraints, departmental changes, and world events can cause a delay in the processing times quoted by the IRS.

As previously mentioned, if you elect to use an incorporation service provider or an attorney when you incorporate your business, these providers will most likely offer to apply for and/or obtain the EIN on behalf of your company. There is typically an additional charge for this service. In some cases, the provider may insert the information it has regarding your corporation into Form SS-4 and provide it to you; you would then supply any additional information that is needed and sign the form. After that, you would either call the IRS or fax or mail the form to the IRS to obtain your EIN. In other cases, the provider may complete most of the form, mail it to you for insertion of any missing information and your signature, and then obtain the number on your behalf.

S Corporation Election

When you form a for-profit corporation, it is automatically created as a standard C corporation. However, if your corporation meets the necessary criteria, you have the option to elect a different tax status with the

FIGURE 11-1

IRS Form SS-4

Form **SS-4**
(Rev. December 2001)
Department of the Treasury
Internal Revenue Service

Application for Employer Identification Number
(For use by employers, corporations, partnerships, trusts, estates, churches, government agencies, Indian tribal entities, certain individuals, and others.)
▶ See separate instructions for each line. ▶ Keep a copy for your records.

EIN

OMB No. 1545-0003

1 Legal name of entity (or individual) for whom the EIN is being requested

2 Trade name of business (if different from name on line 1)   **3** Executor, trustee, "care of" name

4a Mailing address (room, apt., suite no. and street, or P.O. box)   **5a** Street address (if different) (Do not enter a P.O. box.)

4b City, state, and ZIP code   **5b** City, state, and ZIP code

6 County and state where principal business is located

7a Name of principal officer, general partner, grantor, owner, or trustor   **7b** SSN, ITIN, or EIN

8a Type of entity (check only one box)
☐ Sole proprietor (SSN)
☐ Partnership
☐ Corporation (enter form number to be filed) ▶
☐ Personal service corp.
☐ Church or church-controlled organization
☐ Other nonprofit organization (specify) ▶
☐ Other (specify) ▶

☐ Estate (SSN of decedent)
☐ Plan administrator (SSN)
☐ Trust (SSN of grantor)
☐ National Guard ☐ State/local government
☐ Farmers' cooperative ☐ Federal government/military
☐ REMIC ☐ Indian tribal governments/enterprises
Group Exemption Number (GEN) ▶

8b If a corporation, name the state or foreign country (if applicable) where incorporated   State   Foreign country

9 Reason for applying (check only one box)
☐ Started new business (specify type) ▶
☐ Hired employees (Check the box and see line 12.)
☐ Compliance with IRS withholding regulations
☐ Other (specify) ▶

☐ Banking purpose (specify purpose) ▶
☐ Changed type of organization (specify new type) ▶
☐ Purchased going business
☐ Created a trust (specify type) ▶
☐ Created a pension plan (specify type) ▶

10 Date business started or acquired (month, day, year)   **11** Closing month of accounting year

12 First date wages or annuities were paid or will be paid (month, day, year). **Note:** *If applicant is a withholding agent, enter date income will first be paid to nonresident alien. (month, day, year)* . . . . ▶

13 Highest number of employees expected in the next 12 months. **Note:** *If the applicant does not expect to have any employees during the period, enter "-0-."* . . . . ▶   Agricultural   Household   Other

14 Check **one** box that best describes the principal activity of your business. ☐ Health care & social assistance ☐ Wholesale–agent/broker
☐ Construction ☐ Rental & leasing ☐ Transportation & warehousing ☐ Accommodation & food service ☐ Wholesale–other ☐ Retail
☐ Real estate ☐ Manufacturing ☐ Finance & insurance ☐ Other (specify)

15 Indicate principal line of merchandise sold; specific construction work done; products produced; or services provided.

16a Has the applicant ever applied for an employer identification number for this or any other business? . . . . . ☐ Yes ☐ No
Note: *If "Yes," please complete lines 16b and 16c.*

16b If you checked "Yes" on line 16a, give applicant's legal name and trade name shown on prior application if different from line 1 or 2 above.
Legal name ▶   Trade name ▶

16c Approximate date when, and city and state where, the application was filed. Enter previous employer identification number if known.
Approximate date when filed (mo., day, year)   City and state where filed   Previous EIN

Complete this section **only** if you want to authorize the named individual to receive the entity's EIN and answer questions about the completion of this form.

Third Party Designee
Designee's name   Designee's telephone number (include area code) ( )
Address and ZIP code   Designee's fax number (include area code) ( )

Under penalties of perjury, I declare that I have examined this application, and to the best of my knowledge and belief, it is true, correct, and complete.
Applicant's telephone number (include area code) ( )

Name and title (type or print clearly) ▶
Applicant's fax number (include area code) ( )

Signature ▶   Date ▶

For Privacy Act and Paperwork Reduction Act Notice, see separate instructions.   Cat. No. 16055N   Form **SS-4** (Rev. 12-2001)

IRS. Electing to have your corporation taxed under subchapter S of the Internal Revenue Code allows for pass-through taxation. With pass-through taxation, the profits and losses of the business pass through the corporation and are reported on the owners' personal tax returns.

In order to elect S corporation status, you must file Form 2553 with the IRS. This form must be filed no later than the fifteenth day of the third month of the tax year in which the election is to take effect. To put that in simpler terms, if your corporation is a calendar-year taxpayer, and you wish to have it taxed as an S corporation starting in the year 2004, you would need to file Form 2553 with the IRS no later than March 15, 2004. You could still make the election after that date, such as in June or November of 2004, but your corporation would not be taxed as an S corporation until tax year 2005. Page one of Form 2553 is included as Figure 11-2, showing you the information that is required. Page two of Form 2553 is required only if your company will not be a calendar-year taxpayer. Page two is not included in this figure, but both pages and instructions for completing this form can be viewed on and downloaded from the IRS web site.

As Chapter 2 outlined, there are restrictions on becoming an S corporation. In order to be approved for S corporation status, the corporation must satisfy the following requirements:

- It must have fewer than 75 shareholders
- Shareholders must be individuals, estates, or certain qualified trusts
- All shareholders must consent in writing to the election of S corporation status
- Shareholders cannot be nonresident aliens
- The corporation can have only one class of stock (disregarding voting rights)

You will need to apply for an EIN for your corporation prior to filing Form 2553 to make the S corporation election. Form 2553 requires your EIN, but the IRS allows you to put "applied for" in this area if you have not yet received the number.

To file Form 2553, you must either mail or fax the original form to the IRS service center responsible for the state in which your corporation's principal business office is located. You will receive notification from the IRS as to whether the election was accepted and, if so, when it will take effect. Generally, you will receive notice from the IRS approximately 60 days after your form is received, unless you select a tax year ending on a date other than December 31. If you choose a noncalendar tax year, additional information must be included on the form, and the IRS processing time may be lengthened.

As with the paperwork for the EIN, incorporation service providers and attorneys often offer preparation of Form 2553 as an additional service.

FIGURE 11-2

IRS Form 2553

Form **2553** (Rev. July 1999) Department of the Treasury Internal Revenue Service	**Election by a Small Business Corporation** (Under section 1362 of the Internal Revenue Code) ▶ See Parts II and III on back and the separate instructions. ▶ The corporation may either send or fax this form to the IRS. See page 1 of the instructions.	OMB No. 1545-0146

Notes: 1. This election to be an S corporation can be accepted only if all the tests are met under **Who may elect** on page 1 of the instructions; all signatures in Parts I and III are originals (no photocopies); and the exact name and address of the corporation and other required form information are provided.
2. Do not file **Form 1120S**, U.S. Income Tax Return for an S Corporation, for any tax year before the year the election takes effect.
3. If the corporation was in existence before the effective date of this election, see **Taxes an S corporation may owe** on page 1 of the instructions.

Part I   Election Information

Please Type or Print

	Name of corporation (see instructions)	**A** Employer identification number
	Number, street, and room or suite no. (If a P.O. box, see instructions.)	**B** Date incorporated
	City or town, state, and ZIP code	**C** State of incorporation

D Election is to be effective for tax year beginning (month, day, year) . . . . ▶   /   /

E Name and title of officer or legal representative who the IRS may call for more information

F Telephone number of officer or legal representative
(   )

G If the corporation changed its name or address after applying for the EIN shown in **A** above, check this box . . . . ▶ ☐

H If this election takes effect for the first tax year the corporation exists, enter month, day, and year of the **earliest** of the following: (1) date the corporation first had shareholders, (2) date the corporation first had assets, or (3) date the corporation began doing business . . . . ▶   /   /

I Selected tax year: Annual return will be filed for tax year ending (month and day) ▶. . . . .
If the tax year ends on any date other than December 31, except for an automatic 52-53-week tax year ending with reference to the month of December, you **must** complete Part II on the back. If the date you enter is the ending date of an automatic 52-53-week tax year, write "52-53-week year" to the right of the date. See Temporary Regulations section 1.441-2T(e)(3).

J Name and address of each shareholder; shareholder's spouse having a community property interest in the corporation's stock; and each tenant in common, joint tenant, and tenant by the entirety. (A husband and wife (and their estates) are counted as one shareholder in determining the number of shareholders without regard to the manner in which the stock is owned.)	**K** Shareholders' Consent Statement. Under penalties of perjury, we declare that we consent to the election of the above-named corporation to be an S corporation under section 1362(a) and that we have examined this consent statement, including accompanying schedules and statements, and to the best of our knowledge and belief, it is true, correct, and complete. We understand our consent is binding and may not be withdrawn after the corporation has made a valid election. (Shareholders sign and date below.)		**L** Stock owned		**M** Social security number or employer identification number (see instructions)	**N** Shareholder's tax year ends (month and day)
	Signature	Date	Number of shares	Dates acquired		

Under penalties of perjury, I declare that I have examined this election, including accompanying schedules and statements, and to the best of my knowledge and belief, it is true, correct, and complete.

Signature of officer ▶   Title ▶   Date ▶

For Paperwork Reduction Act Notice, see page 2 of the instructions.   Cat. No. 18629R   Form **2553** (Rev. 7-99)

Typically, these providers will complete Form 2553 with as much information as they have for your corporation, then give the form to you. You must then insert any missing information, obtain the signatures of all shareholders of your corporation, and send the form to the IRS.

CORPORATE KIT

The corporate kit, also called a corporate binder, is a group of materials that has been created to assist you with your corporate formalities and help you to keep your corporate records in one place. There are a variety of corporate kits; however, standard materials that are typically included are:

- A binder and often a matching slipcase (which may be customized with your corporate name), varying in cost and quality
- A number of stock certificates for your corporation
- A stock transfer ledger for recording stock transactions
- A metal seal for stamping corporate documents with the corporation's official seal
- Sample forms, such as sample bylaws and directors' or shareholders' meeting minutes

While having a binder customized with your corporate name is not a necessity, it can help you differentiate this book from the other binders and books that you may have in your office or that the secretary of your corporation might keep.

The most inexpensive corporate kits may not include stock certificates that have been customized with your corporation's name and state of incorporation. They may, however, include standard stock certificate templates in which you insert the necessary information. You present stock certificates to the owners of your company as they purchase shares in your corporation. The certificates include the date on which the shares were purchased, the name of the purchaser, the number of shares purchased, and the signature of an authorized officer or director of the company.

The stock transfer ledger is a book used for recording transfers, meaning both sales and purchases, of shares in your corporation. For example, the directors of Strong Builders Corp. decide to issue 50 shares of stock to each of the officers they elected. The directors would record in the stock transfer ledger the names of those officers, the dates on which the stock was issued, and the number of shares issued. If one of these officers leaves the company and is required to sell the shares back, this transaction will also be recorded in the stock transfer ledger.

If you purchase a very basic corporate kit—for example, from a legal supply store—it may not include the corporate seal. In that case, you may have to special-order that item. The corporate seal includes your corporate name and the state, month, and year of incorporation. When you press a document with the seal, it leaves an imprint of the seal on that document, thereby signifying that it is an official corporate document. Some areas of the country, such as New York City, require a corporate seal to open a bank account. Other states do not require corporations to have a corporate seal at all. Seals come as handheld metal seals or stand-alone desk seals.

Corporate kits often include sample forms, such as bylaws, that business owners can use as a template when customizing these documents for their businesses. If you use an attorney for your incorporation needs, it is possible that bylaws and forms customized for your corporation will be included as part of the attorney's service fee.

If you use an incorporation service provider to file your incorporation documents, that company will probably either offer a corporate kit as part of an incorporation package or allow you to select a corporate kit as an add-on item to a standard service. If you prepare and file your own incorporation paperwork, and you decide you would like to purchase a corporate kit, you can do so at legal supply stores or at some office supply stores. You can also do a keyword search on an Internet search engine, such as Google or Yahoo!, on the words "corporate kit" to find providers of this product. Most incorporation service providers will let you purchase a corporate kit from them even if they did not process your incorporation. As mentioned previously, attorneys typically include a corporate kit as part of their service fee; however, if you use an attorney to prepare and file your incorporation documents, you may wish to ask about this in order to ensure that a corporate kit will be included in the materials you receive.

The use of a corporate kit to help you comply with a corporation's required formalities will be discussed in more detail in Chapter 18.

LOCAL BUSINESS LICENSES

Depending on your type of business, you may be required to obtain state and local business licenses. Examples of local business licenses include liquor licenses and sales permits. Some states require most businesses to obtain business licenses, while other states require only certain types of businesses to be licensed.

Business licenses can be mandated at both the state and the local (either city or county) level. At the state level, there is often a body called the Department of Licensing, or something similar, that regulates and issues business licenses. At the local level, the city or county recorder often has this responsibility. Requirements differ from state to state, and often even between counties within a state. It is advisable to research the types of licenses your business may need, and to learn ahead of time what must be done to obtain these licenses.

Some states provide business license information online. In other states, you must call the appropriate state and local bodies for this information. A good example of a state where the necessary information is accessible online is California. The CalGold web site at www.calgold.ca.gov helps business owners learn what licenses are required for their businesses and how to obtain them. When you use this site, you first enter a keyword that describes your business type. The site will then display matches for that keyword within its system. You select the match that best describes your business, select your county, select your city, and then receive a list of business licenses and other information. For each item included on the list, the appropriate agency and its address and phone number are given. The list also displays information on items such as state income taxes and workers' compensation.

STATE TAX FILINGS

There are a couple of filings that you may be required to make at the state level for tax purposes. A few states require businesses to obtain a state tax identification number. Just as the IRS requires businesses to have an identifier (the EIN), some states require businesses that are incorporated or transacting business in that state to obtain a state tax identification number. This number does not replace the EIN issued to you by the IRS. It is used for creating a record for your company with the state's tax department.

A state tax filing that new corporations are often required to make is a sales tax permit filing. "Sales tax permit" is one of the many names states have for this document. The name differs by state, with other names including "sales tax number," "sales tax license," or "reseller's permit." The sales tax permit is required in order for businesses to collect sales taxes, which are taxes that states impose on retail sales. The permit is typically filed with the state department of revenue or department of taxation. The detailed state information tables on Business Filings' web site provide information on some of each state's tax requirements.

If your corporation makes the S corporation election with the IRS, you may be required to file a separate state S corporation election. States that require a separate state S corporation election, such as California, will not recognize a corporation's S corporation status until this separate election has been received and approved by the state. There are also some states, such as Texas, that do not recognize the S corporation election at the federal level. When a state does not recognize S corporation status, the corporation must pay state taxes at the corporate level.

The states' requirements for licenses and tax filings differ greatly, as do the fees imposed by the states. Costs are typically low, but they vary both by state and by type of license. It is advisable that you research your state and local license and taxation requirements, either when your business is still in the conceptual stage or once you've started the incorporation process. You should obtain any necessary licenses after the incorporation of your business is completed, to ensure that licenses and tax permits are obtained using your state-approved corporate name.

DIVISIONS AND SUBSIDIARIES

While this isn't a filing that businesses typically need to undertake upon incorporating, it is another item to consider. There may come a time in the life of your business when you wish to operate a second business or multiple businesses out of your existing corporation or to have your business start on a new path through a separate division. No separate state filing is required in order to create a division. Commonly, divisions focus on different types of business from the parent, and therefore different names are often desired. In these cases, your corporation could file for a DBA (doing business as) name, which is often called an assumed name or fictitious name, for each of your divisions. This allows your divisions to transact business under a name other than your corporate name. Corporate DBA filings were introduced in Chapter 7. They are often undertaken at the county level, but some states require corporations to file DBAs at the state level.

If your state of incorporation is one that requires a specific business-purpose clause (rather than a general-purpose clause) in the articles of incorporation, you may need to amend your articles of incorporation to account for the different type of business that your corporation will now be engaging in. For example, suppose you own a restaurant and you wish to offer T-shirts, mugs, and hats for sale both in your restaurant and from a kiosk at the airport. You could create a division focused on selling the merchandise. If the specific business-purpose clause in your articles of incorporation reads "eating establishment," you will need to change your business purpose to reflect the new business activity your corporation is engaging in. In order to amend the articles of incorporation, a certificate of amendment must be filed with the secretary of state and the necessary filing fees paid.

Another option would be to incorporate a new corporation that would be owned by your existing corporation. The newly formed corporation is commonly called a subsidiary corporation, because it is owned and controlled by the existing or "parent" corporation. The primary advantage to forming a subsidiary is the separation of liabilities. For example, if the subsidiary is forced into bankruptcy, the assets of the parent corporation typically cannot be used to pay the debts of the subsidiary corporation (just as your personal assets typically cannot be used to pay the debts of your corporation). If the same situation occurred in a corporation with multiple divisions using DBAs, the assets of the different parts of the corporation's business would not be considered separate, and all the corporation's assets could therefore be used to satisfy the debts of the failed division.

The expense of forming a subsidiary corporation is the primary disadvantage of this method, but, as you can see, there are limited liability benefits for your existing corporation. This may not be relevant to your business when you are in the start-up phase, or even if you are incorporating an existing business that was a sole proprietorship or partnership, but you may encounter a need for it later in the life of your business. Therefore, we wanted you to have information on divisions and subsidiaries in the back of your mind.

CHAPTER 12

Incorporation Case Studies

The first 11 chapters of this book were aimed at helping you to understand what a corporation is and how it functions, and what the incorporation process entails. This chapter presents two case studies that tie this information together, taking you through the process from start to finish. The previous chapters often included general information and price ranges. This chapter focuses on two specific states and uses information specific to those states.

> *Major topics covered: This chapter includes case studies on a home-state incorporation in Oregon and an incorporation in Delaware. Both step through the incorporation process from deciding which entity to form through filing the necessary paperwork with the states.*

These case studies are completely fictitious. Also, although the fees quoted were current at the writing of this book, they may have changed by the time you are reading it.

CASE STUDY 1: HOME-STATE INCORPORATION IN OREGON

Andrew and Julie are planning to start a business. They would like to open a small store that buys and sells used children's clothing and associated products, particularly baby clothing and items such as cribs, high chairs, and car seats. They first had to decide which type of business entity to form.

Andrew and Julie researched each type of business structure available to them, and decided that protecting their personal assets is important. Since C and S corporations and limited liability companies (LLCs) all offer limited liability, they narrowed their choices to these entities. Additionally, they felt that pass-through taxation would be advantageous in their situation, and therefore they eliminated the C corporation.

They considered their long-range goals: If the initial store is successful, they would like to expand into other markets. They thought that their expansion would initially be geographic within the state of Oregon, but they didn't want to rule out the possibility of expanding into other states as their business grows. They also felt that if they needed to seek outside funding, they would turn to friends and family rather than outside investors. They wanted to keep the ownership of their company relatively small, and therefore, if they selected the S corporation, they planned to authorize a relatively low number of shares.

Up to this point, the LLC and the S corporation were close contenders. However, the S corporation proved more advantageous because of its treatment of self-employment taxes (FICA taxes). As Chapter 2 highlighted, with S corporations, the salaries paid to employee-owners are subject to FICA taxes; however, distributions from corporate profits typically are not subject to FICA taxes, as long as the salaries are reasonable. With LLCs, in most circumstances, all distributions to member-employees are subject to FICA taxes.

Andrew and Julie concluded that the S corporation would be the best option for their new venture. It afforded them limited liability, which was their top concern, as well as pass-through taxation, which they felt would be advantageous. The S corporation still allowed them to easily raise capital for their venture through the sale of stock, if they chose to follow that path. The unlimited life aspect of the corporation was also appealing to them. If either of them decided to leave the business, the company could continue to operate.

The state of incorporation was a harder decision to make. Andrew and Julie planned to locate their initial store in their home state of Oregon. While their business would initially transact business primarily within their home state, they hoped their venture would prove successful enough to allow them to eventually expand into other states. They researched the cost of incorporating in their home state versus incorporating in Delaware. The filing fees were similar: The state filing fee to form a corporation in Oregon was $50, and that in Delaware was $74. If they incorporated in Delaware, they believed that they would probably need to foreign-qualify in Oregon. If they did expand into other states, they would probably also need to foreign-qualify in those states.

After further discussion and review, they decided that incorporating in their home state was the best option. While they hoped to expand geographically in the future, it would be quite some time before that became a reality, if it ever did. Also, they planned to limit the number of shareholders of their corporation and to authorize a small number of shares, with the result that they would have a simple capitalization structure. Because of these aspects, they didn't consider the benefits of Delaware to be that advantageous to their corporation, and they did not want to incur the increased cost of incorporating in Delaware and also registering as a foreign corporation in Oregon.

Their next decision was whether to prepare and file their own incorporation documents or to seek assistance. Having researched the state fees, they knew that the cost of undertaking the process themselves was minimal; however, the time involved was a bigger concern. They preferred to spend their time on preparing to open the store, rather than on paperwork. Their attorney offered to handle this process for them, quoting a fee in the range of $500 to $700.

They also researched incorporation service providers like Business Filings Incorporated. They found that if they used Business Filings, they would incur a service charge of $130 plus the Oregon state filing fee, bringing the total to $180 for a basic corporation formation. Business Filings also offered a complete formation service that included expedited filing service, a corporate kit, the preparation of the S corporation election document, the obtaining of the EIN, and a disk with sample forms to help them comply with corporate formalities. The cost of this option would be $310 plus the Oregon state fee, bringing the total to $360. Business Filings would not assist them in obtaining their state or local business licenses, but since the company provided the other elements that Andrew and Julie sought, they decided to use Business Filings.

Andrew and Julie had formulated their incorporation road map; however, before beginning the process, they needed to determine a few other items. What would they name their company? They came up with a list of names and sought feedback on those names. Of the names on their list, the name Rerun Kids was their favorite. Since Oregon required a corporate ending of *corporation, company, incorporated, limited,* or an abbreviation of one of those words, they decided to name their corporation Rerun Kids, Inc.

While they did not plan to sell any of their products online initially, they still felt that a web presence was necessary. They checked the availability of the domain name www.rerunkids.com and found that it was available. They also ran a free trademark search on the U.S. Patent and Trademark Office's web site. This search showed no registered or pending marks on the name Rerun Kids, Inc. Knowing that Business Filings would conduct a preliminary name check in the state of incorporation once they placed their order, they decided not to undertake the name search on their own. They purchased the domain name, ordered a comprehensive trademark search, and prepared to place their order with Business Filings.

While evaluating incorporation service providers, they reviewed Business Filings' online order form to see what information was required. Figure 12-1 illustrates Business Filings' order form questions for corporation formations in any state. Prior to ordering, they determined who would act as the directors for the corporation, how many shares of stock they wished to authorize, and the par value of those shares. Business Filings also asks for officer information on the order form. Even though Massachusetts is currently the only state that requires officer information to be included in the formation document, Business Filings collects this information in all states, if it has already been determined. (With small businesses, one or two people often hold all officer positions. With many closely held companies, such as this one, the same person or persons are shareholders, directors, and officers.) Even though officers are typically not appointed until the initial meeting of directors, many owners of small businesses determine who will hold these positions prior to holding the meeting and officially appointing the officers.

Andrew and Julie also determined that they would order the complete formation package, meaning that Business Filings would prepare the IRS documents for making the S corporation election and for obtaining the EIN. The package also included expediting the filing with the state of Oregon. Andrew and Julie had their state-approved articles of incorporation in 8 business days.

CASE STUDY 2: DELAWARE INCORPORATION

While Ben was a college student, he worked part-time testing and reviewing various products and technologies for companies in order to earn money. By the time he was finishing college, demand for his services had become quite high. After graduating, he decided to start a company and make this his full-time job.

Considering the high demand for his services, Ben felt that if he marketed his testing services correctly, he could get national and possibly international customers. He believed that companies were always in

Sample Business Filings Incorporated Order Form Questions

Assuming you have selected to form a for-profit corporation using Business Filings Incorporated, these are the questions you would incur during the order process. Service options would also be selected at the time of ordering, but are not included in this example.

Company Name: Your company name will be filed with the state exactly as it is entered below. The name must include a corporate identifier such as Incorporated, Corporation, Company, Limited, or an abbreviation thereof.

First choice:_____   Second Choice:_____

State of incorporation:_____

Principal Business Activity/Purpose:_____
_____

Order contact information
Name:_____
Address:_____
City, State, Zip:_____
Phone number:_____   Fax number:_____
Email:_____

Legal Address for order: (This is asked incase the order contact address is not the same as the legal address of the corporation–for example, if an accountant is placing orders on behalf of clients.)
Name:_____
Address:_____
City, State, Zip:_____
Phone number:_____

Directors: (Only one director is required in most states.)
Name:_____   Name:_____
Address:_____   Address: _____

Name:_____   Name:_____
Address:_____   Address: _____

Company Officers:
Pres._____   Vice Pres._____
Sec._____   Treas. _____

Stock: Unless you instruct otherwise, the corporation will be authorized to issue up to 2000 shares of $0.01 par value common stock. Please note: in some states an increase in the number of shares may affect the state filing fees.
Shares:_____   Par Value:_____

Registered Agent: States require corporations to have a registered agent within the state of incorporation. The registered agent is responsible for accepting service of process and other important documents for the corporation.
___ Check here to select Business Filings as your registered agent.
___ If registered agent will not be Business Filings, include name and address (no P.O. boxes).

Name:_____
Address: _____

need of an outside opinion regarding their new developments. His objectivity and his previous testing experience had provided a solid list of customers who were interested in retaining his services. Understanding that some testing might need to be conducted in person, Ben decided to focus on tests that could be done from remote locations, such as testing software products. He could arrange it so that companies could ship their products to him for testing and review.

Being a recent college graduate, Ben did not have much capital available for marketing his business or for hiring additional testers. He determined that he would need to seek funding from outside investors. Considering the company's growth potential, he felt that seeking venture capital (VC) funding would be the best way to raise the money necessary to get his business off the ground. Because of this, Ben decided to seek the advice of an attorney regarding how to best structure his business.

As Ben researched the VC funding process, he also researched the different types of business structures. When he met with his attorney and discussed his business plans, the attorney advised him to form a C corporation in Delaware. Ben's attorney advised him to create a more complex capitalization structure by having a larger number of authorized shares and different classes of stock, as this would allow him to offer different types and levels of ownership in his corporation to outside investors. Because of this more complex capitalization structure, Ben's attorney advised incorporation in Delaware. Additionally, because of Delaware's potentially lower costs for corporations with a large number of authorized shares and its corporate-friendly laws and court system, many venture capitalists prefer to have the companies in which they invest formed as Delaware corporations. Ben accepted his attorney's advice and decided to incorporate his business in Delaware.

Because of Ben's desire to attract outside investors, his attorney advised him to authorize a larger number of shares and to authorize both common and preferred shares of stock. Common stock is the primary stock of the corporation; it gives shareholders ownership and voting rights and the right to receive a proportionate share of any dividends distributed by the corporation and of the corporation's assets should it dissolve. Preferred stock generally provides the shareholder with preferential payment of dividends and assets upon dissolution, but does not provide the shareholder with voting rights. (Common and preferred stock will be discussed in more depth in Chapter 16, on capitalization.) Ben's attorney recommended that Ben's corporation authorize a total of 10,000,000 shares, with 8,500,000 being shares of common stock and 1,500,000 being shares of preferred stock. All shares would have a par value of $0.01.

Since Ben worked with an attorney for advice on starting and structuring his business, and planned to seek his attorney's assistance in customizing the contracts he would be using with his outside investors, he decided to have the attorney prepare and file his incorporation paperwork. Ben considered doing this himself and just using his attorney for the document customization; however, he opted to ask his attorney to assist with customizing the certificate of incorporation in Delaware to prepare for the director and shareholder roles that future investors would most likely take in Ben's corporation. Since Ben planned to seek funding relatively soon after incorporating his business, he felt that it was important to include this in his formation paperwork.

Because Ben would initially be running the business from his apartment in Colorado, his attorney also advised him to foreign-qualify his business there. Ben envisioned serving most of his clients from this location and taking most of his orders over the phone or through his web site. He would have at least one employee in the state (himself), and he would be accepting and fulfilling orders from this location. In addition, it was likely that Ben would be opening a bank account for his business in the state of Colorado. Reviewing these factors, his attorney advised that his operations met the definition of transacting business within the state of Colorado. Therefore, foreign qualification in Colorado was necessary.

Deciding to name his company Test Venture Corp., Ben performed an availability search for the domain name www.testventure.com and found that it was available. He also performed an initial trademark search on the U.S. Patent and Trademark Office's web site. There were no live or pending marks on this name, but Ben felt that it was also necessary to undertake a comprehensive trademark search. After taking these steps, Ben contacted his attorney to begin the incorporation process.

One issue that Ben needed to consider was the registered agent. Since he was located in Colorado, he could not act as his own registered agent, and his attorney did not offer this service. Ben checked the Delaware Division of Corporations web site and found a list of registered agents in Delaware. After researching a few companies, Ben selected Business Filings Incorporated because it offered registered agent services to companies even if the incorporation process was carried out by another provider.

After selecting his name and finding a registered agent, Ben was ready to proceed with the incorporation process. He was not under any time pressure to have the corporation formed, and therefore he did not request his attorney to expedite the filing.

Because his corporation planned to authorize a greater number of shares of stock in anticipation of future VC shareholders, he was subject to higher state filing fees. The large number of shares caused the standard Delaware corporation formation fee of $74 to increase by $30, to $104.

Because Delaware is a state that ties filing fees and annual franchise taxes to the number of authorized shares a corporation has, Ben may incur higher annual franchise taxes for his corporation as well. As the Delaware page on Business Filings' web site outlines, if a corporation has over 10,000 authorized shares, the franchise tax can be calculated in two ways. One way is based on each increment of 10,000 shares, and the other is based on the total gross assets of the corporation and factors in the par value of the shares. Until Ben knows the total gross assets, it is unclear which method his corporation should use for calculating annual franchise taxes. It is fairly common, however, for a corporation with a large number of shares, a low par value, and a relatively small amount of assets to use the gross asset method for calculating annual franchise taxes. This method can provide a lower tax than the shares-only method. It may also provide a lower tax than other states might charge for the same number of authorized shares, had Ben decided to incorporate in another state.

The attorney's fee for the incorporation was approximately $2000, which included the legal advice that Ben received, the preparation and filing of Ben's certificate of incorporation in Delaware, a corporate kit, and the customization of Ben's corporate bylaws. Ben's attorney filed with Delaware by fax, which speeds the standard turnaround time, and Ben had the state-approved documents in about 2 weeks.

Figure 12-2 is the state-approved certificate of incorporation for this fictitious company. Because this document uses the official format of Delaware's fax-filed certificates of incorporation and was provided for use in this book by the Delaware Secretary of State Division of Corporations, the word *sample* appears across the document.

As previously mentioned, the attorney in this case study filed the certificate of incorporation with Delaware by fax. In states that allow electronic or fax filing, such as Delaware, the approved documents are typically returned by fax, and thus may not look as "formal" as you might expect. The state approval is included in the upper right-hand corner of the document, as you can see in Figure 12-2, and this electronic "stamp" signifies the official nature of this document. However, if a certified copy of the certificate of incorporation is obtained, or if the filing is submitted by mail, a certification page on Delaware letterhead will be attached to the certificate of incorporation attesting that the certificate of incorporation is a true and correct copy.

FIGURE 12-2

State of Delaware Sample Certificate of Incorporation

STATE OF DELAWARE
SECRETARY OF STATE
DIVISION OF CORPORATIONS
FILED 09:00 AM 08/08/2002
022002613 – 2405329

CERTIFICATE OF INCORPORATION
OF
Test Venture Corp.

FIRST: The name of the corporation is: **Test Venture Corp.**

SECOND: The address of the registered office of the corporation in the State of Delaware is located at:

9 E. Loockerman St., Suite 205
Dover, Delaware 19901
Located in the County of Kent

The name of the registered agent at that address is:
BUSINESS FILINGS INTERNATIONAL, INC.

THIRD: The purpose of the corporation is to engage in any lawful act or activity for which corporations may be organized under the Delaware General Corporation Law.

FOURTH: The total number of shares that the corporation is authorized to issue is 10,000,000 shares, consisting of 8,500,000 shares of common stock, par value $0.01 per share, and 1,500,000 shares of preferred stock, par value $0.01 per share. The board of directors is hereby expressly granted the authority to issue the preferred stock from time to time in one or more classes or series and by resolution or resolutions to establish the number of shares to be included in each such class or series and to fix the designations, powers, preferences and rights of the shares of each such class or series and the qualifications, limitations and restrictions thereof.

FIFTH: No director of the corporation shall be personally liable to the corporation or its stockholders for monetary damages for breach of fiduciary duty as a director; provided, however, that the foregoing clause shall not apply to any liability of a director (i) for any breach of the director's duty of loyalty to the corporation or its stockholders, (ii) for acts or omissions not in good faith or which involve intentional misconduct or a knowing violation of law, (iii) under Section 174 of the General Corporation Law of the State of Delaware, or (iv) for any transaction from which the director derived an improper personal benefit. This Article shall not eliminate or limit the liability of a director for any act or omission occurring prior to the time this Article became effective.

SIXTH: The name and address of the incorporator is My Attorney, My Attorney's Law Firm, 1000 Fictitious Street, Fictitious City, CO 80000.

SEVENTH: The board of directors shall consist of not fewer than 3 and not more than 9 directors, as fixed from time to time by vote of a majority of the entire board of directors. The number of directors shall be 3 until otherwise fixed. Any director elected to fill any vacancy on the board of directors, whether created by reason of death, resignation, removal or increase in the number of directors, shall hold office for the remainder of the full term of the class of directors in which the vacancy occurred or the new directorship was created. Notwithstanding that some lesser percentage may be specified by law, this certificate of incorporation or the bylaws, a director may be removed from office only for cause and then only with the affirmative vote of the holders of at least 75% of the voting power of all outstanding shares of capital stock of the corporation then entitled to vote generally at an election of directors.

I, the undersigned, being the incorporator, for the purpose of forming a corporation under the laws of the State of Delaware do make, file, and record this Certificate of Incorporation and do certify that the facts herein are true.

My Attorney
My Attorney's Law Firm

Dated: August 7, 2002

As you will see, this document follows much the same format as the sample Delaware certificate of incorporation shown in Figure 8-1. However, the certificate of incorporation for Test Venture Corp. incorporates provisions that were addressed during this case study. The registered agent is listed as Business Filings. A general-purpose business clause was utilized, which is standard for corporation filings in Delaware. The fourth clause outlines the larger number of shares this corporation will authorize and sets the par value for these shares. An indemnification clause is included. The incorporator's information in included in the sixth clause; in this case, it is the fictitious address for our fictitious attorney. The seventh clause includes information on the number of directors, director vacancies, and director removal (this is not required information, but it was included for this case study because of Test Venture Corp.'s desire to seek venture capital funding). While Chapter 8 included sample articles of incorporation for several states, this figure is meant to provide a more realistic example of filed documents.

YOU'VE INCORPORATED; NOW WHAT?

Now that both Rerun Kids, Inc., and Test Venture Corp. are incorporated, they need to address items such as holding the initial meeting of directors and shareholders, creating and ratifying bylaws, and establishing a bank account. Part Three of this book addresses the steps business owners should take after incorporating their businesses, and also a number of the annual requirements that corporations face.

After Incorporating

Initial Meetings

One of the first steps a business should take after incorporating is to hold its initial meetings of directors and shareholders. These meetings, particularly the initial meeting of directors, complete the formation process, since major corporate actions, such as appointing officers and adopting the corporate bylaws, take place at these meetings. Also, the directors lay the groundwork that enables the corporation to begin business. Even if you've operated your business prior to incorporating, the initial meeting of directors is still important.

> *Major topics covered: This chapter addresses the initial meeting of directors and the initial meeting of shareholders. It includes information on the procedures for calling, holding, and documenting these meetings, and also outlines the items typically addressed during these meetings.*

State law requires corporations to comply with a number of formalities. Holding initial meetings of directors and shareholders is part of these requirements, as is holding annual meetings thereafter. Documenting these meetings and the actions taken at them is another requirement. This and the following chapters are aimed at helping you understand the requirements that businesses face after incorporating. As you read the chapters in this section of the book, remember that small corporations differ from publicly traded corporations. If you operate a corporation with only one shareholder who also acts as a director and officer, you still need to comply with corporate formalities, such as initial and annual meetings of directors and shareholders. However, these requirements do not need to be as time-consuming or intimidating as they might at first sound. Throughout this chapter and this section of the book, we will address the differences between public companies and closely held companies with regard to undertaking these necessary steps.

INITIAL MEETING OF DIRECTORS

The initial meeting of directors, often called the organizational meeting, is extremely important, as fundamental corporate actions are defined and approved at this meeting. Three primary actions taken at the initial meeting of directors are to approve and adopt the corporation's bylaws, to name the corporation's officers, and to issue shares of the corporation's stock. Since the bylaws are the road map for internal corporate governance, and the officers manage the day-to-day affairs of the corporation, having these in place immediately following state approval of your incorporation is typically desired.

Calling the Meeting

If the corporation's directors were listed in the articles of incorporation, the organizational meeting may be held immediately upon incorporation. If the directors were not listed there, the corporation must first obtain a written statement from the incorporator that names the directors. Once the directors of the corporation have been officially named, the initial meeting of directors may be held.

The procedure for calling, holding, and documenting directors' and shareholders' meetings is quite formal. To call meetings, notice must first be sent to all directors or shareholders, depending upon the type of meeting being held. In the case of the organizational meeting, notice would be sent to all of the corporation's directors. Notice is sent in writing, typically by mail. The notice document outlines the date, time, and place of the meeting, and should be signed and sent by one of the corporation's directors. The corporation also often includes an "Affidavit of Mailing of Notice for the Initial Meeting of Directors" with its corporate records. This document formally states that the notice was sent to directors on a certain date, and also states the means by which it was sent—for example, by U.S. mail. An example of this document is included as Figure 13-1, which you can use as a template for creating your own affidavit document.

F I G U R E 13-1

Affidavit of Mailing of Notice of Initial Meeting of Directors

State of:_____
County of:_____

<Secretary's name> being duly sworn according to law deposes and says:

I am the secretary of <name of corporation>. On <date> I personally deposited in a post office box in the city of <city name,> county of <county name,> copies of the attached notice of initial meeting of directors, each enclosed in a sealed, postage paid envelope. A notice was addressed to each person whose name appears below:

<Name of director 1>
<Name of director 2>
<Name of director 3>

Sworn to before me this day of <date>

_____
Secretary

_____
Notary Signature

Directors have the ability to waive notice. If this is done, the directors draft a formal document agreeing that they waive notice for the initial meeting of directors and declaring the date, time, and place of the meeting. Use of the waiver is fairly common among small businesses, because small businesses often have only a small number of directors who regularly communicate with one another. Waiving notice saves the step of drafting documents and mailing them to a small number of people who may see each other every day.

For example, if Top Security Limited has three directors, all living in the same city, it may wish to waive the notice requirements. Let's say that the three directors meet over dinner and decide to hold their initial meeting of directors on the upcoming Saturday. Since they are all aware of the date and have agreed upon the date, time, and location, there is no need to send each of them a formal notice outlining the date and time of the meeting. Instead, they draft a waiver of notice document that specifies the date and time they have agreed upon.

The title of the waiver document would be "Waiver of Notice of Organizational Meeting of Board of Directors of <corporation's name>." The waiver of notice document is typically brief with straightforward wording. For Top Security Limited, the waiver document could read:

> WE, THE UNDERSIGNED, being all the members of the Board of Directors of Top Security Limited, a Corporation incorporated under the laws of Vermont, hereby waive notice of the time, place, and purpose of the initial meeting of the Board of Directors of said Corporation, and do fix Saturday, July 5, 2003, at 12:00 P.M. as the date and time, and the offices of the Corporation, 1234 Security Street, as the place of said meeting.
>
> We hereby waive the requirements of the statutes of the Vermont as to notice of said meeting and the publication thereof; and we consent to the transaction at said meeting of such business as may come before the meeting.

All three directors would then sign this document and file it in the corporate records or the corporate minute book. It is important for corporations to designate where all corporate records will be kept and who will be responsible for these records. It is often the secretary that has this responsibility. Keeping corporate records together can prevent hassles later, should the corporation ever be required to produce documentation of meetings held and actions taken.

Holding the Meeting

As previously stated, three primary tasks are addressed at the organizational meeting: approving and adopting the bylaws, appointing officers, and issuing corporate stock. However, a number of other items may also be addressed at that time. There are no guidelines for meeting locations. For example, meetings may be held at the corporation's office or in a conference facility. Depending on what the bylaws outline, it is possible for meetings to be held electronically via videoconference or teleconference. Furthermore, a meeting is not required if the agenda items are approved via "unanimous written consent," which is explained later in this chapter.

With small corporations, particularly when there are only a few directors and they are also shareholders and officers, the directors are very involved in the incorporation process and the establishment of the business. As they begin conceptualizing the business, they commonly determine who will fill the roles of shareholders, directors, and officers. They also often work together in creating the corporation's bylaws, and they typically know all the information that will be addressed at the organizational meeting. When an attorney provides customized bylaws for the corporation, a copy of that document is typically provided to the directors prior to the organizational meeting, so that they have a chance to review it before the meeting takes place. For small businesses, the steps taken at the organizational meeting are often formalities, since the directors are often issuing shares to themselves, appointing themselves as officers, and approving bylaws that they worked together to create or have already reviewed. This is another reason why many small corporations approve the items typically addressed at the organizational meeting by unanimous written consent in lieu of holding a meeting.

Should you decide to hold your corporation's initial meeting of directors, instead of utilizing unanimous written consent, having an agenda prepared prior to the meeting will help it to progress quickly and run smoothly. An agenda for an organizational meeting could include:

- Roll call (to ensure that a quorum exists)
- Discuss and approve corporate bylaws
- Issue shares of stock to shareholders
- Appoint corporate officers
- Discuss and vote on other business items (such as approval of the articles of incorporation, corporate seal, S corporation election, etc., and the issuance of a resolution to open the corporate bank account)
- Set date and time for annual meeting of directors
- Adjourn

Since many small corporations do not have a chairman of the board, you should determine which of your board members will be responsible for overseeing and running the meeting. You should also designate a board member to prepare the minutes of the meeting. If the person who was appointed to the role of corporate secretary is also a board member, he or she could assume this role, as this duty typically resides with the secretary.

Approving and Adopting Bylaws
The bylaws are the second most important corporate document, after the articles of incorporation, as they establish the rules for internal corporate governance. Because corporations are not required to file their bylaws

with the state, this document can be amended more easily than the articles of incorporation. Therefore, the majority of the information on internal structure and governance is included in the bylaws.

The bylaws outline items such as procedures for directors' and shareholders' meetings, voting rights, and transfer of shares of stock. They also define such items as the number of directors the corporation will have, the powers of the directors, and the duties of the corporate officers. It is standard across all corporations that bylaws must be approved and adopted by the directors. Once they have been approved by the directors, they typically are also approved by the shareholders during the initial meeting of shareholders.

The next chapter focuses on a corporation's bylaws, outlining the type of information commonly included within this document. Chapter 14 also includes a template that you can use when drafting the bylaws for your corporation.

Appointing Officers

Unless you incorporated your business in Massachusetts, where officers are listed in the articles of incorporation, appointment of the corporation's officers is typically done during the initial meeting of directors. The bylaws outline the types of offices a corporation will have and the duties of each of these offices; however, the officers themselves are appointed at the organizational meeting.

Corporations routinely have the offices of president, vice president, secretary, and treasurer; however, the bylaws can define other corporate offices as well. If a corporation chooses to use other names for certain officers, such as the combination title of president and chief executive officer, or to have other officers, such as a chief technology officer, this should be outlined in the bylaws. Those officers are also appointed during the organizational meeting.

Issuing Corporate Stock

During the organizational meeting, the directors may authorize the issuance of corporate stock to designated shareholders. Corporations are not required to issue the full number of authorized shares provided for in the articles of incorporation. When only a portion of the authorized shares will be issued, the directors determine the number of shares to be issued and then approve the issuance of those shares.

A directors' resolution should be created that outlines the number of shares that will be issued, to whom they will be issued, and for what consideration. Consideration is what the corporation receives in return for the shares. This can be cash, physical assets (such as equipment or real estate), or possibly services. For example, Bernie might provide $1000 in cash, Todd might provide $1000 worth of equipment for the corporation to use, and Katherine might provide $1000 worth of consulting time to the corporation. The directors would then determine the number of shares to provide to each of these three shareholders. In this case, maybe they will receive 500 shares each. The directors' resolution would then specify that 500 shares will be issued to Bernie, Todd, and Katherine in return for the specified consideration.

Directors also approve the corporation's stock certificates, and one of those certificates is included with the minutes of the organizational meeting, signifying that it is the approved certificate. Bernie, Todd, and Katherine would each be issued a stock certificate indicating that he or she owns 500 shares of the corporation's stock. Stock certificates, which provide physical proof of a shareholder's ownership of the corporation, should be issued any time that shares are issued, whether it be to new or existing shareholders.

Additionally, the directors would ensure that the corporation's stock transfer ledger is updated to reflect the number of shares issued, to whom they were issued, and the date on which they were issued. Keeping the stock transfer ledger up-to-date by entering all stock issuances and/or repurchases is important; the ledger should be updated not only at the initial meeting of directors, but also whenever stock changes hands throughout the life of the corporation.

Other Items

The other points of business addressed at the organizational meeting vary greatly. If a company has been in business for quite some time before incorporating, the initial meeting may be used to formally document relationships that are already in place, such as banking relationships, key vendor relationships, and so on. Agreements governing these relationships would then need to be reissued in the name of the corporation.

For businesses that are beginning operations, other items that are commonly addressed during the initial meeting of directors include:

- *Approval of the articles of incorporation.* This is a formality, since the articles have already been approved by the state; however, it is still proper for the board of directors to approve the articles. A copy of the articles is typically included with the minutes of the organizational meeting.

- *Approval of the corporate seal.* By approving the corporate seal at the organizational meeting, the directors designate it as the official seal of the corporation. After the approval, the meeting minutes are stamped with the seal to illustrate the mark.
- *Determination of the corporation's fiscal year.* The directors may determine at their initial meeting the fiscal year the corporation will use. This is often outlined in the bylaws as well.
- *Authorization to open a bank account.* During the organizational meeting, the board may authorize the president, or any other officer it deems fit, to open a bank account on behalf of the corporation.
- *Approval of S corporation election.* If the corporation plans to elect S corporation status with the Internal Revenue Service (IRS), the directors often will approve this action during their initial meeting.
- *Approval of the intention to have 1244 stock.* Section 1244 of the Internal Revenue Code provides for special treatment of losses on "small business corporation stock," allowing individuals to deduct as ordinary losses any losses that result from the sale or exchange of the stock of a small business. This concept is further defined in Chapter 16, on capitalization.

Note that in order to hold any directors' or shareholders' meeting, a quorum is required. A quorum is the minimum attendance required in order to conduct business at meetings. In the case of directors' meetings, a quorum is typically achieved if a majority of the directors are present; however, a corporation may set its own quorum requirement and define this requirement in the bylaws.

For example, we'll say that Blue Mark Consulting Incorporated has five directors. The bylaws for this corporation specify that a quorum is achieved if 60 percent of the directors, or three of them, are present at any directors' meeting. As long as at least three directors are present for the initial meeting of directors for Blue Mark Consulting, a quorum has been achieved. The directors in attendance vote on each of the organizational meeting's agenda items. When voting at the meeting, a majority of those present need to vote together to constitute an act. For example, if only three of Blue Mark Consulting's directors attended the meeting, and two of them voted in favor of an item, the majority vote has been cast, and the item would be adopted.

Unanimous Written Consent in Lieu of Holding a Meeting

Directors can approve the items that would have been discussed and voted on during the organizational meeting without physically holding an organizational meeting. If the directors unanimously consent to the resolutions that would be made at the meeting, they can adopt these resolutions without holding the initial meeting of directors. This is a method that is often utilized by closely held corporations, especially those with a small number of directors, all of whom are involved in the day-to-day operation of the business. For example, Tommy and Peggy own Subs Online Inc., and they are the only shareholders, directors, and officers of the corporation. They can approve the ratification of the corporate bylaws, the issuance of shares to themselves, and the appointment of themselves as the officers of the corporation through unanimous consent.

Just as items voted on at the organizational meeting are recorded in the minutes, resolutions made by unanimous consent must be formally documented. This formal document is called the "Unanimous Consent of Directors in Lieu of an Initial Meeting." All directors sign this document, signifying their unanimous consent. The document should then be placed in the corporate records. In the case of Tommy and Peggy, they would draft this document outlining the approved resolutions, sign it, and place it with their corporate records.

Documenting the Meeting

It is imperative that you document the results of the organizational meeting or those items approved by unanimous consent. This provides a written record that each item was approved and adopted by the corporation's directors. The standard way to document the actions taken during the organizational meeting is through meeting minutes that are signed by the directors present and are then kept with the corporate records in a corporate minute book.

The minutes should also document the time and place of the meeting, who was in attendance, and each of the actions taken. Figure 13-2 includes sample minutes for an organizational meeting. In this figure, you can see the official and more formal format that minutes of directors' and shareholders' meetings follow. Note that while this figure may help you structure your own minutes, it is not meant to be an absolute rule for documenting your organizational meeting. Your corporation's situation will most likely vary, and different items may need to be

F I G U R E   13-2

Minutes of Initial Meeting of Directors

MINUTES OF INITIAL MEETING OF DIRECTORS
<CORPORATION'S NAME>

The initial meeting of the Board of Directors of <corporation's name> was held at
the principal office of the company at <company address>, at 12:00 PM on
Saturday, July 5, 2003.

<Person's name> chaired the meeting and <person's name> served as secretary
of the meeting.

The secretary reported that notice of the meeting had been properly given or waived
by each Director in accordance with the Bylaws. Upon a motion made, seconded
and approved, the Secretary was directed to attach the appropriate Notice of
Meeting and Affidavit, or the Waiver of Notice, document to these minutes.

The following Directors were present: <Names of directors present>
These directors were sufficient to constitute a quorum.

The undersigned, being all of the Directors of <corporation's name,> a <state of
incorporation> Corporation, hereby consent, pursuant to State Law, to the adoption
of the following resolutions:

RESOLVED, that the Articles of Incorporation, together with the bylaws of this
Corporation, both attached hereto, are approved.

RESOLVED, that the proper officers of the Corporation are hereby authorized to
execute and issue stock certificates for <number of shares> shares of the
Corporation's common stock to <shareholder's name>. These shares shall be
deemed fully paid and non-assessable by the Corporation (except as otherwise
provided for in State corporate law).

RESOLVED, that the form of certificate for the Common Stock of this Corporation,
a copy of which is annexed hereto, be, and it hereby is, adopted as the form of
stock certificate to be issued to represent shares of the Common Stock of this
Corporation.

RESOLVED, that the form of seal impressed on the margin is approved and adopted
for use as the corporate seal of this Corporation.

RESOLVED, that the following individuals are elected to the offices set forth below
opposite their respective names, each to hold office until the first meeting of
directors following the next annual meeting of shareholders of this Corporation or
until his/her successor shall have been duly elected and qualified:

President   <President's name>
Vice President   <Vice President's name>
Secretary   <Secretary's name>
Treasurer   <Treasurer's name>

F I G U R E   13-2

(Continued)

MINUTES OF INITIAL MEETING OF DIRECTORS
<CORPORATION'S NAME> *page 2 of 2*

RESOLVED, that the Board of Directors, having determined that the Corporation has complied with the requirements of Section 1244 of the Internal Revenue Code of 1986, as amended, does hereby declare its intention that the Corporation's common stock be deemed "Section 1244 stock." This 1244 election enables shareholders who are individuals and who purchase their stock directly from the Corporation to obtain ordinary loss treatment for losses realized upon the sale or worthlessness of their stock.

RESOLVED, that the President is hereby authorized on behalf of the Corporation to open such bank accounts as he/she in his/her discretion shall deem necessary or convenient to the conduct and affairs of the Corporation. The authorized signer or signers of checks or withdrawal orders shall be any person whose name and signature shall have been certified to such bank by the President, and any such bank shall be fully protected in relying upon any such certification until it shall have received written notice of a change in such signing authority.

RESOLVED, that the fiscal year of this Corporation shall start on <start month and date> and end on <end month and date>.

RESOLVED, that the Corporation hereby elects under section 1362(a) of the Internal Revenue Code to be treated as an "electing small business corporation" for income tax purposes. This election allows the taxable income or loss of the corporation to be taxed directly to the shareholders rather than to the Corporation itself. The Board of Directors hereby recommends to the shareholders of the Corporation that they execute and consent to, and authorize and direct the proper officers of the Corporation to complete, execute and file at such time as they deem appropriate an Election by Small Business Corporation on Form 2553 (a copy of which is to be attached hereto).

RESOLVED, that for the purpose of authorizing this Corporation to do business in any state, territory, or possession of the United States or any foreign country in which it is necessary or expedient for this Corporation to do business, the officers of this Corporation be, and they hereby are, authorized to appoint and substitute all necessary agents or attorneys for service of process, to designate and change the location of all necessary statutory offices, and to make and file all necessary certificates, reports, powers of attorney, and other instruments as may be required by the laws of such state, territory, possession, or country to authorize this Corporation to do business therein, and whenever it is expedient for this Corporation to cease doing business therein and withdraw therefrom to revoke any appointment of agent or attorney for service of process and to file any necessary certificate, report, revocation of appointment, or surrender of authority of this Corporation to do business therein.

Dated: _____

_____ (Director)

_____ (Director)

_____ (Director)

addressed during your initial meeting of directors and subsequently recorded in the minutes. It is also possible that some of the items included in this figure are not applicable to your corporation.

As previously mentioned, a copy of one of the corporation's stock certificates should be included with the minutes, and the minutes are typically impressed with the corporate seal to show that the seal was approved during the meeting. A copy of the corporation's bylaws and articles of incorporation should also be included. If any other items that lend themselves to being copied are approved, a copy of each of those items should be included with the minutes.

INITIAL MEETING OF SHAREHOLDERS

A corporation's board of directors has the primary role in laying the corporate groundwork upon completion of the incorporation process; however, shareholders also have a role. As the owners of the corporation, shareholders can exert influence over the corporation and its policies. During the initial meeting of shareholders, however, their role is basically to approve the steps taken by the directors at the organizational meeting. Technically, there are no shareholders of the corporation until the organizational meeting has been held, since the directors issue shares to the shareholders during that meeting. Therefore, the initial meeting of shareholders takes place after the initial meeting of directors.

Calling the Meeting

Calling the initial meeting of shareholders is similar to calling the initial meeting of directors. All shareholders must be given notice of the upcoming meeting; this is typically given by means of a written document, most often sent by mail.

As with all formal notices, the secretary of the corporation should formally document this action by completing the "Affidavit of Notice of Initial Meeting of Shareholders" form. This form, which is signed by the secretary, documents the date and method of providing notice. Sample wording for this form would be

> <Secretary's name> being duly sworn according to law states:
> I am the secretary of <name of corporation>. On <date> I personally deposited in a post office box in the city of <city name>, county of <county name> copies of the attached notice of initial meeting of shareholders, each enclosed in a sealed postage-paid envelope.

A notice was addressed to each person whose name appears on the list of shareholders and to their respective post office addresses as therein set forth.

As you can see, this document is similar to the "Affidavit of Mailing of Notice of Initial Meeting of Directors" document, which is included in this chapter as Figure 13-1. Many of the standard minute, notice, and waiver documents used for shareholders' meetings are similar to those for directors' meetings.

Like directors, shareholders can waive notice for shareholders' meetings. This is more common in corporations with a small number of shareholders. The shareholders can select a date, time, and place for the initial meeting of shareholders, then formally document this decision, thereby waiving official notice. The name of this document is "Waiver of Notice of Initial Shareholders' Meeting." The wording is very similar to the sample wording provided earlier in this chapter for the "Waiver of Notice of Organizational Meeting of Board of Directors."

Holding the Meeting

The primary items that are commonly addressed during the initial meeting of shareholders are the approval of the incorporation, acceptance and approval of the board of directors, and approval of the directors' resolutions from the organizational meeting. In many respects, the initial shareholders' meeting is simply a formality, since the corporation's directors have already approved each of these items. As with the initial meeting of directors, there are no regulations governing when or where the initial meeting of shareholders is to take place. If all the shareholders of your corporation are also the only directors, you can opt to hold these meetings concurrently; this is common with closely held corporations.

Like directors, shareholders may consent in writing to the items that would be discussed during the initial meeting in lieu of holding the meeting. With shareholders, however, only majority written consent is required, provided that all the shareholders received timely written notice of the meeting and that notice of the consent is promptly provided to all nonconsenting shareholders. In many small companies, the shareholders are also the directors of the corporation, and in such cases, unanimous consent in lieu of holding an initial meeting of shareholders is common. Since the directors and shareholders are the same group of people, and the directors have already approved the items to be presented at the initial shareholders' meeting, the likelihood of the shareholders' not approving the items is slim.

If you decide to hold an initial meeting of shareholders instead of approving the items by unanimous or majority written consent, having an agenda will help the meeting progress quickly and run smoothly. Sample agenda items for the initial meeting of shareholders could include:

- Roll call (to ensure that a quorum exists)
- Approval of the articles of incorporation
- Approval of the appointment of corporate directors
- Approval of corporate bylaws
- Approval of the appointment of officers
- Receipt of shares (share certificates)
- Approval of other resolutions created and approved during the organizational meeting
- Adjournment

The corporate secretary commonly attends all shareholders' meetings in order to document the actions taken and prepare the meeting minutes. In many small businesses, the corporate secretary is often a shareholder as well, and so would normally attend these meetings anyway.

Documenting the Meeting

As with directors' meetings, documenting the outcome of all shareholders' meetings is extremely important. Keeping these records is a required formality for all corporations. This requirement is met by generating meeting minutes for every shareholders' meeting and keeping the minutes with the corporate records. As previously mentioned, it is often the secretary of the corporation who is charged with compiling the minutes, signing them, and keeping the corporate records.

The minutes should document the time and place of the meeting, who was in attendance, and each of the action items taken. When action items can be further documented by including attachments, this should be done. In the case of the initial meeting of shareholders, copies of the minutes of the organizational meeting, the articles of incorporation, the corporate bylaws, and a stock certificate are typically attached to the minutes.

If the action items are approved by unanimous or majority consent of the shareholders, this should also be formally documented. Figure 13-3 shows an example of a "Unanimous Consent of Shareholders in Lieu of an

F I G U R E 13-3

Unanimous Consent of Shareholders Form

**UNANIMOUS CONSENT OF SHAREHOLDERS IN LIEU OF
AN INITIAL MEETING**

The undersigned, being all of the initial shareholders of <corporation's name>, a
<state of incorporation> Corporation (the "Corporation"), do hereby adopt the
following resolutions by written consent in lieu of an initial meeting of the
shareholders pursuant to <state of incorporation> corporate law, such action to
have the same effect as if taken at a duly constituted meeting of shareholders
held on <date of incorporation>.

RESOLVED, that any and all notice to take any action in adopting the following
resolutions is hereby waived by the undersigned pursuant to the <state of
incorporation> corporate law.

RESOLVED, that the Articles of Incorporation, together with the bylaws of this
Corporation are adopted and approved.

RESOLVED, that the following individuals shall be, and hereby are, appointed to
the Corporation's Board of Directors to serve in such capacity until their death,
resignation, renewal, or reelection:

<Director's name>
<Director's name>
<Director's name>
<Director's name>

RESOLVED, that all actions taken by the Board of Directors by way of the
Organizational Meeting held on <meeting date> are hereby in all respects ratified
and approved.

RESOLVED, the following documents, as attached to the meeting minutes from
the above approved Organizational Meeting are hereby approved and adopted:

    (A) Articles of Incorporation
    (B) Bylaws of the Corporation
    (C) Common Stock Certificate
    (D) <Any other attachments to the mintues>

IN WITNESS WHEREOF, this instrument has been executed by the undersigned as
of the aforementioned date to be filed as part of the minutes of the Corporation.

<Corporation's Name>
a <State of Incorporation> Corporation

By: _____
<Person's Name, Person's Title>

Initial Meeting" document. This can be used as a template for creating your own form, should your corporation's shareholders approve all action items by this means. Remember that shareholders may approve items by majority vote, as long as notice of the consent is promptly provided to all nonconsenting shareholders. With closely held corporations that have only a few shareholders, it is relatively easy to obtain the unanimous consent of the shareholders, instead of only majority consent. Like meeting minutes, the unanimous or majority consent form includes resolutions approving certain actions or items. In Figure 13-3, the shareholders approve the articles of incorporation, the corporate bylaws, and those serving as the corporation's directors, and also approve the items previously approved at the initial meeting of directors. An officer of the corporation then signs this form and files it with the attached documents in the corporate record book.

Because the initial meetings lay the groundwork that enables your business to begin its existence as a corporation, they are important steps for all corporations to take. As previously noted, approval by unanimous consent of the directors or shareholders is a tool that helps to simplify the meeting requirements for closely held corporations. As you've learned in this chapter and will continue to see in the following chapters, a number of the steps required of corporations are quite formal. These steps are just as important for a corporation with one director and one shareholder as they are for large corporations with 10 directors and thousands of shareholders. The primary difference lies in the procedures available to small corporations to make complying with these formalities easier.

CHAPTER 14

Bylaws

A corporation's bylaws are the second most important corporate document, after the articles of incorporation, as the bylaws set the rules governing the corporation's internal affairs. For example, bylaws set the requirements for shareholders' and directors' meetings and define the roles of the officers. If there is a choice between putting certain information in the bylaws and putting it in the articles of incorporation, it is often a good idea to put the information in the bylaws. Since the bylaws are not filed with the state, they are easier to amend than the articles of incorporation. Also, there are no state filing fees for making such amendments.

> *Major topics covered: This chapter outlines the basics of creating and updating corporate bylaws, including information on what is typically included in this document, resolutions for amending it, and how to document any changes. This chapter also includes sample bylaws, which you can use as a template for creating the bylaws for your corporation.*

A question that many entrepreneurs have concerning incorporation is how to create the bylaws for their corporation. If you prepare and file your own incorporation paperwork, you can often purchase sample bylaws from a legal supply store. If you purchase a corporate kit, sample bylaws are often included. If you utilize the services of an incorporation service provider, the provider will often have sample bylaws that small business owners can use as templates for creating their own document. Attorneys can also provide customized bylaws for your corporation, whether or not you utilized their services for the preparation and filing of your incorporation paperwork. While having your bylaws prepared by an attorney is the most comprehensive option, it is also the most expensive.

The importance of creating and updating your bylaws cannot be overstated. There are a number of formalities that corporations must comply with in order to maintain the limited liability that they afford shareholders, and the bylaws outline the corporation's rules for carrying out these formalities. As Chapter 18 will discuss, failing to carry out these formalities can have serious consequences for your corporation. Having detailed bylaws that are kept accurate with well-documented changes is a key step in complying with these formalities.

CREATING YOUR BYLAWS

The bylaws are typically a fairly extensive document that addresses both high-level operations and a number of details on the required processes. Bylaws outline everything from the principal office address of the corporation to how and when the corporation can pay dividends to shareholders. There is no set rule for what information must be included in the bylaws, and their composition can vary greatly. This chapter will outline the information that is commonly included.

Bylaws consist of a number of articles that address certain corporate topics, such as shareholders, directors, officers, and common stock. Each article contains a number of subsections that break the topic down further, such as annual meetings of shareholders, compensation of directors, and duties of officers. In this chapter we discuss common subsections, lending insight into why corporations make rules covering certain internal actions. At the end of this section, we've also included sample bylaws to demonstrate the way these topics are often addressed. You can use the sample as a template for creating bylaws for your corporation if you choose to handle the incorporation paperwork yourself. If you use an incorporation service provider, the provider will typically offer sample bylaws and other corporate forms as an add-on item to its formation service. If you use an attorney for your incorporation, it is likely that the attorney will customize the bylaws for your corporation as an included part of his or her fee.

Principal Office

Not all states require the corporation's principal office address to be included in the articles of incorporation. Therefore, it is commonly provided in the first article in the bylaws. This article typically lists only the principal office or headquarters address for the corporation, but it may also include general wording covering the establishment of other offices at a later date. Including that type of general wording decreases the need for amending the bylaws if your corporation expands.

Meetings of Shareholders

The bylaws dictate the who, what, when, where, and why for shareholders, directors, and officers. One factor that is unique to corporations is the requirement for holding annual meetings of directors and shareholders. The bylaws outline the governing logistics for these meetings, as well as for the roles of these corporate players in general.

Location of Shareholders' Meetings

As previously mentioned, there is no set requirement covering where or when shareholders' meetings are held. Smaller corporations often hold these meetings at the corporate office. Public corporations often rent conference facilities to hold their shareholders' meetings, because of the large number of shareholders they have. Your bylaws can list a specific location for shareholders' meetings or utilize general language that allows the directors to set the location.

Annual Meeting of Shareholders

All corporations are required to hold an annual meeting of shareholders. During these meetings, shareholders typically elect directors and vote on any corporate actions that require shareholder approval. A subsection of the bylaws typically includes information on the date and location for the annual meeting. It is not uncommon for corporations to hold this meeting on the same day each year—for example, the first Thursday in the month of May. This consistency is often beneficial for companies with a large number of shareholders, as it means that shareholders do not have to await the corporation's notice of the date of the meeting. For corporations with a small number of shareholders, the directors can decide whether to have a consistent date or to have the flexibility to pick a date that is best for all shareholders.

Special Meetings of Shareholders

When business arises that needs shareholder approval and that cannot wait until the next annual meeting, a special meeting of shareholders can be called. In this case, the notice to shareholders must outline the items that will be discussed at the special meeting, and no other business may be addressed. This subsection typically outlines who can call a special meeting of shareholders: for example, the board of directors, the president of the corporation, a majority of the shareholders, and so on.

Notice of Shareholders' Meetings

As discussed in Chapter 13, corporations are required to provide directors and shareholders with formal notice of a meeting, unless that notice is waived. This subsection outlines how notice of all shareholders' meetings must be given to shareholders. Each corporation sets its own rules for how long before the meeting the notice must be sent. A corporation can set separate guidelines for the different types of shareholders' meetings, or it can set the same guidelines for all shareholders' meetings. For example, a corporation may decide that it wishes to provide 6 weeks' notice for a special meeting of shareholders and 12 weeks' notice for the annual meeting, or it may decide to provide 8 weeks' notice for all types of shareholders' meetings.

Quorum

In regards to shareholders' meetings, a quorum is the minimum number of shares that must be represented in order to conduct business at a meeting. Since most items at shareholders' meetings require a vote of the shareholders, it is important to establish what constitutes a quorum. The typical quorum requirement is a majority of the total number of issued shares; however, a corporation may set its quorum requirement at any amount it sees fit. The number of issued shares your corporation currently has and the number you envision it having in the future may be factors in the decision as to what constitutes a quorum. For example, if you have 1000 authorized shares, but only 400 are issued at the time you draft your bylaws, setting your quorum at 400 shares may cause the need to amend your bylaws at a later date. The number of shares issued can change often with some corporations. In this case, setting the quorum at 75 percent of issued shares could help eliminate the need to amend this section of your bylaws regularly.

Voting

Your bylaws should also outline the voting procedures allowed by your corporation. For example, since 100 percent attendance at shareholders' meetings is not always realistic, your bylaws may allow for voting by proxy. With proxy voting, another individual is given the power to vote on a shareholder's behalf. Information concerning the record date for determining who is considered a shareholder with voting rights and the actual procedure for submitting votes by proxy is also often addressed in this subsection.

Order of Business

The bylaws also typically set the order in which business is to be conducted during shareholders' meetings. The use of general language in this subsection gives the board of directors the right to change this order. A standard order of business for shareholders' meetings could be:

- Roll call
- Proof of notice of meeting or waiver of notice
- Reading and accepting minutes from a previous meeting
- Reports from the corporation's officers
- Reports from the board of directors' committees (if applicable)
- Election of directors (if required)
- Unfinished business
- New business
- Closing of the meeting

Informal Action by Shareholders

As Chapter 13 discussed, it is possible for shareholders to offer written consent in lieu of holding shareholders' meetings. To do this, a majority of the shareholders must approve each of the points of business that would be discussed at the meeting, and notice of the consent must be promptly provided to the nonconsenting shareholders. The bylaws can outline the majority written consent procedure. In smaller corporations (with only a handful of shareholders), the corporation may wish to specify that unanimous written consent of shareholders is required unless this is prohibited by the law of your state of formation.

Directors

At a high level, the bylaws address and define most of the rights of corporate directors and of the board of directors as a whole. When it comes to directors' meetings, the bylaws provide much of the same information as is provided for shareholders' meetings. The bylaws also typically cover such things as directors' compensation and provision for indemnification of the corporation's directors.

General Powers

The general powers subsection typically outlines the corporate affairs for which the directors have responsibility, as well as how they are to govern the corporation. This often includes general language stating that the directors will manage and control the business, affairs, and property of the corporation, and that the majority of the board of directors present at duly called meetings must approve all decisions.

Number of Directors

The number of directors that a corporation will have may also be stated in the bylaws, instead of being declared in the articles of incorporation. Most states require corporations to have a minimum of one director, but the states typically do not specify the maximum number of directors. Closely held corporations often have only a few directors, and wish to keep that structure. In this case, the bylaws may specify that the number of directors is three, and that this number cannot be increased without both board and shareholder approval.

Bylaws for corporations that are anticipating growth or that intend to seek funding from venture capitalists, who typically take a seat on the board of directors of a corporation that they fund, may allow for growth of the board of directors within this subsection. One thing to keep in the back of your mind as you set the number of directors in your bylaws is that having an odd number of directors helps to prevent tie votes on the board.

Election and Removal of Directors

This subsection details when and how directors may be elected and removed from their positions, and defines the length of time that directors will serve in that role. Typically, directors are elected or reelected during an annual meeting of shareholders. Addressing how a vacancy can be filled, if one should arise between annual meetings, is also important. That can be done within this subsection or by creating a separate subsection on vacancies.

Quorum

The bylaws also outline what constitutes a quorum for the board of directors, just as they did for the shareholders. With directors, a quorum is the minimum number of directors required to be in attendance in order to conduct business at a meeting. The quorum can be defined generally, such as a simple majority of the board of directors, or be defined more specifically, such as 80 percent of the board of directors.

Annual and Special Meetings of Directors

The corporate structure also requires that directors, like shareholders, hold annual meetings. The bylaws outline the logistics for calling and holding these meetings. Since all or most directors are typically present for the shareholders' meeting, it is not uncommon for the annual meeting of directors to be held on the same date and in the same place as the shareholders' meeting. The sample bylaws included in Figure 14-1 have a provision for holding the annual meeting of directors in conjunction with the annual meeting of shareholders.

Like special meetings of shareholders, special meetings of directors can be called and held when the board must take action on items that cannot be postponed until the next annual directors' meeting. In addition to detailing the procedure for calling and holding special meetings of directors, this subsection also typically outlines who can call such a meeting.

Notice

Notice must be given for directors' meetings, just as it must for shareholders' meetings, and the notice requirements for directors' meetings are also outlined in the bylaws. If the corporation decides to hold the directors' annual meeting in conjunction with the annual meeting of shareholders, this subsection may address only providing notice for special meetings of directors. Smaller companies often include a provision in this section allowing a meeting to be called without notice if all directors are present. For example, if a corporation has only three directors and all three are employed by the corporation, this provision helps to lessen the formality required for these directors to hold a meeting to conduct official business.

Directors' Compensation

The bylaws typically include rules governing directors' compensation; however, the amount of detail included in this subsection can vary greatly. In public companies, directors often are not employed by the company. It is possible that the company's CEO will be the only employee on the board. It is also common for executives or retired executives of a corporation to serve on another corporation's board. Because this is an outside commitment for the directors, they are often compensated for being a part of the board of directors. Compensation varies, but it may include company stock, coverage of all expenses related to their duties as a board member, or possibly direct monetary compensation. The bylaws of public companies may outline in detail the compensation offered to board members.

With smaller companies, the directors often are also the shareholders and officers of the corporation. In these cases, it is common for board members' only compensation to be reimbursement of expenses that relate directly to their functions as directors. They will already be receiving compensation from the company as employees. The sample bylaws in Figure 14-1 include wording for this type of situation.

Manner of Acting

This can be a very brief subsection. It often simply states that any action taken by a majority of the directors present at a meeting at which a quorum is present is a valid act of the directors. If the quorum subsection includes a percentage instead of just general language, this subsection often requires approval by a certain percentage of the directors present at the meeting in order to constitute a valid resolution or act.

Electronic Meetings

The directors may wish to insert a subsection allowing for electronic meetings. With electronic meetings, a director may be present at the meeting via telephone or videoconference. For corporations with directors located in different areas, this could be a benefit. If all directors of the corporation are located in the same city, this may not be as necessary.

Executive and Other Committees

A board of directors may establish smaller committees that are responsible for overseeing specific areas of the corporation's business or specific projects as they arise. Committees are particularly beneficial if the corporation has a larger number of directors, because as the number of directors grows, bringing them together to approve time-sensitive business items becomes more difficult. Committees are discussed in more depth in Chapter 15, on the roles of shareholders, directors, and officers.

With regard to the information on committees that is included in the bylaws, the bylaws may specify the names and roles of certain committees. Alternatively, the bylaws may simply state that the directors have the right to create committees. Because committees often have the power to make decisions on behalf of the entire board of directors, the bylaws may also include language outlining certain areas over which committees would not have approval authority. Common items that committees cannot approve include changes in the articles of incorporation or bylaws and filling a vacancy on the board of directors, both of which would need full board approval and approval of the shareholders.

Informal Action by Directors

Like the shareholders, the directors can be given the right to approve actions by unanimous consent in lieu of holding a meeting; however, for directors, this consent must be unanimous. This is beneficial for companies that have directors in multiple locations or for corporations with a small number of directors. Having this provision may eliminate the need to call a special meeting of directors if all directors are in agreement on the action to be taken.

Indemnification

As discussed in Chapter 8, the articles of incorporation may include a director indemnification clause. If the articles of incorporation do not include this language, it is typically included in the corporation's bylaws. It is not necessary to include indemnification language in both a corporation's articles of incorporation and its bylaws.

Officers

As the previous chapter outlined, the board of directors typically appoints a corporation's officers during the initial meeting of directors. Outside of this initial appointment, the standard procedure for electing, reelecting, and removing officers is covered in the bylaws. The bylaws note what officers the corporation will have, and also include a general description of these officers' duties.

Election of Officers and Their Terms

Within this subsection, the bylaws typically list the officers that the company will have, such as president, vice president, secretary, and treasurer. It also typically defines the procedures for electing officers and the length of each officer's term. If the corporation allows one person to hold multiple offices, such as president and secretary, this may be addressed in this subsection.

Removal of Officers and Vacancies

It is possible that a corporation may face the need to remove an officer from a position or to fill an office that has been vacated when an officer has been promoted to another office before the expiration of his or her term. This subsection should outline the corporation's procedure for removing officers and filling vacancies.

Resignations

It is not uncommon for officers of the corporation to resign their posts prior to the end of their term. Bylaws often include provisions allowing officers to resign as long as they give proper notice. It is also possible for the corporation to address the issue of resignations in the same subsection in which removing officers and filling vacancies are addressed. The sample bylaws in Figure 14-1 include resignations as a separate item.

Officers' Duties

As previously mentioned, the standard officer positions in a corporation are president, vice president, secretary, and treasurer. It is possible that a corporation will have a chief executive officer, a chief technology officer, a chief information officer, and so on. The bylaws should include a descriptions of the basic duties of each officer, including to whom or which body the officer reports and for which corporate functions the officer has responsibility. For example, the subsection on the duties of the president may state that the president has the authority to sign documents such as contracts, deeds, or mortgages on behalf of the corporation. The subsection on the duties of the secretary may state that this officer shall be responsible for recording the events of all directors' and shareholders' meetings, and must maintain corporate records such as meeting minutes, reports, company contracts, and other important documents. Corporations have flexibility in defining officers' duties as outlined in the bylaws, and the roles of officers may vary among corporations.

Compensation

Like the compensation subsection in the article on directors, this subsection can be as detailed or as general as you wish. The board of directors determines the compensation of officers and oversees any changes in the compensation structure. The bylaws may simply state generally that the directors will determine the officers' compensation, but in today's world, with corporations often providing stock options, bonus structures, and other benefits to their officers, it is fairly common for the compensation parameters to be more thoroughly defined in the bylaws.

Capital Stock

If a company plans to offer multiple classes of stock, with or without different voting rights, that information is included in the bylaws. The capital stock article of the bylaws also dictates how a corporation will record stock transactions, how it will handle lost or damaged stock certificates, and whether there are any restrictions on the transfer of shares.

Certificates

Corporations issue stock certificates to prove stockholders' ownership of the company. When shares are bought, sold, or awarded as compensation, a stock certificate should be issued to prove the recipient's ownership, and the transfer should be recorded in the corporation's stock transfer ledger or through some other recording mechanism. This subsection defines the procedures governing these processes.

Lost or Destroyed Certificates

Given human nature, it is certain that at some point in the life of a corporation, shareholders will lose their stock certificates or certificates will be damaged or even destroyed. The corporate bylaws should deal with this inevitability by noting the procedure for replacing stock certificates.

Transfer of Shares

Even small companies are likely to encounter the need to transfer shares. It is advisable to have a documented policy for this process. For example, if a shareholder leaves shares to a family member by means of a will, the shares must be transferred to the name of the new holder. The bylaws often outline the transfer procedure. They may also outline any restrictions on who is allowed to transfer or facilitate the transfer of shares; however, such restrictions are often included in a shareholder agreement instead of fully being defined in the bylaws. Shareholder agreements are discussed in the next chapter.

Consideration for Shares

Bylaws often include language allowing the corporation to issue shares when the consideration is something other than cash. For example, if a corporation plans to enter into a partnership with another company that it feels will be extremely beneficial to its business, the corporation may wish to issue shares of its stock to that partner, thereby providing the partner with additional incentive to make the partnership succeed. The bylaws may grant this power to the corporation, but they will often put checks and balances in place by requiring approval by the board of directors to ensure that the transaction is not a detriment to the corporation.

Record Date

The record date is a date selected for the purpose of determining which corporate shareholders are entitled to notice of and the right to vote at a corporation's shareholders' meetings. The bylaws can set a specific date as the record date, or they can leave this to the board of directors to determine. If the record date is not specified, the bylaws often impose a limit on how far in advance of a particular action the record date might be.

For example, if the company always holds its annual meeting of shareholders on the first Thursday of May, and the notices subsection of the bylaws states that notice must be given 5 weeks prior to the annual meeting, a corporation may wish to select a date 7 weeks prior to the annual meeting as the record date. If a corporation prefers to go with more general language, it may wish to stipulate in the bylaws that the record date cannot be more than 60 days before the date of the particular meeting or action.

Miscellaneous Provisions

Included in this section are miscellaneous provisions that are typically included in a corporation's bylaws. Other provisions beyond those discussed here may also be included, particularly those addressing conditions affecting your particular business or industry.

Corporate Seal

As noted in Chapter 11, the corporate seal can be used to signify that a document is official. A corporation may wish to approve the corporate seal and outline in the bylaws the appearance of the corporate seal. If a corporation decides not to have a seal, this would also be outlined in the bylaws.

Fiscal Year

The bylaws typically address the corporation's fiscal year. You can set a specific end date, such as December 31, or provide both the start date and the end date, such as January 1 through December 31. Another option is to use general language in order to give the board of directors the right to specify this date. This provides some additional flexibility, particularly for changing the tax year. If the fiscal year is not specified in the bylaws, it can be set or changed by a committee of the board of directors. If it is stated in the bylaws and the corporation wishes to change it, the entire board of directors will need to approve the change.

Authorization of Checks, Notes, and Drafts

The bylaws often indicate which officers have the right to sign important corporate financial documents, such as checks, notes, and drafts. While this may also be addressed in the subsection outlining the duties of the officer(s) who are granted this right, this information is typically included in its own subsection as well.

Amendment of Bylaws

It is likely that the bylaws will need to be amended at some point in time; therefore, the original document should outline the procedures for bylaw amendments and the proper documentation of approved amendments. It is standard practice to require the board of directors to approve any amendments. Beyond that, the corporation can decide whether additional approvals are required for all or some amendments. For example, your bylaws may state that only amendments to those sections of the bylaws covering directors need shareholder approval, or possibly they will specify that any amendment to the bylaws should have shareholder approval. The process of amending bylaws is discussed in more detail in the next section of this chapter.

Dividends

The bylaws also often include a subsection on the distribution of dividends. The distribution of dividends will depend on a number of factors, and you may decide to include general language governing this practice. Figure 14-1 includes such general language. Your bylaws can outline the specific circumstances that would lead to the distribution of a dividend, or they may specify that your corporation will not issue dividends.

Sample Bylaws

Figure 14-1 is an example of corporate bylaws that include each of the articles and subsections that have been discussed in this chapter. It can be used as a template for creating your corporation's bylaws, if you did not receive customized bylaws or sample bylaws from an attorney or incorporation service provider when you incorporated. This figure is not meant to be an absolute standard to follow. Each corporation's situation is different. Some of the subsections in this figure may not apply to your corporation. Likewise, your corporation may have specific needs that you prefer to address in the bylaws that are not included in this example.

UPDATING YOUR BYLAWS

Corporations need to adapt over time, and adapting may necessitate changing the corporate bylaws. Since the bylaws are such an important document, the amendment process should be formal and well documented.

As previously mentioned, the bylaws typically include provisions regulating the amendment process. The board of directors must approve all amendments, but whether shareholders must also approve some or all amendments varies from corporation to corporation. Given the need for the board of directors' approval, proposed amendments are typically included as agenda items for a corporation's annual meeting of directors. If the need for the amendment is urgent, a special meeting of directors may be called to act upon it.

If your bylaws stipulate shareholder approval in addition to director approval, once the board of directors approves an amendment, it then goes to the shareholders for approval. This approval can be gained either at the annual meeting of shareholders or by calling a special meeting of shareholders. Approval can also be gained by obtaining majority consent in lieu of holding a shareholders' meeting.

Documenting Changes

Once the corporation's board of directors has approved an amendment to the bylaws, this action is finalized in the form of a corporate resolution. Resolutions are formal corporate decisions that have been adopted either by the board of directors or by shareholders. Formally documenting a resolution makes the change in the bylaws official.

For example, a corporation's bylaws include a provision stating that the corporation will have three directors. A few years after incorporating, there is a desire to increase this number to five directors. A meeting of the three existing directors must be called to approve the change. If the directors approve it, a formal resolution document would be drafted to formalize the decision to approve the change in the bylaws increasing the number of directors from three directors to five. If the bylaws also state that amendments regarding directors must have shareholder approval,

F I G U R E   14-1

Bylaws

ARTICLE I. Principal Office

1.1 Office
The address of the principal office of the Corporation shall be _____ in
the city of _____ and state of _____. The Corporation may
have other offices, either within or without of the State of Incorporation as the Board
of Directors may designate or as the business of Corporation may require.

ARTICLE II. Meetings of Shareholders

2.1 Place of Meetings
The meetings of the shareholders shall be held at such place, either within or without
of the state of _____, as may be fixed by the Board of Directors.

2.2 Annual Meetings
The annual meeting of the shareholders, for the election of Directors and transaction
of any other business that may come before the meeting, shall be held in each year
at the corporate offices or at any other place within or without of the state
of _____ as may be determined by the Directors and as may be designated
in the notice of that meeting. If that date is a legal holiday, the annual meeting shall
be held on the next succeeding day that is not a legal holiday.

2.3 Special Meetings
A special meeting, other than those regulated by statute, of the shareholders for any
purpose or purposes may be called at any time by the President, by a majority of the
Board of Directors, by designated officers of the Corporation, or by shareholders
together holding at least 20% of the number of shares of the Corporation at the time
outstanding and entitled to vote with respect to the business to be transacted at such
meeting. At a special meeting no other business shall be transacted and no corporate
action shall be taken other than that stated in the Notice of the meeting.

2.4 Notice of Meetings
Written or printed notice stating the place, day, and hour of every meeting of the
shareholders and, in case of a special meeting, the purpose or purposes for which the
meeting is called, shall be mailed not less than five nor more than 60 days before
the date of the meeting to each shareholder of record entitled to vote at such
meeting, at his/her address which appears in the share transfer books of the
Corporation. If mailed, notice shall be deemed to be delivered when deposited in the
United States mail. Such further notice shall be given as may be required by law,
but meetings may be held without notice if all the shareholders entitled to vote at
the meeting are present in person or by proxy or if notice is waived in writing by
those not present, either before or after the meeting.

2.5 Quorum
Any number of shareholders together holding at least a simple majority of the
outstanding shares of capital stock entitled to vote with respect to the business to
be transacted, who shall be present in person or represented by proxy at any
meeting duly called, shall constitute a quorum for the transaction of business.
If less than a quorum shall be in attendance at the time for which a meeting shall
have been called, the meeting may be adjourned by a majority of the shareholders
present or represented by proxy without notice other than by announcement at
the meeting.

F I G U R E   14-1

(Continued)

2.6 Voting

At any meeting of the shareholders, each shareholder of a class entitled to vote on any matter coming before the meeting shall have one vote, in person or by proxy, for each share of capital stock of such class standing in his/her name on the books of the Corporation on the date, at least 30 days prior to such meeting, fixed by the Board of Directors as the record date for the purpose of determining shareholders entitled to vote. Every proxy shall be in writing, dated, and signed by the shareholder entitled to vote or his/her duly authorized attorney-in-fact.

2.7 Order of Business

The order of business at all meetings of shareholders shall be as follows, unless otherwise adopted by the Board:

1. Roll call
2. Proof of notice of meeting or waiver of notice
3. Reading and accepting of preceding meeting minutes
4. Reports of officers
5. Reports of committees
6. Election of directors, if required
7. Unfinished business
8. New business

2.8 Informal Action by Shareholders

Unless otherwise provided by law, any action required to be taken at a meeting of shareholders or other action which may be taken at a meeting of the shareholders, may be taken without a meeting if the shareholders give unanimous written consent setting forth the action to be taken and signed by all shareholders entitled to vote on the action.

ARTICLE III. Directors

3.1 General Powers

The property, business, and affairs of the Corporation shall be managed and controlled under the direction of the Board of Directors, and, except as otherwise expressly provided by law, the Articles of Incorporation or these Bylaws, all of the powers of the Corporation shall be vested in such Board. Such management and general control will be by majority vote of the Board of Directors, with each Director having equal vote.

3.2 Number of Directors

The number of Directors constituting the Board of Directors shall be _____.

3.3 Election and Removal of Directors

(A) Directors shall be elected at each annual meeting of shareholders to succeed those Directors whose terms have expired and to fill any existing vacancies.

(B) Directors shall hold their offices for a term of one year and until their successors are elected. Any Director may be removed from office at a meeting called expressly for that purpose by the vote of shareholders holding not less than a majority of the shares entitled to vote at an election of Directors.

F I G U R E   14-1

(Continued)

(C) Any vacancy occurring in the Board of Directors may be filled by the affirmative vote of the majority of the remaining Directors, even though less than a quorum of the Board may exist, and the term of office of any Director so elected shall expire at the next shareholders' meeting at which Directors are elected.

3.4 Quorum
A majority of the number of Directors proscribed in these Bylaws shall constitute a quorum for the transaction of business. The act of a majority of Directors present at a meeting at which a quorum is present shall be the act of the Board of Directors. If less than a majority is present at a meeting, the majority of those present may adjourn the meeting without further notice.

3.5 Regular Meetings of Directors
An annual meeting of the Board of Directors shall be held without notice other than this bylaw immediately after, and at the same place as, the annual meeting of shareholders.

3.6 Special Meetings of Directors
Special meetings of Directors may be called at the request of the President, other duly authorized officer, or any two Directors. The person or persons authorized to call special meetings of Directors may designate the place and time for holding any special meeting of Directors.

3.7 Notice
Notice of any special meeting shall be given at least 10 days previously thereto by written notice delivered personally or mailed to each director at his/her business address. If mailed, notice is deemed to be delivered when deposited in the United States mail. The attendance of a Director at a meeting shall be deemed to be a waiver of notice of such meeting unless the Director attends the meeting for the express purpose of objecting to the transaction of business at the meeting because the meeting is not properly called or convened. Meetings may be held at any time without notice if all of the Directors are present, or if those not present waive notice in writing either before or after the meeting.

3.8 Compensation
By resolution of the Board, Directors may be allowed a fee and expenses for attendance at all meetings, but nothing herein shall preclude Directors from serving the Corporation in other capacities and receiving compensation for such other services.

3.9 Manner of Acting
The act of the majority of the Directors present at a meeting at which a quorum is present shall be the act of the Directors.

3.10 Electronic Meetings
Members of the Board of Directors may participate in regular or special meetings by, or through the use of, any means of communication allowing all participants to simultaneously hear each other, such as teleconference or videoconference. If a meeting is conducted by such means, the presiding officer shall inform all participating directors at the commencement of such meeting that a meeting is taking place at which official business may be transacted. Any participant in a meeting by such means shall be deemed present in person at such meeting.

F I G U R E   14-1

(Continued)

3.11 Executive and Other Committees
The Board of Directors may designate committees made up of Directors from time
to time as the Directors see fit. The purpose for which the committees are formed
are to be designated by the Board. The committees may be dissolved by affirmative
vote of the Board of Directors. A committee may be authorized to exercise the
authority of the Board of Directors, except that a committee may not do the
following: (a) authorize distributions, (b) fill vacancies on the Board of Directors,
(c) amend the corporations articles of incorporation, (d) adopt, amend, or repeal
these bylaws, (e) approve a plan of a merger not requiring shareholder approval,
and/or (f) authorize or approve issuance or reacquisition of shares, except according
to a method already prescribed by the Board of Directors.

3.12 Informal Action by Directors
Unless otherwise provided by law, any action required to be taken at a meeting of
Directors, or other action which may be taken at a meeting of the Directors, may
be taken without a meeting if the directors give unanimous written consent setting
forth the action to be taken and signed by all Directors entitled to vote on the action.

3.13 Indemnification
The Corporation shall indemnify each of its directors, officers, and employees whether
or not then in services as such, against all reasonable expenses actually and
necessarily incurred by him or her in connection with the defense of any litigation
to which the individual may have been made a party because he or she is or was a
director, officer, or employee of the Corporation. The individual shall have no right to
reimbursement, however, in relation to matters as to which he or she has been
adjudged liable to the Corporation for negligence or misconduct in the performance
of his/her or her duties, or was derelict in the performance of his/her or her duty as
director, officer, or employee. The right to indemnity for expenses shall also apply to
expenses of suits which are settled if the court having jurisdiction of the matter shall
approve of the settlement.

ARTICLE IV. Officers

4.1 Election of Officers; Terms
The officers of the Corporation shall consist of a President, a Secretary, and a
Treasurer. Other officers, including a Chairman of the Board, Chief Executive Officer,
Chief Operating Officer, one or more Vice-Presidents, and assistant and subordinate
officers, may from time to time be elected by the Board of Directors. All officers shall
hold office until the next annual meeting of the Board of Directors and until their
successors are elected. Any two officers may be combined in the same person as the
Board of Directors may determine.

4.2 Removal of Officers; Vacancies
Any officer of the Corporation may be removed summarily with or without cause,
at any time, by the Board of Directors. Vacancies may be filled by the
Board of Directors.

4.3 Resignations
Any officer may resign at any time by delivering notice to the Corporation that
complies with state law. The resignation shall be effective when the notice is
delivered, unless notice specifies a later effective date and the Corporation accepts
the later effective date.

F I G U R E 14-1

(Continued)

4.4 Duties

The officers of the Corporation shall have such duties as generally pertain to their respective offices, as well as such powers and duties as are prescribed by law or are hereinafter provided or as shall be conferred by the Board of Directors.

4.5 Duties of the President

Unless otherwise defined by the Board, the President shall be the Chief Executive Officer of the Corporation and shall be primarily responsible for the implementation of policies of the Board of Directors, and shall have authority over the general management and direction of the business and operations of the Corporation and its divisions, if any, subject only to the ultimate authority of the Board of Directors. In the absence of the Chairman and the Vice-Chairman of the Board, or if there are no such officers, the President shall preside at all corporate meetings. The President may sign and execute, in the name of the Corporation, share certificates, deeds, mortgages, bonds, contracts, or other instruments except in cases where the signing and the execution thereof shall be expressly delegated by the Board of Directors or by these Bylaws to some other officer or agent of the Corporation or shall be required by law otherwise to be signed or executed. In addition, the President shall perform all duties incident to the Office of the President and such other duties as may be assigned by the Board of Directors.

4.6 Duties of the Vice Presidents

Each Vice President, if any, shall have such powers and duties as may be assigned to him or her by the President or the Board of Directors. Any Vice President may sign and execute, in the name of the Corporation, deeds, mortgages, bonds, contracts, or other instruments authorized by the Board of Directors, except where the signing and execution thereof shall be expressly delegated by the Board of Directors or the President to some other officer or agent of the Corporation or shall be required by law or otherwise to be signed or executed.

4.7 Duties of the Treasurer

The Treasurer shall have charge of and be responsible for all funds, securities, receipts, and disbursements of the Corporation, and shall deposit all monies and securities of the Corporation in such banks and depositories as shall be designated by the Board of Directors. The Treasurer shall be responsible for maintaining adequate financial accounts and records in accordance with generally accepted accounting practices; for the preparation of appropriate operating budgets and financial statements; for the preparation and filing of all tax returns required by law; and for the performance of all duties incident to the office of Treasurer and such other duties as may be assigned to him or her by the Board of Directors, the Finance Committee, or the President. The Treasurer may sign and execute in the name of the Corporation share certificates, deeds, mortgages, bonds, contracts, or other instruments, except in cases where the signing and the execution thereof shall be expressly delegated by the Board of Directors or by these Bylaws to some other officer or agent of the Corporation or shall be required by law or otherwise to be signed or executed.

F I G U R E   14-1

(Continued)

4.8 Duties of the Secretary
The Secretary shall act as secretary of all meetings of the Board of Directors and shareholders of the Corporation, and when requested, shall also act as secretary of the meetings of the committees of the Board of Directors. The Secretary shall keep and preserve the minutes of all such meetings in permanent books; see that all notices required to be given by the Corporation are duly given and served; have custody of the seal of the Corporation and shall affix the seal or cause it to be affixed to all share certificates of the Corporation and to all documents the execution of which on behalf of the Corporation under its corporate seal is duly authorized in accordance with law or the provisions of these Bylaws. The Secretary shall have custody of all deeds, leases, contracts, and other important corporate documents; have charge of the books, records, and papers of the Corporation relating to its organization and management as a Corporation; see that all reports, statements, and other documents required by law (except tax returns) are properly filed; and in general perform all the duties incident to the office of Secretary and such other duties as may be assigned by the Board of Directors or the President. The Secretary may designate such subordinate officers or administrative personnel, as desirable, including Assistant Secretary, with the consent of the Board of Directors to carry out the duties of the office.

4.9 Compensation
The Board of Directors shall have authority to fix the compensation of all officers of the Corporation.

ARTICLE V. Capital Stock

5.1 Certificates
Certificates shall represent the interest of each stockholder of the Corporation. They shall be numbered and entered in the books of the Corporation as they are issued. They shall exhibit the holder's name and the number of shares and shall be signed by the President or a Vice-President and the Treasurer or the Secretary and shall bear the corporate seal.

5.2 Lost, Destroyed, and Mutilated Certificates
Holders of the shares of the Corporation shall immediately notify the Corporation of any loss, destruction, or mutilation of the certificate thereof, and the Board of Directors may in its discretion cause new certificates for the same number of shares to be issued to such shareholder upon the surrender of the mutilated certificate or upon satisfactory proof of such loss or destruction.

5.3 Transfer of Shares
The shares of the Corporation shall be transferable or assignable only on the books of the Corporation by the holder in person or by attorney on surrender of the certificate for such shares duly endorsed and, if sought to be transferred by attorney, accompanied by a written power of attorney to have the same transferred on the books of the Corporation. The Corporation will recognize, however, the exclusive right of the person registered on its books as the owner of shares to receive dividends and to vote as such owner.

F I G U R E 14-1

(Continued)

5.4 Consideration for Shares

The Board of Directors may authorize shares to be issued for consideration consisting of any tangible or intangible property or benefit to the Corporation, including cash, promissory notes, services performed, contracts for services to be performed, or other securities of the Corporation. Before the Corporation issues shares, the Board of Directors shall determine that the consideration received or to be received for the shares is adequate.

5.5 Fixing Record Date

For the purpose of determining shareholders entitled to notice of or to vote at any meeting of shareholders or any adjournment thereof, or entitled to receive a dividend payment, or in order to make a determination of shareholders for any other proper purpose, the Board of Directors may fix in advance a date as the record date for any such determination of shareholders. Such date may not be more than 60 days prior to the date on which the particular action, requiring the determination of shareholders, is to be taken. If no record date is designated for the determination of shareholders entitled to notice of a meeting shareholders or to vote at a meeting of shareholders, or shareholders entitled to receive payment of a dividend, the date on which notices of the meeting are mailed or the date on which the resolution of the Board of Directors declaring such dividend is adopted, as the case may be, shall be the record date for such determination of shareholders. When a determination of shareholders entitled to vote at any meeting of shareholders has been made as provided in this section, such determination shall apply to any adjournment thereof.

ARTICLE VI. Miscellaneous Provisions

6.1 Seal

The seal of the Corporation shall consist of a flat-faced circular die, of which there may be any number of counterparts, on which there shall be engraved the word "Seal" and the name of the Corporation.

6.2 Fiscal Year

The fiscal year of the Corporation shall end on such date and shall consist of such accounting periods as may be fixed by the Board of Directors.

6.3 Checks, Notes, and Drafts

Checks, notes, drafts, and other orders for the payment of money shall be signed by persons authorized by the Board of Directors. When the Board of Directors so authorizes, however, the signature of any such person may be a facsimile.

6.4 Amendment of Bylaws

Unless proscribed by the Articles of Incorporation, these Bylaws may be amended or changed at any meeting of the Board of Directors by affirmative vote of a majority of the number of Directors fixed by these Bylaws. The shareholders entitled to vote in respect of the election of Directors, however, shall have the power to rescind, amend, alter, or repeal any Bylaws and to enact Bylaws which, if expressly so provided, may not be amended, altered, or repealed by the Board of Directors.

6.5 Dividends

The directors may declare, and the Corporation pay, dividends on its outstanding shares in the manner and upon the terms and conditions provided by law.

the shareholders would then be asked to approve the directors' resolution. To gain shareholder approval, the board of directors could either call a special meeting of shareholders or add the resolution to the agenda for the next annual meeting of shareholders. Figure 14-2 is a sample board of directors' resolution to amend the bylaws. It specifies the section of the bylaws to be amended and also includes the amended verbiage. This particular example also includes wording regarding the calling of a special meeting of shareholder to approve the amendment.

If the shareholders do not approve the proposed amendment, the corporation must maintain the provision that was originally established in the bylaws. In the example given here, this would mean that the corporation would continue to have only three directors. If the shareholders approve the change, the bylaws must then be formally amended, and all steps leading to the change should be formally documented. Documentation of approved resolutions and changes to the bylaws is a formality that is imposed on all corporations. As Chapter 18 will discuss, corporations run the risk of losing the limited liability afforded to shareholders if the formalities are not properly carried out.

Because of the risks associated with not properly complying with corporate formalities, it is highly advisable that you document all resolutions made by shareholders and directors, and that you keep these resolutions with your corporate records. Some business owners view the paperwork requirements that corporations face as a disadvantage. While the proper documentation of corporate actions may be time-intensive, it beats the alternative of possibly losing the limited liability that shareholders enjoy.

A number of steps should be taken to properly document the process of amending the bylaws. If a special meeting of directors is called to address the change, the notice document must include the reason for which the meeting is called. A copy of this document should be saved and included with the corporate records. If the change is accepted by unanimous consent of the directors, without formally holding a meeting, the consent document must include the resolution language. If a meeting is held, the meeting minutes should indicate whether or not the change was accepted. The unanimous consent document or the meeting minutes should also be included with the corporate records.

The process is similar in those cases in which shareholder approval is also necessary. If a special meeting of shareholders is called, the notice of meeting must include information on the action to be discussed. That notice should be kept in the corporate records. The action

F I G U R E   14-2

Board of Directors' Resolution to Amend Bylaws

Upon a duly made and seconded motion, the resolution that follows below was duly adopted by the directors:

RESOLVED, that Section <section number> of the Bylaws of the Corporation, <corporate name>, be changed to read as follows:

<Insert new text for the particular bylaw section being changed>

FURTHER RESOLVED, that the President of this Corporation is hereby directed to convene a special meeting of the shareholders on <date> at <time,> to consider and take action on the proposed amendment of the Bylaws of this Corporation.

The undersigned, <name,> certifies that I am the duly appointed Secretary of this Corporation and that the above is a true and correct copy of a resolution duly adopted at a meeting of the directors thereof, convened and held in accordance with law and the Bylaws of said Corporation on <date,> and that such resolution is now in full force and effect.

IN WITNESS THEREOF, I have affixed my name as Secretary of this Corporation and have attached the seal of this Corporation to this resolution.

_____
Secretary

Dated:
<stamp document with corporate seal>

taken by the shareholders, whether it be to approve or to reject the directors' resolution, should be included in the minutes of the shareholders' meeting. If the resolution is approved by majority consent without holding a meeting, the consent document should be drafted, signed by all shareholders, and included with the corporate records. Notice of the consent must also promptly be sent to all nonconsenting shareholders.

After amendments to the bylaws have been approved and adopted, the bylaws should be updated to include the new language. When bylaws are amended, they should be given a new title that shows that they are different from the original bylaws. For example, the first time the bylaws are revised, when the amended text is added, the document may become "Restated and Amended Bylaws of XYZ Corporation." Such titling allows the numbers to be changed each time an amendment is integrated. Over the course of time, this corporation may reach its "Fifth Restated and Amended Bylaws of XYZ Corporation." Keeping the bylaws up-to-date and documenting all changes made in them is a very important aspect of being a corporation.

CHAPTER 15

The Roles of Shareholders, Directors, and Officers

Shareholders, directors, and officers have defined roles in the corporate structure; however, in small companies, these standard roles often apply to a lesser degree. The role of a director of a Fortune 100 public company differs greatly from the role of a director of Charlie's Bar and Grill, where two people each act as a director, a shareholder, and an officer of the corporation. Furthermore, if the corporation has elected statutory close corporation status, it is possible that directors may be eliminated entirely. This chapter discusses the traditional roles of these corporate figures and explores their roles within smaller closely held corporations and statutory close corporations.

> *Major topics covered: This chapter outlines who can act as shareholders, directors, and officers in a corporation. It includes information on these groups' traditional roles and how these roles often differ in closely held and close corporations.*

Public companies have a visible role in today's society. The officers, and particularly the CEOs, of many large corporations are not only visible but quite powerful in terms of the influence they exert in the business world. You often read about shareholders suing corporations, or, on a more positive note, about shareholders making profits from an increase in the price of a corporation's stock. Since you are planning to form a corporation, or at least are seriously considering it, it is important that you understand the traditional roles of shareholders, directors, and officers, even if their roles may be different in your corporation. It is also important that you understand how the lines between the traditional roles of these corporate players often blur with small businesses.

SHAREHOLDERS

Shareholders are the owners of a corporation. People and/or entities become shareholders in a corporation when they buy or receive shares of that corporation's stock. There are no rules governing the maximum or minimum number of shareholders that a standard C corporation can have. Publicly traded companies may have tens of thousands of shareholders. Smaller companies may have as few as one shareholder. S corporations are restricted to having no more than 75 shareholders, and statutory close corporations are restricted to having fewer than 50 shareholders.

Who Are Shareholders?

For corporations other than S corporations, there are no restrictions on who can be a shareholder. Individuals, other corporations, limited liability companies (LLCs), partnerships, trusts, or other entities can be shareholders in C corporations. In contrast, with a few exceptions, shareholders of S corporations typically must be individuals.

A person or entity becomes a shareholder upon receiving shares of a corporation's stock. In public companies, this is typically accomplished by buying shares. With privately held companies, shares are not always purchased per se. It is common for these companies to issue shares for consideration other than cash, such as property, ideas, or services rendered to the corporation. As Chapter 14 noted, a corporation's bylaws often include language regarding consideration for shares, and may also require board approval of such issuance to ensure that the transaction is beneficial to the corporation.

Traditional Shareholder Roles

Traditionally, shareholders are primarily responsible for electing and removing directors and for approving or disapproving fundamental changes in the corporation, such as mergers, sales of substantially all of a corporation's assets, changes in the articles of incorporation, or the dissolution of the corporation. Shareholders cannot require directors to take a particular action; instead, they must seek to exert their influence on the directors, which can be done in a number of ways.

Exerting Influence

Traditionally, shareholders have a number of vehicles for influencing the corporation, particularly the corporation's board of directors.

- *Electing and removing directors.* Since the shareholders elect and remove directors, they can use this power to replace directors who they feel aren't acting in the corporation's best interest or who they feel are ineffective. Along that same line, shareholders can also seek to elect directors who they feel will help the corporation achieve particular goals, whether those goals be to increase profits, diversify offerings, accelerate growth, or take the company in a completely new direction.

- *Approving and/or disapproving changes in the bylaws or articles of incorporation.* Not all corporations require shareholder approval of all changes in the bylaws, but shareholders must always approve changes in the articles of incorporation. Typically, shareholders vote on proposed changes after the board of directors has already adopted a resolution to approve the amendment. If the shareholders do not approve and ratify the change, they are not only expressing their dissatisfaction with the board of directors' decision, but also exerting their influence on the corporation's rules and policies.

- *Approving and/or disapproving fundamental changes in the corporation.* Fundamental actions affecting the shareholders, such as mergers, the sale of substantially all assets, or dissolution, must typically have shareholder approval. The directors cannot dissolve a corporation without the approval of the shareholders. Likewise, while officers and directors may approve a proposed merger or acquisition, the merger or acquisition cannot take place until shareholders have also approved the transaction.

- *Approving and/or disapproving of transactions in which the directors and/or officers have self-interest.* Transactions in which directors, officers, or both have self-interest are typically presented to the shareholders for a vote. For example, Global Manufacturing Corporation wishes to enter into a multimillion-dollar deal in which it will subcontract part of its operations to a company owned by the brother of one of Global's directors. Because of the high value of the deal, it requires the approval of the board of directors. Because one of the board members has a self-interest in this deal, the relationship may also be put to a shareholder vote. In addition to being another way in which shareholders can exert influence over corporate actions, this also allows for checks and balances within the corporation, not unlike the executive, legislative, and judicial branches of the U.S. government.

- *Shareholder resolutions.* Most of the actions noted so far relate to steps that were first taken by either the directors or the officers. With shareholder resolutions, shareholders can propose corporate actions, even though these actions will need to be approved by the board of directors as well. For example, if the shareholders adopted a resolution to amend the corporation's bylaws to include a provision to standardize the date for the annual meeting of shareholders, the board of directors would need to approve the shareholder resolution and adopt its own resolution allowing the change before it could occur.

The primary difference between the shareholders of a publicly traded company and those of a privately held company, besides the number of shareholders, is the level of shareholders' involvement. Shareholders in public companies have primarily a passive role, while shareholders of private companies typically have a more active role in the direction and even the day-to-day operation of the business. The more active role of shareholders in privately held companies typically comes about because the shareholders are also directors and/or officers of the corporation.

Meetings

Shareholders' meetings are a formality required of all corporations. As Chapter 13 discussed, there is typically an initial meeting of shareholders, at which the shareholders approve the formation of the corporation, the corporation's bylaws, the appointment of the corporation's directors, and any directors' resolutions approved during the organizational meeting. Annual meetings of shareholders are also required. Chapter 18 discusses annual meetings in more depth, but briefly these are meetings held each year at which the shareholders elect directors and approve or disapprove any actions put forth for their vote.

Previous chapters have also briefly discussed special meetings of shareholders. Special meetings, which are called pursuant to notice of the time, place, and reason for the meeting, address an action that the directors feel cannot or should not be postponed until the next annual meeting of shareholders. As mentioned previously, when a special meeting is called, the notice given to shareholders must include the action item to be addressed. No other business can be conducted during a special meeting of shareholders.

Shareholders of public companies typically do not have regular interaction with one another, the corporation's directors, or the officers. Meetings are the primary medium whereby shareholders learn about the corporation's current status and direction, and exert their influence by voting on the issues at hand.

Shareholder Agreements

Shareholder agreements are designed to help all shareholders or a group of shareholders reach a desired goal or undertake a desired course of action. There are two primary, common types of shareholder agreements—shareholder voting agreements and buy-sell agreements. While voting agreements are more common in larger companies, buy-sell agreements are frequently utilized in small companies.

- *Voting agreements (also called pooling agreements).* A shareholder voting agreement or pooling agreement is one in which two or more shareholders agree to vote together on certain matters or all matters. Shareholder voting agreements are often put in place to give minority shareholders more of a voice. Within this type of agreement, there are two subtypes: specific agreements and general agreements. With specific agreements, the shareholders agree to vote together on a certain issue or group of issues. For example, a group of shareholders may enter into a specific pooling agreement to always vote against an acquisition of the corporation, when or if this possibility arises. With general agreements, shareholders are basically agreeing to agree, but do not specify exactly how votes are to be cast. The primary requirement is that the votes be cast together. If a group of shareholders have a general pooling agreement stating that they will always vote together, those shareholders would most likely communicate before a vote must be taken to ensure that they are voting their shares in the same manner on the issues at hand. For example, Mary, Marcus, and Tom have agreed to always pool their votes on actions brought before the shareholders. The next annual meeting of shareholders will feature a vote on the reelection of two of the corporation's directors. Mary, Marcus, and Tom may communicate prior to the meeting and determine that they wish vote for the reelection of one director but against the reelection of the other.
- *Buy-sell agreements.* These agreements, which are more commonly used by shareholders of small companies, help to control changes in the ownership of the corporation. They basically govern when

and how the shares of a corporation can be sold. This type of agreement often outlines the types of situations that would cause the other shareholders to buy all or part of a shareholder's shares and at what price the shares would be purchased. They also typically outline the course of action to be taken if a shareholder wishes to sell or transfer shares, declares bankruptcy, goes through a divorce in which the spouse might receive the shares in question, dies, or becomes disabled.

Regarding voting agreements, note that shareholders are not required to enter into formal agreements in order to vote together. If Walter, Judy, Charlie, and Elaine are all attending the annual meeting of shareholders and they strike up a conversation before the meeting begins regarding the issues being addressed during the meeting, they can agree to vote in a certain way. In this case, a formal, legal shareholder agreement is not necessary.

Regarding buy-sell agreements, we would like to emphasize the importance of these agreements for small corporations. With closely held corporations, events such as the death, disability, divorce, or bankruptcy of a shareholder or disputes among the owners can have a substantial effect on the corporation. For example, Larry and Cindy have a corporation, and they both act as shareholders, directors, and officers. Larry dies unexpectedly, and his will specifies that his wife and his three children receive equal portions of his shares in the corporation. The corporation has instantly gone from having two shareholders to having five. Reaching an agreement on issues that arise with the business can often be more difficult with five people than with just two. If Larry and Cindy have a buy-sell agreement in place that specifies that an owner will have the chance to buy the other owner's shares in the event of her or his death, this type of situation can be avoided.

As another example, if Larry and his wife divorce and Larry's wife is awarded all of Larry's shares, she now becomes the other shareholder with Cindy in the corporation. If Cindy and Larry's wife do not get along, this could have a negative effect on the corporation. Larry's wife may be open to Cindy's purchasing her shares, but there is no guarantee of that. Having an agreement in place that outlines the steps to be taken if any of these situations should arise can save you potential headaches later. With small corporations that have more than one shareholder, you may wish to seriously consider the implementation of a buy-sell agreement. That way, you can determine, before a crisis occurs, how a number of potential situations should be handled.

Shareholder agreements can be relatively simple or quite complex. They may stay in effect for an extended period of time, or they may be reevaluated and renewed in shorter periods of time. Before entering into a shareholder agreement, it is important to first answer the question, "What is the agreement meant to do or accomplish?" Is the intent of the agreement to influence the way the corporation is run by voting for a certain director or a certain type of director? Maybe the intent is to limit the number of shareholders that the corporation can have. Answering questions and addressing thoughts such as these will help determine both the type and the content of the agreement. Given the potential complexity of shareholder agreements, using an attorney to draft them is sound advice.

DIRECTORS

Directors oversee the affairs of the corporation, but they do not manage its day-to-day operations. The directors appoint officers to run the corporation on a daily basis, but continue in a supervisory role. Directors formulate corporate policy and carry out their business within the setting of annual or special meetings. Together, directors make up a body known as the board of directors, which is often referred to as just "the board."

Who Are Directors?

Directors are individuals who are elected by the shareholders to govern the corporation. Typically, directors can be placed into three categories—insiders, outsiders, and a hybrid of the two.

- *Insiders.* Insiders are people who are employed by the corporation; they usually include the CEO, and possibly other corporate officers.
- *Outsiders.* Outsiders are people who have no direct affiliation with the company. With publicly traded companies, you often see the CEOs, former CEOs, or founders of public companies serving on other companies' boards.
- *Hybrids.* Hybrids are people who have ties to the company, but are not employed by it, such as the corporation's attorney or banker or venture capitalists.

In companies with a larger number of directors, directors are often nominated because of the insight they can provide into a certain area of the corporation's business, such as appointing the CEO of a computer company for technology expertise or a retired executive for general business experience. In smaller companies, directors are again often chosen because of the expertise and experience they can provide, but most often they also have close ties to the corporation, such as being an owner of the company, an owner's relative, or possibly a friend.

Traditional Director Roles

Directors are like the captains of a ship. They help guide the ship and ensure that it's on course, but they do not do the actual steering of the ship. Directors set the rules and policies for the corporation, and then appoint officers to manage the day-to-day aspects of the business.

Meetings

Directors carry out most corporate business through established meetings. Chapter 13 discussed the organizational meeting, or the initial meeting of directors. It is during this meeting that the groundwork for the corporation is laid. Officers are elected, and bylaws are approved. Directors also have annual meetings. These will be discussed more thoroughly in Chapter 18; however, it is during the annual meetings of directors that major corporate decisions are made.

If corporate business arises in between annual meetings, a special meeting of directors may be called and held. As with special meetings of shareholders, notice must be sent to the directors specifying the reason for calling the meeting. For example, if a corporation's bylaws require any contract valued over $100,000 to have board approval, a special meeting of the board could be called should an opportunity of this scope arise at a time when the next annual meeting is months away.

Committees

A corporation's board of directors may be divided into a number of separate committees, each of which is charged with a separate task. Committees are common within the boards of large and/or publicly traded companies; however, most smaller corporations do not have directors' committees. A primary benefit of committees is the ability to have a smaller group of directors who can still act on behalf of the board. For example, if HDM Corporation has nine directors on its board, and the directors live in different areas of the country, it might be beneficial to have committees of three directors that are responsible for overseeing certain aspects of the business.

The board must approve the formation of a committee, determine the authority that committee has, and approve the dissolution of a committee, should that be decided upon. The roles of certain committees may be defined in the corporation's bylaws. The directors may also adopt a resolution creating and defining the role of a committee if a new committee is created at a later date or if committees were not defined in the bylaws but are later desired.

The four committees most commonly found within public companies, but not the only committees, are the audit, compensation, executive, and nominating committees.

- *Audit committee.* The audit committee is probably the best-known committee, especially after the accounting scandals that erupted at a number of public companies in 2002. This committee is responsible for reviewing a corporation's financial statements and for working with the corporation's auditors. Public companies are required by the Securities and Exchange Commission (SEC) both to have an audit committee and to have their financial statements certified by an outside accounting firm. The audit committee often works closely with the corporation's CFO and financial team as well as with the external auditors.

- *Compensation committee.* This committee is responsible for setting the salaries for the corporation's executives and management. When a corporation utilizes noncash forms of compensation, such as stock options, the compensation committee typically must approve this compensation as well. In the case of stock options, the compensation committee will generally have the authority to act on behalf of the entire board to issue new options or make changes to options that are already in existence.

- *Executive committee.* The executive committee performs the functions of the entire board in between meetings. This committee is often composed of the CEO and other insiders, since insiders are closely tied to the day-to-day activities of the corporation. The executive committee must also be able to assemble quickly to hold meetings and take action on items that need prompt approval by the board.

- *Nominating committee.* This committee is responsible for nominating people to fill vacancies on the board of directors. As mentioned previously, large companies often seek outsiders with specific expertise and experience. Finding a person who can enhance a corporation's board by providing the right mix of knowledge, experience, expertise, and availability is often not very easy. The nominating committee researches, contacts, and interviews possible directors prior to making recommendations either to the entire board or to the shareholders. This committee also helps to ensure that the board is well balanced, not including too many insiders, outsiders, or hybrids.

Committees are typically given the power to make decisions on behalf of the entire board, but restrictions may be imposed on their authority. It's possible that a corporation may grant committees the right to make big decisions, such as the appointment or removal of officers, the pursuit of large capital investments, or the taking on of long-term debt. However, there are certain actions that the entire board should approve or that may require shareholder approval. It's common for the corporation's bylaws or the directors' resolution creating a committee to list actions that the committee does not have the authority to undertake. For example, committees may be prohibited from approving actions such as filling board vacancies, amending the bylaws, approving actions that require shareholder approval, or authorizing the issuance of corporate shares.

As mentioned previously, the boards of smaller corporations often have no real need for committees. Small companies typically have fewer directors, and in many cases the directors may live very close to one another or be employed by the corporation. In these situations, the full board can act jointly and quickly on actions needing board approval.

OFFICERS

Officers manage the day-to-day operations of the corporation under the supervision of the board of directors. The board of directors appoints the corporation's officers during the organizational meeting. Officers may have set terms, with the directors evaluating their performance at the end of the term and determining whether to extend the term. More commonly, officers serve in a given position until they are promoted, are terminated from the position, or leave the corporation.

Some states still require corporations to have the four primary officers: president, vice president, secretary, and treasurer. Most states, however, allow corporations to have any number of officers and to give these officers any titles they choose. Common titles today are chief executive officer, chief operating officer, chief financial officer, chief technology officer, chief information officer, executive vice president, and general manager, among others. It is also possible for companies to have executive managers who are not corporate officers. The corporation's bylaws typically outline the officer positions for the corporation and the general duties of each officer.

Who Are Officers?

Basically, any individual can become a corporate officer. Like directors, officers are often selected and appointed because of their knowledge and expertise. CEOs are frequently recruited to become CEOs at other companies. Other individuals move up through the ranks within a company and finally are promoted to an officer position. Current officers may also leave to take higher or different positions with other companies.

Traditional Officer Roles

Since a corporation can have any number of officers with any number of titles, we'll focus on the four traditional officers. There are no rules stating what duties and responsibilities these officers have, but over the course of time many standard ones have been defined.

- *President.* The president is now often called the chief executive officer (CEO) or given the combination title president and CEO. Unless the board of directors specifies otherwise, the president is typically responsible for implementing the policies set by the board of directors and overseeing the general management of the corporation. The president helps define the direction of the business, and the other corporate officers often report directly to the president. The president typically has the authority to sign and execute important documents such as contracts, loans, and real estate mortgages or leases in the name of the corporation.
- *Vice president.* Smaller companies tend to have only one or a very small number of vice presidents, while larger companies may have quite a few. Because of this, the role of vice president may encompass a number of areas of the business, or it can be very targeted, such as a vice president of sales or a vice president of North American operations. The board, or often the president, may assign responsibilities to the vice president. The vice president typically has the authority to sign important documents on behalf of the business, especially those that relate directly to his or her areas of responsibility. For example, a vice president of marketing is likely

to have the authority to sign advertising contracts or advertising agency contracts, since this type of document directly relates to this officer's role in the corporation.

- *Secretary.* The secretary plays an important role, as he or she is typically responsible for documenting major corporate actions. The secretary sends the directors and shareholders notice of annual meetings and of any special meetings that are called. The secretary is also typically responsible for recording what takes place at these meetings and for preparing the meeting minutes. This officer is also often responsible for keeping the corporate records, which typically include the articles of incorporation, the bylaws, all resolutions and meeting minutes, major corporate contracts, property deeds, and any other documents that have been approved by the board of directors and/or the shareholders. Additionally, the secretary typically keeps the corporate seal and is responsible for using it as necessary to signify the official nature of certain corporate documents, such as stock certificates when they are issued.

- *Treasurer.* In publicly traded corporations, the treasurer's role may often be combined with that of the chief financial officer (CFO). This officer is responsible for maintaining the financial records of the corporation and for reporting its financial performance, using generally accepted accounting principles. Publicly traded companies are required by the SEC to publicly report their financial results and earnings per share on a quarterly basis. This is not the case with privately held companies, which are under no obligation to share their financial results. However, the treasurer is often required to provide these results to the board of directors. The treasurer is generally in charge of all corporate funds, securities, receipts, and disbursements. He or she must also typically prepare operating budgets and prepare and file all necessary tax returns. If a corporation has external auditors or if there is a finance committee as part of the board of directors, the treasurer often works closely with these groups. The treasurer may or may not have the authority to sign important corporate documents on behalf of the corporation.

Authority to Act on Behalf of the Corporation

Officers have certain authority to act on behalf of the corporation, but the authority that rests with a particular officer position is not always strictly defined. Officers and their roles vary among corporations; therefore, the authority granted to officers also varies. When the roles of the corporation's officers are detailed in the corporation's bylaws or in a resolution, those officers are given express authority to act on behalf of the corporation in performing those duties. There are three primary types of authority: express authority, implied actual authority, and apparent authority.

- *Express authority.* As mentioned previously, officers are typically granted express authority by having their powers outlined in the bylaws or in a directors' resolution granting the authority to undertake a certain act on behalf of the corporation. For example, if the bylaws of White's Paper Plant Inc. specify that the president may sign documents such as contracts or leases, then the president has express authority to sign and execute these documents on behalf of the corporation. If a project were to arise that was not covered by the powers outlined in the bylaws, the board of directors could adopt a resolution assigning an officer the authority to carry out that project. For example, if White's Paper Plant Inc. needs to expand operations by opening a new paper plant, the board could adopt a resolution granting a particular officer the authority to negotiate and sign all necessary contracts, leases, and/or deeds relating to the new facility.

- *Implied actual authority.* Implied actual authority isn't as concrete as express authority. It is often referred to as the authority inherent in the office. Most people have perceptions of the roles of certain officers. For example, most people believe that all CEOs have the ability to act on behalf of their corporations by signing documents that relate to the ordinary course of business. Examples of this might be signing an agreement with a supplier of raw materials necessary for the manufacture of a corporation's products or signing the corporation's checks. With CEOs in particular, there is a level of implied authority inherent in the position. Also, implied authority may be created in the bylaws or by a resolution of the directors. For example, if a directors' resolution instructs the corporation's president to sell an asset, the president has the express authority to sell the asset and the implied authority to hire lawyers and brokers to negotiate the sale.

- *Apparent authority.* While express and implied authority relate more to internal authority, apparent authority relates more to the outside world's perceptions. While the outside world may reasonably believe that an officer has certain authority, in reality that may not be the case. Apparent authority can exist by virtue of the position alone. For example, the vice president of marketing may not have actual authority to legally bind the corporation by signing contracts on behalf of the corporation, but because of the title, the outside world may believe that this officer can sign marketing-related contracts.

Generally, corporations want their officers to know what they can and cannot do by virtue of their office. A corporation does not want the treasurer acting as the president. Corporations therefore rely on express authority to outline the powers granted to each officer. Since it is unrealistic to believe that the corporation's bylaws can address every aspect of the officers' jobs, corporations also rely on implied authority to fill in the gaps. Apparent authority can have consequences for the corporation if the officers are legally binding the corporation by means of contracts and agreements when they do not have the express or implied authority to do so. Therefore, corporations should communicate to their officers what authority they do and do not have as part of their position, even if this is implied authority.

Closely held corporations present a unique situation when it comes to the authority of officers, since the officers of the corporation often are also the shareholders and directors. It is common for the officers of the corporation to communicate regularly on all facets of the business, and for each of them to know most of what the other officers are doing. Because the officers are also the directors and shareholders, these bodies typically also know what actions the officers are taking. Because of this overlap, closely held corporations may utilize implied authority more often.

Despite the ease of relying on implied authority, defining the roles of your corporation's officers within your bylaws is advisable. This is the safest way to go, in terms of protecting your corporation from an officer who tries to abuse the implied or apparent authority that comes with the title. Defining officers' roles in your bylaws helps to establish more concrete parameters for the authority each person possesses. Remember that bylaws, particularly those of small corporations with only a few directors, are fairly easy to amend, so that the board of directors of your corporation can add or change officers' responsibilities and authority as needed.

THE ROLES OF SHAREHOLDERS, DIRECTORS, AND OFFICERS IN CLOSELY HELD CORPORATIONS

The terms *closely held corporation* and *close corporation* have both been used before in this book. While the two may sound substantially similar, there are differences between them. Because of these differences, the roles of the corporate figures within these types of corporations will be discussed separately.

Note that the term *closely held* is often taken to be synonymous with the term *privately held*. In both situations, the corporation's stock is not traded publicly. In some cases, the term *privately held* may be used to refer to larger corporations in terms of number of employees, whereas the term *closely held* refers to smaller corporations. However, both terms relate to the ownership of the corporation, not its size, and there is no specific number of shareholders that identifies one corporation as closely held and another as privately held.

With closely held companies, there is often no real separation between ownership and control, as there is with public companies. Many, if not all, of the shareholders of closely held companies typically occupy all three corporate roles: shareholders, directors, and officers. Shareholders and directors tend to have more constant interaction among themselves and with each other.

For example, Mr. and Mrs. Individual, the shareholders, approve themselves to serve as directors. Mr. and Mrs. Individual, the directors, appoint themselves to the roles of president and vice president. The same two people now occupy all three corporate roles, and the distinction among these roles has been lost. Realistically, Mr. and Mrs. Individual, the shareholders, are not going to disapprove the appointment of themselves as officers.

Technically, this arrangement also occurs with public companies, where the CEO often serves as a director and typically also owns shares of the corporation's stock. However, the CEO's role as shareholder is a traditional one. For example, Mr. CEO, the shareholder, cannot directly require the board or the officers to undertake a certain act. Conversely, Mr. CEO, the director, can influence corporate actions, but not typically on his own. He would need board or at least board committee approval. Likewise, Mr. CEO, the officer, has responsibility over the day-to-day activities of the business, but the board of directors still oversees his actions.

The corporate structure itself includes inherent checks and balances to try to ensure that abuses of power do not occur. In public companies, the directors are really the "police" for the corporation. They are responsible for overseeing the actions of the officers and reviewing the officers' performance. The directors are also responsible for approving or disapproving major corporate actions. In closely held corporations, this objective body does not exist. (We realize that the directors of public companies may not always be objective, but what we mean is that they do not typically occupy the roles of shareholder and officer as well.) With closely held companies, the role of the board of directors in reviewing the officers' actions and performance may be lost or substantially diminished, since the directors often are also the officers. One thing that the shareholders, officers, and directors of closely held corporations do have is a level of devotion to the company that is often not present with public companies. Owners of small corporations invest more than just capital in their corporations; they also invest a substantial amount of time. Abuses of power in small corporations tend to have a profound effect on the other shareholders, officers, and directors.

As previously discussed, shareholders have greater influence in closely held corporations. Shareholder agreements can be arranged to control the number of shareholders, and also to govern who can be shareholders. In addition, closely held corporations also use the number of shares authorized and issued to help control the ownership size of the company.

Closely held corporations have the ability to issue the total number of authorized shares to a small group of people. For example, Frank is forming The Table Company with 2000 authorized shares. He wishes to limit the number of shareholders to himself, his sister Rebecca, and his brother Douglas. If the board of directors for The Table Company issues all 2000 shares to Frank, Rebecca, and Douglas during its organizational meeting, the company cannot add any additional shareholders without authorizing more shares. Because the number of authorized shares is listed in a corporation's articles of incorporation, a state filing to amend the articles to include a higher number would need to be made. Shareholder approval is typically required to amend the articles of incorporation. As shareholders, Frank, Rebecca, and Douglas would need to approve the authorization of new shares, and this gives them an element of control over the ownership of the corporation.

The roles of directors on the board of a closely held corporation remain similar to the traditional roles. The boards of these corporations are often smaller in size, eliminating the need for committees, and directors often take many formal actions by means of unanimous consent rather than holding meetings. Because of the larger number of directors and their less close geographic proximity in publicly held companies, this is an option that does not often present itself to these boards.

Closely held corporations still face the same formal requirements as public corporations, such as initial and annual meetings of directors and shareholders. All actions taken during those meetings should be formally documented and kept with the meeting minutes. As mentioned previously, the directors of closely held corporations often take actions by means of unanimous consent rather than holding a formal meeting. This is also often the case with the shareholders of closely held companies, who can approve actions by majority consent as long as notice of the consent is promptly given to all nonconsenting shareholders. The majority consent document satisfies the necessity of formally documenting major corporate decisions, without the added steps associated with calling and holding a formal meeting.

THE ROLES OF SHAREHOLDERS, DIRECTORS, AND OFFICERS IN STATUTORY CLOSE CORPORATIONS

As previously discussed, statutory close corporations are corporations formed pursuant to different state statutes from those under which general corporations are formed. Close corporations typically cannot have more than 50 shareholders, and the shareholders must be closely involved in the management and day-to-day operations of the corporation. Not all states have close corporation statutes, and not all corporations that are eligible to elect treatment as a close corporation choose to do so.

In terms of corporate roles, the primary difference between close corporations and closely held corporations is in the role of directors. Because the shareholders are very involved in determining the corporation's direction and play a role in overseeing the management and day-to-day operations, the traditional role of the board of directors is often taken by the shareholders. It is possible for close corporations to eliminate directors or to substantially reduce their role. Eliminating the role of directors decreases the number of formalities the corporation is required to comply with, since directors' meetings will not be held.

Another characteristic of a close corporation is restrictions on the sale of stock. A common practice for restricting the sale of stock of a close corporation is to provide the corporation with the right of first refusal when a shareholder wishes to sell or transfer shares. The right of first refusal serves to tightly control who can be a shareholder of the corporation. For example, Diane is a shareholder of a close corporation. She has acted as an officer of the corporation since its inception, but she has decided to retire, and she wishes to sell her ownership position in the company. The company would have the first right to purchase Diane's shares. Often state statutes provide that the other shareholders of close corporations will have the right to buy shares if the corporation refuses.

If the corporation or the other stockholders do not purchase Diane's total shares, or if they purchase only a portion of them, Diane can then transfer her shares to a family member, or possibly sell them to a third party. If the corporation does purchase Diane's shares, it will then have to determine whether to distribute those shares to the other shareholders or to keep them as authorized but unissued shares. If it keeps the shares as unissued shares, it can issue all or a portion of them to new shareholders or use them to increase the ownership percentage of existing shareholders at a later date. Having authorized but unissued shares does not typically have negative consequences for corporations.

As a reader of this book, you probably have started or are planning to start a small business, but it's always possible for your small business to grow and become a publicly traded company. Whether you plan to form your business pursuant to close corporation statutes or to maintain a closely held company (at least for the time being), understanding the roles that shareholders, directors, and officers play in a corporation is important.

Capitalizing Your Business

The financial logistics of owning a business frighten many would-be entrepreneurs. It's no secret that starting your own business often requires a large investment, both financially and in terms of your time. To put it simply, to start a business, you must provide adequate capital to get the business off the ground. Furthermore, your business needs adequate capital to continue each day. Providing the necessary funds and other assets to start and run your business is called capitalizing your business. While it would be nice if capitalization was as easy as, "Here's some money; the business is capitalized," that's not the case. This chapter seeks to help you understand the basics of capitalization.

> *Major topics covered:* This chapter contains information on getting money into and out of your corporation. It also addresses the need to prohibit the commingling of business and personal assets, the importance of documenting financial transactions, valuing noncash assets, and the logistics of 1244 stock.

Small corporations face a unique situation in terms of capitalization, primarily because the shareholders of closely held corporations are typically very involved in the day-to-day aspects of the business. There are formalities that must be complied with regarding capitalization, and failing to comply with them correctly has consequences. Let's use a corporation with one shareholder as an example. Most likely, this one shareholder is also the sole director and officer of the corporation, and runs the entire business. In cases like this, it is very easy for the owner to purchase something for the business with his or her personal credit card or check. However, doing so, or keeping only one bank account for both personal and business uses, can cause substantial problems for the corporation. The commingling of assets and its potential consequences are discussed later in this chapter; however, keep in mind that corporations are separate from their owners, and that you need to uphold this principle.

GETTING MONEY INTO THE CORPORATION

We hope that the words "getting money into the corporation" painted a picture in your mind of providing your business with the capital it needs at the start and the capital it will need in the future in order to continue to survive. In reality, of course, businesses need more than just money as they start and grow. They need items such as computers, machinery, office equipment, furniture, employees, and so on. To secure all of these assets, the corporation needs to have capital.

For example, Curt has $10,000 of capital to start his e-commerce business. Because of the technological nature of his business, he needs to have a server for running his web site and accepting online orders, as well as computers, a phone system, desks, a fax machine, office supplies, letterhead, and so on. As you can see, businesses incur a number of start-up costs, and without proper capitalization, a business will probably never get off the ground.

There are a few ways in which you can get capital into your corporation. The most common are by accepting contributions in return for stock, thereby creating shareholders in your corporation, or by taking out business loans. Both of these methods are described in the following subsections.

Note that the examples used in this chapter often simplify the process of obtaining the capital necessary to start and run your business. We understand that this can be a very stressful and often difficult task for entrepreneurs. To help illustrate various capitalization concepts, we will use some basic examples. There are often a number of additional factors that you should consider and weigh when capitalizing your business. For questions regarding this rather complex subject, it is best to contact an accountant or an organization that specializes in providing financial advice to small business owners.

Contributing Money or Property in Return for Stock

One of the most common ways to get money into the business is for you and/or others to contribute money or other items in return for stock, thereby creating shareholders or owners of your corporation. In closely held companies, which typically have only one or very few shareholders, each shareholder normally contributes something to the company, whether it be cash, property, equipment, or services, in return for stock.

For example, Jill and Lisa are starting a printing business. Jill contributes a new printing press, and Lisa contributes cash. In return for their contributions, both Jill and Lisa receive stock in the corporation. The printing press will be used for printing needs, and the cash will be used for the corporation's other expenses, such as rent, supplies, phones, computers, and advertising. These contributions provide the capital necessary for this fictitious printing business to begin operations. In return for their contributions, both Jill and Lisa will receive stock in the corporation.

Valuing these capital contributions can prove challenging. With cash, there is no question as to the value of the contribution. The value of a $1000 cash contribution is $1000. When assets such as equipment (particularly used equipment), real estate, and services are contributed, however, establishing a value is more difficult. Valuing noncash assets is discussed later in this chapter, but briefly, a fair market value must be established for the items contributed.

If the printing press Jill contributed was previously owned, a fair market value would have to be established in order to determine the amount of Jill's contribution and therefore the number of shares she should receive. To determine a fair market value for this used printing press, Jill might be able to contact the manufacturer or a distributor of printing presses. Another option would be to have the press appraised.

If there were a third shareholder in Jill and Lisa's corporation, Jack, and Jack contributed 40 hours of his time to set up the corporation's computer systems, the corporation would need to issue shares in return for Jack's contribution of his services. Again, the complexity comes in valuing the time Jack spent on this project. Fair market value might be established by obtaining a quote for similar services from a company specializing in the installation of computer systems.

One concept to keep in mind is that ownership in a corporation, whether it is publicly held or privately held, is proportionate to the shareholder's contribution. To continue with the example, we'll say that Jill contributed a new printing press that cost $10,000 to the corporation and

Lisa contributed $5000 in cash. If Jill and Lisa are the only two shareholders, their ownership percentages would not be equal, because Jill contributed more capital to the corporation than Lisa did. If each of them is to hold 50 percent of the outstanding shares of the corporation's stock, Lisa will need to contribute an additional $5000 to equal Jill's $10,000 worth of machinery.

While our examples thus far have focused on contributions made when the business is started, contributions can be made at any time during the life of the business. After Jill and Lisa's print shop has been in business for 2 or 3 years, they may decide that it's time to add a smaller printing press in order to be able to run two presses simultaneously. If they cannot purchase this new press with money from corporate profits, Jill and/or Lisa will again need to contribute a new press (or the money to buy it) to the business. However, each could contribute $2500 for the $5000 printing press, and in return the corporation would issue them additional shares of stock.

Note that there are many items to consider when analyzing how much start-up capital is needed. The owners of closely held corporations are often hesitant to give up part or all of their authority to external parties, such as potential outside investors or the originators of loans. To avoid this loss of control, the owners may need to either contribute additional capital or use preferred stock. In addition, the start-up process often takes more time and more money than the owners originally anticipated. Owners should factor this into their decision making regarding their initial capital needs.

Basis

In terms of stock, the concept of *basis* needs to be introduced. *Basis* is an accounting concept that represents the cost of the stock, generally meaning the amount contributed in order to receive the stock. With a C corporation, a shareholder's basis is typically equal to the amount the shareholder contributed in return for his or her shares and does not increase or decrease based on the financial results of the corporation. With an S corporation, however, a shareholder's basis can increase or decrease as a result of the corporation's taxable profits and losses, because the S corporation is a pass-through tax entity. Basis becomes very important when a shareholder wishes to sell shares in the corporation, because basis helps determine the gain or loss, and consequently the tax (if any) that will be imposed on the sale.

For example, when Jill contributes a $10,000 printing press and Lisa contributes $10,000 in cash, each has a basis of $10,000. With a C corporation, their basis would remain at $10,000 regardless of whether the corporation posts a profit or a loss. With an S corporation, however, this is not the case. For example, Jill and Lisa now have a basis of $10,000, but if the corporation passes through a $4000 loss to each shareholder's tax return, both Jill and Lisa's basis would be reduced to $6000.

As previously mentioned, basis is important for figuring gains or losses when shareholders sell their shares. Let's return to the initial $10,000 basis. If Lisa decides to sell her shares for $15,000, she will incur a taxable gain of $5000. Conversely, if she sells her shares for $5000, she will incur a loss of $5000 on the sale.

Basis can be a complex subject, particularly when the corporation's earnings and expenses are factored into the equation. To learn more about basis, and how it specifically applies to C and S corporations, it is best to research this subject on the IRS web site at www.irs.gov or to contact an accountant or tax adviser.

Common versus Preferred Stock

C corporations can issue multiple classes of stock that may allow certain groups of shareholders to receive preferential treatment over other shareholders. Not all corporations, particularly closely held corporations, choose to have multiple classes of stock; however, the terms *common stock* and *preferred stock* are often heard, and should be explained. Remember that S corporations cannot have more than one class of stock (disregarding voting rights). This is a restriction placed on corporations that file for subchapter S tax treatment with the IRS. Creating another class of stock would invalidate an S corporation's status as such.

If a corporation chooses to have multiple classes of stock, this must be reflected in the articles of incorporation. You can also add additional classes of stock after you incorporate your business, should the need arise. To do so, you will need to file an amendment to your articles of incorporation with the secretary of state that includes the information on the different classes of stock and their par value. You will also need to pay a fee to the state to amend your articles of incorporation. Furthermore, if your state figures franchise taxes on number of shares and par value, changing the stock structure for your corporation, particularly if you are increasing the overall number of shares, could increase the franchise taxes that your corporation owes to the state.

If a corporation has only one class of stock, it is deemed by default to be common stock. Common stock gives shareholders the right to vote on corporate matters posed to them, and to receive a proportionate share of dividends and of the corporation's assets upon dissolution. There can be multiple classes of common stock, each with different voting rights. For example, Class A stock may allow shareholders to vote for directors, while Class B stock carries no voting rights, but both classes may still have the right to receive a proportional share of dividends. When a corporation has multiple classes of common stock, information on each class is typically included in the articles of incorporation.

Corporations often add multiple classes of common stock when they plan to seek a number of outside investors. This allows the corporation to bring more money into the corporation, but to restrict the voting rights of these new shareholders, thus limiting the amount of influence the new shareholders can exert over the company.

Preferred stock generally provides shareholders with preferential payment of dividends and preferential rights to the corporation's assets upon dissolution, but does not necessarily carry voting rights. Typically, investors who are granted preferred stock pay more for these shares because of these preferential rights. If a company pays dividends to shareholders, it will often pay all the owners of preferred shares before paying any owners of common shares and/or pay the owners of preferred shares more than it pays common shareholders. Additionally, in the event that the corporation dissolves, the corporation's assets would typically be used to repay preferred shareholders' equity before what remains is distributed to common shareholders.

In exchange for this preferential treatment, owners of preferred shares occasionally give up their voting rights, meaning that they do not vote on any items requiring shareholder approval, such as electing directors. Sometimes preferred shares can be convertible to common shares upon the request of the shareholder. This is becoming a more common feature of stock given to outside investors, such as venture capitalists. When a company has preferred stock, the directors may set the parameters and rights associated with these shares. If the directors set the parameters of the stock, this can be done in the bylaws or by a directors' resolution. This information should be documented and kept with the corporate records. The preferences may also be given in the articles of incorporation. Owners of preferred shares should also be provided with information regarding their rights as preferred shareholders of your corporation.

For example, a corporation may determine that preferred shareholders receive 75 percent of any dividends paid to shareholders, and that those owning common stock receive the remaining 25 percent. The corporation could also outline that in the event of the corporation's dissolution, the preferred shareholders would receive a certain amount or percentage over their original investment paid out of the assets of the corporation, prior to any remaining assets being distributed to the owners of common shares. For additional information on preferred stock and whether it would be a benefit to your corporation, it is best to seek the advice of an attorney.

Loans to the Business

The second primary method of getting money into the business is through loans. Loans made to businesses are fundamentally no different from the loans we secure as individuals, such as car loans or school loans. Money is provided to the business for a certain purpose, whether it be to provide the business with working capital for a certain period of time, to buy new equipment, or to enter into a new contract. In return, the business must pay back the amount of the loan and pay interest on the loan amount.

Contributions made to the business in return for stock are often the preferred method for capitalizing a business. The primary reason for this is that shareholders do not expect to be repaid in a certain time frame—or at all, for that matter. Of course, when most shareholders invest in companies, whether they be publicly held or closely held companies, they hope to make a profit on their investments. They know, however, that this does not happen overnight, and that there are risks involved. It is possible that you may lose your investment if the corporation fails (in the case of closely held companies) or the stock price tumbles (in the case of public companies).

In addition, contributions made by shareholders do not put your company in debt. Just as individual loans put individuals in debt, business loans put businesses in debt. The business is obligated to pay back its loans and the interest associated with them. Just as a college student with large school loans may find, when starting his or her first full-time job, that it is quite difficult to repay the loans on top of his or her other standard monthly expenses, businesses face the same situation. It may be hard for a business, particularly a start-up business, to repay loans while also paying the other required monthly expenses.

Banks, investors who are not interested in corporate ownership, and the owners' family and friends are often sources of loans to entrepreneurs' businesses. While a loan may be able to instantly provide the cash you need for your business, keep in mind that loans are often hard to secure. For a bank loan, you will need to complete a lot of paperwork and meet certain requirements. In addition, most banks require the owners of new businesses to personally guarantee the loan. In doing so, you as the owner become personally responsible for the repayment of the loan, should your business not be able to repay it. When you personally guarantee something for your business, the limited liability afforded to you by the corporate entity will not shield you from this personal guarantee. You will be held personally responsible for any business debts you guarantee.

There's no need to dwell on the horror stories concerning the bad feelings that develop when friends and family members of an entrepreneur lend money that is never repaid. Almost everyone knows someone to whom this has happened, so your friends and family may be hesitant to provide your business with a loan. It is not our intention to scare you away from securing a business loan—we just want to outline the potential negative aspects of these loans.

GETTING MONEY OUT OF THE CORPORATION

Let's be realistic. Business owners do not start businesses for their health, especially considering the time, effort, and capital that most business owners put into their businesses. Their ultimate motivation is to make a profit. That having been said, most business owners want to know at least the basics of how to get money out of the corporation.

Salaries and Bonuses

Corporations can pay salaries to owners who are employed by the corporation in some capacity, as long as the amount of the salary is considered reasonable by the IRS. Typically, a salary is considered reasonable if it is comparable to the market value of wages for similar positions. Because salaries are listed separately on the corporation's tax return, it is advisable to ensure that the salaries paid by your corporation are at fair market value and therefore are considered to be reasonable by the IRS.

There are web sites, such as www.salary.com, that can help you discern the fair market value of salaries by position and geographic area.

Your local chamber of commerce may also have general salary information for the city or region it serves. Because of the consequences of paying salaries to employee-shareholders that are deemed to be too high, it is advisable that you research salaries as you are starting your business.

Chapter 3 introduced the concept of a deemed dividend payment. When the IRS deems a salary paid by the corporation to an employee-shareholder to be unreasonable, these payments are no longer tax-deductible to the corporation, which has a negative effect on the corporation's taxable income. The corporation will probably be held responsible for additional or back taxes.

Along with salaries, corporations can also pay bonuses to employees, including owner-employees. Bonuses, and the method of determining the amount of each employee's bonus, should be well documented, in case any questions arise. With regard to the deemed dividend concept, the IRS reviews the overall compensation package for the employee-owner, which includes both salary and bonuses. While we have discussed deemed dividends thus far only in relation to salary, note that bonuses are also part of the compensation whose value is assessed by the IRS.

Distributions and Dividends

Distributing funds and paying cash dividends are both ways of getting money out of the corporation. Cash distributions are payments made to the owners of the corporation that do not represent payments of salaries or reimbursement for expenditures. Dividends are a type of distribution that is unique to corporations. As earlier chapters discussed, dividends are optional distributions of cash or property that the corporation pays to shareholders out of its profits. Most often, distributions made to shareholders are made in the form of a dividend.

It's important to remember that dividends must be distributed to shareholders pro rata, meaning that they must be in proportion to the shareholders' ownership shares. To return to our example of Jill and Lisa and their printing company, we'll say that the corporation plans to distribute a dividend totaling $2000 to shareholders. Since Jill and Lisa are the only shareholders, this distribution needs to be made in proportion to their ownership percentages. If each of them owns 50 percent of the shares, each should receive $1000. However, if Jill owns 75 percent of the shares and Lisa owns 25 percent, Jill should receive $1500 of the distribution and Lisa should receive the remaining $500.

OTHER ITEMS TO CONSIDER

There are other items that business owners should consider when it comes to capitalizing the corporation. Some of these are more complex in nature, but warrant being mentioned. For any questions regarding the financial aspects of your business, it is always best to seek the advice of an accountant or tax adviser.

No Commingling of Assets

This chapter has talked mostly in terms of a corporation's cash, but businesses have numerous assets, of which cash is only one. Generally, an asset is anything owned that has a monetary value. Assets include cash, property, stock, inventory, equipment, and so on. Remember that corporations exist separately from their owners; therefore, the assets of the business and the personal assets of the shareholders need to be kept separate.

One of the problems small businesses often encounter is making a complete separation between the owners and the corporation, particularly in terms of finances; however, this is a necessity. When personal and business assets are "commingled," a number of problems can arise. This can complicate the accounting and tax preparation process, and potentially cause the corporate veil to be pierced, leading to shareholders' losing the limited liability that the corporation provides. (Piercing the corporate veil will be discussed in Chapter 18.)

We'll provide an example of how commingling assets can have a detrimental effect on the corporation and its owner(s). Jim owns his own business, Jim's Driving School Inc., in which he is the sole shareholder. He has one checking account that he uses for both business and personal expenses, instead of maintaining separate business and personal checking accounts. If Jim's Driving School is sued, a judge may consider all the cash in the checking account to be assets of the business rather than personal assets of the business owner. The judge could award all the money in Jim's checking account to the plaintiff in the suit.

Another possibility is that the judge may determine that because of this commingling of assets, it is not possible to separate Jim the business owner from Jim's Driving School Inc., meaning that Jim's Driving School is functioning more like a sole proprietorship than like a corporation. The judge may rule that Jim is therefore personally liable for any debts or liabilities of the business.

There are a number of actions you can take to segregate your business and personal assets. The more diligent you are in separating and properly documenting your business assets, the better off your corporation will be in the long run. You can use any or all of the following methods for separating and tracking business assets:

- *Separate checking accounts.* Maintain separate checking and/or bank accounts for your business and personal expenses. Use the business account only for purchases that relate to your business, and use it for all such purchases.

- *Physically segregate business assets.* If you have a separate office for your business, keep only business assets in the office and keep all personal assets in your home. If you operate a home-based business, try to keep all business assets in one room of the house, such as a room designated as your home office.

- *Log all business usage on assets that receive both business and personal use.* With a computer, for example, log the amount of time the computer is used for business purposes. If the personal usage is insignificant, the computer can be classified as a business asset.

- *Tag items that belong to the business.* In the case of home-based businesses where it is impossible to segregate all business items in one room, it's advisable to tag all items used by the business. This helps to demonstrate the separation of personal and business assets. While physically tagging your business assets may seem a bit extreme, if your home-based business should ever be audited, it is one way to demonstrate that you have taken steps to segregate your business and personal assets.

- *Document decisions regarding corporate assets made by the board of directors and shareholders.* Having records showing that the corporation made formal decisions regarding corporate assets also helps to establish the separation. If a directors' resolution approves the purchase of a computer to be located at the home of a shareholder (who is also a director and officer of the corporation) to enable him to work from home, this demonstrates that the corporation views the computer as a business asset.

The reality is that in many closely held companies, the shareholders are very involved in the day-to-day activities of the corporation. Keeping a distinct separation on the financial side of the business is imperative. Limited liability is not inherent in corporations for the duration of their existence, and corporations must take certain steps to preserve this advantage. Proper segregation of assets is one of these steps.

Documentation

It is important that all assets contributed to and distributed from the corporation be adequately documented. We have stated before the importance of documenting items such as decisions made by directors and shareholders, and keeping this documentation with your corporate records. Properly documenting money coming into and going out of the corporation is also very important. Part of this is for tax purposes. Because of the complexity of this issue, we won't go into details; however, you will save yourself a number of headaches at tax time if you adequately document all financial transactions, including distributions to shareholders, contributions from shareholders, loans, leases, and the valuation placed on noncash assets, from the start.

The type of documentation that is necessary varies depending on the type of asset. In the case of property, you should ensure that the legal transfer of ownership is documented. Examples of this could include transferring the title of a car to or from the name of the corporation, or conveying a deed for land or real estate owned by or being transferred to your corporation.

In terms of cash, documentation could include bank deposit slips for cash proceeds contributed to the corporation and canceled checks for cash payments made by the corporation. With stock, documentation could include a notation on the stock certificate as to the amount of money paid for the shares purchased. If dividends are to be paid to shareholders, the corporation's board of directors typically must approve the distribution and the amount of the dividend. This action should be documented in the minutes for that board meeting, or in the unanimous consent document if the decision was made without holding a meeting.

Be sure to keep the proper documentation for all asset transfers with the financial records of your corporation. If your board of directors needed to approve the transfer of the asset to or from the corporation, a copy of the board of directors' resolution approving the transfer should be keep with your corporate meeting minutes.

Valuing Noncash Assets

This chapter deals mostly with cash, but contributions to and distributions from the corporation can also be made in the form of noncash assets, such as equipment, machinery, cars, and real estate. A value needs to be placed on these assets, and this is typically the fair market value of the asset. The standard employed by the IRS for fair market value is the price that property will garner when it is offered for sale by a willing seller to a willing buyer. A willing seller and a willing buyer means that neither is obligated to buy or sell.

There are a number of ways in which you can determine the fair market value of your noncash assets. If an item has been purchased recently and has not significantly lost value (for example, through extensive use), fair market value can be documented by the purchase receipt for that item. Fair market value can also be documented by noting the cost to purchase a similar item. For example, noting the blue book value for the year, make, and model of a corporate car would establish fair market value. Having items appraised also establishes fair market value. There are also industry guidelines for the value of used merchandise. Organizations such as Goodwill must constantly value used items and merchandise. IRS Publication 551 includes additional information on valuing used assets.

It is best to consult the IRS web site at www.irs.gov or an accountant or tax adviser for additional information or advice on valuing your corporation's noncash assets.

1244 Stock

Section 1244 stock is something that is unique to small businesses. It can be beneficial when a corporation is planning to be acquired or to cease operations, but it can also be linked to getting money out of the corporation. Section 1244 of the Internal Revenue Code allows for special treatment of losses on "small business corporation" stock. A corporation's stock is considered to be small business corporation stock, which is also often called 1244 stock, if it meets the following criteria:

- The value of property and money contributed to the corporation in return for stock must be less than $1 million at the time of the contribution.
- The stock must be issued by the corporation in exchange for money or property, and not for other stock or securities.
- Less than half of the corporation's gross receipts during the previous 5 taxable years (or the entire time of the corporation's existence, if that is less than 5 years) must be from investment-type sources, such as interest, dividends, rent, and gains from securities.
- The stock must be issued to an individual or a partnership.

Section 1244 of the Internal Revenue Code allows individuals to deduct any losses resulting from a sale or exchange of small business corporation stock as ordinary losses. If the stock becomes worthless, treatment of the loss as an ordinary loss is also allowed. The maximum amount of this deduction is currently $50,000 per year, or $100,000 per year if filing jointly. Conversely, if stock is not classified as 1244 stock, the losses can only be subtracted from capital gains.

A corporation does not need to make an election with any government body to have 1244 stock. It also does not need to adopt a plan to issue 1244 stock. As long as the four criteria previously mentioned are met, the corporation's stock is automatically treated as Section 1244 stock. It is not uncommon, however, for a corporation's directors to note in the bylaws or in a resolution that the corporation's stock meets the criteria of Section 1244 of the Internal Revenue Code.

Capitalizing a corporation and other financial issues, particularly those relating to taxes, can be quite complex. As the end of Chapter 3 noted, there are organizations that provide small businesses with financial information and tax assistance. It is also recommended that you seek the advice of an accountant or tax adviser for questions relating to your particular business situation.

Post-Incorporation Business Steps

Once you've incorporated your business, there are a number of common steps that you should research and complete. You've learned that corporations have a number of traits and requirements specific to this entity type, such as requirements involving directors and shareholders. This chapter addresses certain items that are common to most small businesses, regardless of entity type. Understanding these items will help you get your corporation off the ground.

> *Major topics covered: This chapter includes information on opening a bank account, addressing day-to-day financial issues, securing the different types of insurance that businesses require, and complying with government requirements for employers. It also addresses general business items such as leasing office space and equipment, researching zoning requirements, and creating identity materials for your business.*

Processes such as opening a bank account, securing the necessary insurance for your business, and developing identity materials should be undertaken or at least considered shortly after incorporation. Also, the day-to-day financial issues, which can be a business owner's least favorite responsibilities, are quite important in starting and growing a business. While this chapter outlines the basics that you should know when you start your business, some of the points covered are also applicable to business owners who have incorporated a preexisting business.

OPENING A BANK ACCOUNT

As Chapter 16 discussed, it is very important that you keep your personal and business assets and expenses separate. With large companies, this is not an issue. With closely held companies, this task is not always easy, but it is vital. In companies with only one or a few owners, it is often convenient for owners to make business-related purchases or pay business expenses from their personal checking accounts; however, in these cases, the owners should take particular care to document reimbursements for business-related expenditures with actual receipts. Furthermore, the business account should never be used to pay for personal items. As the previous chapter noted, commingling of assets can lead to piercing of the corporate veil (a concept that will be discussed in the next chapter) and the loss of the limited liability afforded by corporations to their shareholders.

One of the first steps a new business owner should take after incorporation is to open a bank account for the business. Most banks have offerings that are specifically targeted to small businesses. Also, there are a number of online banking options available to small business owners today. Whether a business owner opts to open an account with a bank in the city in which the business is located or to establish an account with an online bank is really a matter of personal preference. Depending on your particular business situation, there could be advantages and disadvantages to each. For example, if you anticipate a need to make deposits to your account daily, such as depositing cash received from sales each day, having a local bank may be preferable. If you do not feel that having your bank physically located near your business is a necessity, an online bank may offer advantages over a local bank branch. It is advisable to research the offerings of a number of banks to find the one that is best suited to your needs.

The items that a bank requires for opening a business bank account often vary. Common items and information requested include the following:

- *General information.* The bank will probably request general information about your business, such as the legal name of the business, the type of business, the address, and the business purpose.
- *Employer identification number (EIN).* The bank will typically ask for your employer identification number. As Chapter 11 outlined, this is the number assigned to all corporations by the Internal Revenue Service (IRS) for tax purposes. It is like a social security number for your business.

- *Copy of the business's articles of incorporation.* Banks often require you to present a copy of the articles of incorporation for your business, to prove that your company is indeed incorporated.
- *Information on the person opening the account and a corporate resolution authorizing the account.* The bank will most likely seek additional information about the person who is seeking to open the account and those who will have the authority to sign on behalf of the account. The bank may require the name(s), contact information, title(s) in the company, driver's license state(s) and number(s), and social security number(s) for this person or persons. Often a corporate resolution showing that the person has the power to open the bank account on behalf of the corporation will be required.

As noted previously, the information required typically varies by bank, but it can also vary by area. For example, banks in New York City currently require a corporation opening a bank account to have a corporate seal. The corporate seal is stamped on the signature card held by the bank, denoting that the information on that card is official and true. It is advisable for you to research the bank's requirements prior to attempting to open your account. Coming prepared, or being prepared if you're applying online, will make the process flow more smoothly.

DAY-TO-DAY FINANCIAL ISSUES

Business owners often say that the financial aspects of owning their own business are the most onerous. Many entrepreneurs are idea generators, and business skills are not necessarily their strong point. In these cases, it is easy to focus on the company's vision and neglect its finances. Considering the high number of small businesses that fail every year, keeping on top of the financial aspects of your business is imperative. The amount of accounting, bill paying, invoicing, and collecting on past due accounts that you will have to do varies greatly by type of business and even from business to business in the same general industry. There are a number of steps that business owners should take to help them with this time-consuming and often burdensome task.

Accounting

One of the first steps regarding day-to-day finances that you should take is to set up your account books properly. This makes sound business sense, and the earlier you set up standard accounting practices, the easier it will be to make these a part of your business routine. No business owner wants to imagine this, but should the IRS audit your business, having detailed accounting records from the inception of your business will help you deal with the situation. In addition, shareholders have the right under corporate law to access pertinent financial records of the business. Public companies are required to publicly announce their financial results quarterly; however, that is not the case with privately held companies. In closely held corporations where not all shareholders are substantially involved in the day-to-day activities of the business, the corporation needs to have methods of informing these shareholders of the financial state of the business. Maintaining proper accounting records will assist with this requirement.

Whether you are responsible for the financial aspects of your business or a co-owner or employee handles this function, you should ensure that a minimum set of information is diligently tracked and recorded. Be sure to record the following:

- *All disbursements.* Record all payments that your corporation makes, whether they be for salaries, services rendered to your business, purchase of products, petty cash disbursements, or travel and entertainment. Documentation should not be limited to check stubs or canceled checks. Be sure to retain the original copies of vendor invoices or statements, as these may be required in order to provide additional information about the disbursements. For example, in a sales and use tax audit by the state or local government, the auditor will seek documentation to support all disbursements made by your corporation.
- *Payments received.* Be sure to record any money coming into your business, whether it be from customers, partners, or lenders. It is often advisable to maintain photocopies of checks received from customers or signed credit card sales slips for a reasonable period of time.
- *Invoices/accounts receivable.* Record all invoices that your corporation issues. Once an invoice is issued, it is a receivable until it is paid.
- *Accounts payable.* Likewise, be sure to record all invoices or bills that your corporation has received, but not yet paid.

For each of these items, you should also be sure to keep all supporting documentation. It is advisable to keep all bills, invoices, receipts, and check records for a period of 7 years. Records like salary and retirement information, proof of ownership (such as deeds and titles), and federal and state tax returns should be retained indefinitely.

You will want to have more than a general idea of whether the amount of cash coming into your business is greater than your business expenses. Accurately tracking all the items listed here will give you a clear idea of your company's profitability. You should always know whether your business is making or losing money, and how much. With diligent tracking of the items noted, you will be able to project, over time, revenues and expenses for any given month or for any given year. Having numbers to back up these projections beats making educated guesses as to whether your business can afford the new equipment you'd like to purchase or the new staff you'd like to hire. In those often cash-strapped first months of existence, good record keeping will also help you determine whether you will be able to pay the bills.

Working with an accountant or having an accountant on staff can help to alleviate the headaches that are often associated with day-to-day finances; however, many businesses, particularly those that are just starting, cannot afford this. Another option is to hire a tax adviser at the end of the year for tax compliance work. At a minimum, we recommend that you invest in accounting software that is specifically targeted to small businesses. Today's accounting software practically runs the financial side of your business. Once you enter the necessary information, the software helps you track disbursements and payments received. It also often helps to automate the time-consuming tasks of invoicing and issuing checks.

In addition, many small business accounting solutions are compatible with automated tax preparation software. Tracking disbursements and receipts throughout the year will make the preparation of your tax returns that much easier. It's advisable for you to research the software options available to you, and to find the one that best meets the needs of your business. One offering that is particularly targeted to the needs of small businesses is QuickBooks from Intuit; however, a number of different solutions are available.

Checks and Credit Cards

To reiterate, it is absolutely necessary to keep business and personal expenditures separate; business checks are a must, and business credit cards are advisable. Once you establish a bank account for your business, you will most likely be given business checks. Be sure to use these checks for paying all business-related expenses. If a situation arises in which you must pay a business expense with a personal check, you should include your receipt with the corporate accounting records once a business check has been issued to reimburse you for this expense.

Likewise, it is advisable for you to have either a business credit card or a separate personal credit card that you use solely for business expenses. In today's world, it is no longer practical to pay all business expenses by check. If you'll be traveling for your business, you'll want a credit card for all travel-related expenses. Also, if you plan to order any products or services for your business online, credit cards are often required for these purchases. Keeping separate credit cards for business and personal expenses also helps on the accounting side. If you commingle expenses on a credit card, they will have to be separated for corporate accounting purposes before the corporation can reimburse you for expenses related to the business. Also, if you do commingle expenses in this way, be sure to maintain a copy of your personal credit card statements with your corporate accounting records. Sifting through credit card statements to separate business from personal expenses creates an extra step for you or the person responsible for your corporation's accounting.

Establishing a Line of Credit

It is also important for your business to establish a line of credit. This is beneficial for two primary reasons. First, once you establish a line of credit, your corporation will not be required to prepay for products and services. Second, the credit your company has established can be reviewed by other businesses, and a positive business credit history may result in additional orders, new relationships, and/or new contracts.

When your business first establishes relationships with suppliers and vendors, it is common for those companies to require prepayment for the goods or services they supply. Before they will agree to invoice you, businesses will probably require you to complete a credit application. Credit applications help vendors ensure that your company can indeed pay its bills and do so in a timely manner. Credit applications typically ask for both banking information on your business and trade references. It is possible that a prospective supplier or vendor will contact your banker for information regarding the amount of money in your business bank accounts, to ensure that you have the funds to pay its invoices. A prospective vendor will also check with trade references to ensure that you pay the bills and invoices generated by these companies in a timely manner. Until your company can provide good trade references, it may not be extended credit.

Once vendors and suppliers begin to invoice you, it's important for you to pay those invoices within the terms. By doing so, you build both favorable relationships with these companies and a line of credit with them. Businesses are often like credit card companies in that they may extend your business a relatively low line of credit at the onset, until you demonstrate the ability to pay. Then they may increase your credit limit, giving you greater freedom to purchase their products or services. Also like credit card companies, many businesses impose penalties for late payments, which is another reason to pay on time.

As you establish more relationships in which your business is invoiced for the products and services it purchases, ask these vendors and suppliers whether they are willing to act as trade references for your business. If they are, this will assist you in establishing credit with other companies as the need arises.

Prospective vendors, suppliers, and partners can also track the creditworthiness of your corporation. The primary means for doing this is to obtain a report on a business from D&B (formerly called Dun & Bradstreet). D&B's Data Universal Numbering System (or D-U-N-S number) has become a de facto standard for tracking businesses and their relationships. You may be required to have a D&B D-U-N-S number if you wish to do business with certain companies or agencies. For example, the U.S. government requires the companies with which it does business to have one.

The D&B D-U-N-S number is a nine-digit number that is unique to your business. There is currently no charge for obtaining a D&B D-U-N-S number for your business. When you do so, your business becomes part of the D&B business information database; this allows information on your company to be accessed by other companies when they seek to verify the viability of your corporation. While you may ask why you would want to provide information about your company to D&B, the D&B database is extensively used by companies in determining whether to do business with another company or to approve that company's credit application. Having no record with D&B could mean that your business has to go through extra steps in order to obtain credit or to be awarded a new contract. It could also cause you to lose a new contract or account. Generally, unless your business has something to hide, having a D&B D-U-N-S number and being included in the D&B information database is considered an advantage; however, the decision as to whether to do this ultimately rests with you. You can learn more about the D&B D-U-N-S number by visiting the D&B web site at www.dnb.com.

INSURANCE AND GOVERNMENT REQUIREMENTS

In our personal lives, most of us do not want to go without certain types of insurance, such as homeowner's insurance, renter's insurance, car insurance, and medical insurance. Your business is no different. You'll want to ensure that your business risks are properly covered. While most types of business insurance are not mandated, certain types of insurance, such as workers' compensation and unemployment insurance, may be. Depending on its size, your business may also face certain government requirements. For example, the federal Family & Medical Leave Act, which requires paid leave for maternity and family care, applies to companies with over 50 employees. While your business may not face requirements such as this today, it may do so as it grows. You should be aware of some general points regarding business insurance and government requirements, and then perform the necessary research to learn to what extent they apply to your business.

Business Insurance

There are numerous types of business insurance. Some policies are more general in nature, but most insurance companies also have offerings that are specifically targeted to certain businesses or industries. For example, suppose you're planning to open a child-care center, running it either from your home or in a business facility. Businesses dealing with small children face a number of potential liabilities. Most insurance companies have types of insurance geared specifically toward child-care providers.

This section addresses some of the more common types of business insurance; however, it is advisable to contact your insurance agent regarding the specific types of coverage recommended for your business.

- *Business owner's policy.* This policy often combines property and liability insurance. Property insurance typically covers damage to or theft of your business's physical assets, such as your building, equipment, computers, furniture, inventory, and so on. The liability portion is designed to protect the assets of your business from a lawsuit.
- *Commercial auto insurance.* Most insurance companies offer commercial auto insurance, which covers vehicles used for company

business. It is possible that an accident that occurs while you are using your personal car on company business might not be covered by your personal auto insurance policy. If you plan to have company vehicles or to have employees use their own vehicles during work, having commercial auto insurance is advisable.

- *Errors and omissions policy.* This policy protects you against allegations that an error or omission on your part caused someone harm or cost her or him money. For example, suppose you're a graphic designer who is responsible for the design and maintenance of a client's web site, and the site cannot accept orders correctly for a period of time. If the client sues you, saying that it was your fault that the order process did not work properly and that the client lost money because of this, an errors and omissions policy would help to cover your liability.

- *Home business coverage.* Homeowner's insurance typically does not include coverage for home-based businesses. Most companies either have separate insurance policies or have additional coverage that can be purchased if you are planning to operate a business out of your home. This type of insurance typically covers theft or damage to your business's physical assets and also provides business liability coverage.

As your company adds outside investors, you may wish to consider directors' and officers' (or D&O) liability insurance. While this type of insurance is a necessity for public companies, where directors and officers are routinely named in shareholder lawsuits, it is not very common for closely held corporations to carry this type of insurance. D&O insurance is used to indemnify the directors and officers in the event of a shareholder lawsuit. Because the shareholders of closely held corporations are often also its directors and officers, the need is not as great. The directors and officers of a corporation can be held liable for all of their acts and errors, as well as potentially being held responsible for the acts of company employees. In addition, directors and officers can be personally liable for legal fees and other expenses incurred in defending claims made against them. D&O insurance helps to protect directors and officers from lawsuits solely against them and those in which they might be named as a party.

Unemployment Insurance

The way unemployment insurance works is that all employers, except those specifically exempted by each state, are required to "contribute" premium payments to an unemployment trust fund that pays unemployment compensation to those who qualify. Each state typically administers its own unemployment insurance and compensation program; therefore, the requirements vary. The premium charged will also vary by state, but it is often affected by the number of employees a business has and the organization's work history, such as its hiring and firing history. Contact your state government for more information on what is necessary for your business to comply with your state's unemployment insurance requirements.

Workers' Compensation

Workers' compensation insurance covers employees' medical and rehabilitation expenses for injuries sustained on the job, and also typically covers lost wages resulting from the injury. The amount of workers' compensation insurance that businesses are required to have varies by state. Also, in some states, companies may be exempt from having workers' compensation insurance if they employ less than a certain number of people (often fewer than three to five employees). It is advisable to consult your insurance agent regarding your state's workers' compensation insurance requirements.

OSHA

Under the provisions of the Occupational Safety and Health Act of 1970 (OSH Act), employers must provide a workplace that is free from recognized hazards that cause or may cause death or serious physical harm to employees. This applies to businesses of all sizes, and it is enforced by the Occupational Safety and Health Administration (OSHA). One requirement is that all companies must post OSHA information in a centrally located area of the business, such as in a kitchen or in all break rooms. There are a number of OSHA regulations governing industries such as construction, mining, and manufacturing. Also, any company dealing with chemicals or hazardous waste must comply with a number of OSHA requirements. For many small businesses, hanging the OSHA informational posters and being familiar with OSHA's recommendations regarding ergonomics in the workplace are their only exposure to this agency. To learn more about OSHA requirements and how they pertain to your business, visit the OSHA web site at www.osha.gov.

Information Display Requirements

Most states require all businesses to display within their offices and stores certain state and federal information pertaining to employees. Just as all businesses must display the OSHA posters, most states mandate that companies display information on topics such as the minimum wage and requirements for employees under 18 years of age. There are posters available that combine the necessary state, federal, and OSHA information all on one poster; these are especially useful to small businesses. Business owners can typically obtain these posters from the department responsible for labor and workforce issues in their state. It is possible for your business to be fined if this information is not posted in an area where all employees have access to it, or if the information is not kept up-to-date.

GENERAL BUSINESS ITEMS

There are other general business items that you may have already researched or considered, but if you have not, doing so after incorporation is a good idea. If you've just incorporated a new business, whether you will open an office or store or operate from your home is something to consider. Additionally, one question that always faces business owners, particularly new business owners, is how to announce a business to the public. The creation and standard usage of identity materials are steps in this process.

If you've incorporated a preexisting business, the items addressed in this section may not apply to your particular situation. If you've incorporated a business that you have been operating as a sole proprietorship or partnership, it is advisable for you to notify the persons or entities with which your business has trade relationships of your change to corporate status. As the early chapters of this book noted, one of the benefits to incorporating your business is that doing so often increases your credibility with potential customers, vendors, suppliers, and organizations. Letting entities with which you currently have relationships know of your business's change in status could be advantageous in this regard. Also, if you have formal contracts or agreements in place with other entities, you should amend those contracts to reflect the fact that your company is now a corporation in whichever state you incorporated. For example, changing a contract to read, "This agreement is between vendor X and My Company, a <state of incorporation> corporation" demonstrates this change of status. The revised contract should then be approved by the other party, signed, and kept by both parties.

Leasing Space and Equipment

Since a number of entrepreneurs today incorporate their businesses while those businesses are still in the conceptual stage, or at least research incorporation while they are conceptualizing their businesses, we wanted to discuss leasing. It is also possible that you have been operating your business from your home, and you have decided to incorporate as the business grew. As your business grows, you may need to lease space and hire additional employees.

Leasing office or store space can often be a daunting task for business owners. This step can bring home the reality of the fact that you now own your own business. One thing you should consider when preparing to lease office or store space is location. If your business is retail in nature, you may wish to look for space near other stores that target the same audience. That is one reason why you often see a large number of retail stores located close to shopping malls. Locating your store near a building or a site frequented by your target audience can also be advantageous. For example, if you're starting a sporting goods store, selecting a location near a school could be advantageous, since young athletes are often looking for the necessary clothing and equipment for their sports. If parents drive past your store every day while taking their kids to school, they might be apt to shop at or at least visit your store, since the location is convenient.

Finding space within your price range may complicate your plans. You should take care not to financially overextend your new business just to be in the newest, hottest building in your town. After all, we assume that your goal is to run a successful and profitable business for a number of years, not for only a few months.

Often, small business owners will use a Realtor or lease broker to locate suitable office space. These professionals can help you perform cost assessments and determine if a particular space will meet your business needs. As you review possible locations, you should consider both cost per square foot for the leased space and access to such facilities as rest rooms, kitchens, and waste disposal. If you are considering shared lease spaces, which are spaces in a building with multiple tenants, be aware that the owners of these buildings typically assess annual fees for common area maintenance, such as snow removal, waste disposal, and signage. Often, these annual fees are included as an additional cost per square foot at the end of each calendar year.

Because of the hefty investment required to modify space to suit your needs, small businesses should consider factors like the term of the lease and the availability of expansion space. The term of the lease is important for two diametrically opposing reasons: the possibility of success and the possibility of failure. Short-term leases give the owners flexibility in the event of restructuring or failure. Long-term leases give the owners a chance to recoup refurbishment fees or to establish a presence in one locality. If you are evaluating space in a building with other tenants, you may wish to consider requesting "right of first refusal" on property within that building to facilitate future expansion. With the right of first refusal, you will have the option of leasing vacated space in the building before that space is offered to another company.

Much like vendors or suppliers whom you are asking for credit, landlords will be very interested in your corporation's credit history. They will ask for credit references (including banking references), financial records (such as tax returns or financial statements), and other documentation for your business. If your business is new, the landlord will often ask for a personal guarantee of the lease. This guarantee requires the shareholder(s) to pay for the lease if the corporation is unable or unwilling to do so.

Many businesses today opt to lease rather than buy certain types of office equipment, such as computers and copiers. Most of the major computer manufacturers now have leasing divisions. While the prices of computers have dropped substantially over the past few years, outfitting a new office with a number of computers is quite different from buying a single computer for home use. The time and expense involved in setting up a company's computers and network may be considered a burden. In this case, leasing the necessary equipment either from the manufacturer or from a local company that specializes in leasing may be preferable.

Copying machines are also frequently leased by businesses. Copiers are one of those items that all businesses need, but that no one wants to be responsible for fixing. Also, a business's copying needs can change relatively quickly. Leasing a copier typically allows businesses to upgrade or downgrade as necessary. Remember that maintenance of the equipment is not automatically included in lease contracts. Before signing any lease document, you should read and understand the terms of the lease. Often, there is a separate maintenance contract that covers equipment repair and ongoing service.

Depending on the needs of your business, leasing equipment such as a fax machine or postage meter may be advantageous. Cost is one factor, but service, support, and keeping the technology up-to-date are also often factors in a business owner's decision as to whether to purchase or lease office equipment. Also, the amount of cash you have available for the purchase of equipment may be low, particularly if you are just starting your business. Many owners prefer to make monthly lease payments rather than pay the full purchase price initially so that they can use their cash to cover other business expenses. Performing a cost-benefit analysis on leasing versus buying equipment will help you determine the best option for your business. The Business Owner's Toolkit includes additional information on leasing versus buying. You can find this information at www.toolkit.cch.com/text/P06_6700.asp.

Zoning Restrictions

If you plan to operate a home-based business, you should contact your city regarding zoning restrictions. Some municipalities have restrictions on the types of businesses that can be operated within residential zones. It's advisable for you to research this sooner rather than later. If you establish your business within your house and begin distributing that phone number and using that address in your trade relationships, only to learn that your business is in violation of local zoning restrictions, you will probably incur more headaches and expense in the long run.

Identity Materials

One of the challenges that many small business owners face is letting potential customers know about their business and its offerings. We understand that the topic of marketing your business is really the subject for an entire book. However, one aspect of marketing is the use of identity materials, such as a logo and your business cards and letterhead. Consistent usage of these materials is important. For example, if you use letterhead only for some correspondence and use plain paper for the rest, not only is this inconsistent, but it may impede your efforts to find new business.

It is important that you do not develop identity materials until after your business has been incorporated. It is possible that the name you wish to use for your corporation will not be available in your state of formation—in which case, if you have already spent time and money on creating a logo, letterhead, and business cards, these materials will be unusable, and your efforts will have been wasted. You should wait until you are sure that your company name is available in your state of incorporation. Because corporate names are issued on a state-by-state basis, it is possible that the name you want is already in use in another state. Because of this, as you are selecting the name of your business, it is important that you ensure that no trademarks exist on this name.

Networking often plays a substantial role in business, particularly for those businesses with a local target audience. Having business cards to hand out whenever you meet a prospective customer, as well as to other business owners, helps get the word out about your business. Also, many local chambers of commerce or business organizations have regular meetings that are specifically geared toward a business card exchange. This allows owners of local small businesses to meet and greet one another in an attempt to match up suitable vendors and clients or banking relationships. In addition, you should provide some of your business cards to your friends and family. You never know when a coworker of your sister may state that she needs a product or service that you happen to sell. If your sister can provide her coworker with your business card, you may have gained a new customer.

Providing people with something tangible by which to remember you, your business, or your offering will take you further than just telling them about it. To continue with the coworker example, if your sister only tells her coworker about your offering, chances are that the coworker will forget the name of your business within minutes of hearing it. However, if your sister provides your business card, her coworker now has something tangible by which to remember your company. When your business cards and other identity materials include your company's name, address, phone number, fax number, email address, web site address, and a brief description of what you do, the chances of your gaining a customer or a sale increase.

Likewise, using business letterhead for all of your correspondence helps to establish your business in the minds of others. Use your letterhead not only for letters, but also for thank-you letters, invoices, and fax cover sheets. Let your customers, suppliers, and vendors know exactly who you are and how they can reach you. Even if you're invoicing a current customer, there is no harm in using letterhead or an invoice format that includes your logo and full contact information. It will further solidify the image customers have of your corporation.

If you have a web site, be sure to include your domain address on all of your identity materials. Even if your web site does not allow people to purchase your products and services online, potential customers may try to access your site in order to learn more about your business and your offerings. People also turn to web sites to find a business's location and/or hours of operation. Furthermore, you should ensure that your email correspondence includes your company name, contact information, and web site address. This can be accomplished by establishing an autosignature that always appears at the bottom of your emails. Given the amount of communication that is handled digitally today, your digital identity cannot be neglected.

Enlisting the services of a graphic designer to create a logo and related identity materials for your business may not be in your budget as you are starting your business. While the professionalism that a graphic designer brings to these materials cannot be disputed, you also do not want to break the bank in creating these items. If you choose to enlist the services of a graphic designer, there are relatively inexpensive options available. You can search for a freelance graphic designer or even a student of graphic design in your area or online. Freelance designers are often designing on the side or just starting their own businesses themselves. As they are seeking to grow their portfolio or expand their clientele, they may offer their services at relatively inexpensive rates. Also, if you live near a college or school that offers graphic design courses, students may be willing to work on projects at little cost to you, to further build their experience in this field.

You can also create these materials on your own. All office supply stores carry business card paper that you can run through your printer, just as you do with mailing labels. If you use the business card paper created by Avery, Microsoft Word typically recognizes the brand and assists you in formatting your items to fit within the business card perforations. Creating letterhead can be as easy as including your logo and contact information at the top of the page. Creating a logo on your own can be more challenging, but you can buy graphic design software programs that will assist you with this task. Whether you create your own materials or enlist the services of a designer, remember that consistency in look and usage is key.

ITEMS PREVIOUSLY HIGHLIGHTED

Chapter 11 detailed a number of items that you should consider as you undertake the incorporation process. We want to briefly reiterate some of those items, in case you have not yet completed these steps.

- *Obtain an employer identification number (EIN).* The EIN is the number assigned to a business by the IRS for tax purposes. Any business with employees is required to have an EIN. Also, as noted earlier in the chapter, you most likely will have to have an EIN in order to open a bank account.

- *Make the S corporation election.* If you plan to elect to have your corporation taxed as an S corporation, you need to file the application with the IRS. Form 2553 should be filed with the IRS no later than the fifteenth day of the third month of the tax year in which the election is to take effect. If your state has a separate S corporation election process, be sure to complete and file the necessary paperwork with your state in addition to the federal paperwork.

- *Obtain state, county, and city business licenses.* Be sure to research the types of business licenses required for your particular type of business. Remember that business licenses may be required at the state, county, city, and even the municipality level. It's advisable that you contact each government agency regarding its requirements and the process for applying and paying for these business licenses.

- *Issue stock certificates.* While you probably did this when you held your organizational meeting, it deserves mention here as well. Once you've incorporated and held your initial meetings of directors and shareholders, or all the business that would have been accomplished at those meetings has been approved by unanimous written consent of directors and shareholders in lieu of holding the initial meetings, stock certificates should be issued to all shareholders, and the amount of stock that each shareholder owns should be recorded in your stock transfer ledger. Properly recording stock transactions, including the initial issuance of shares, is an important formality that all corporations should comply with. Additional formalities, and the risks incurred if they are not properly followed, are discussed in the next chapter.

Beyond the post-incorporation steps, corporations face a number of requirements on an annual basis. Chapter 18 addresses these requirements and provides a checklist for helping you comply with them.

Annual Requirements and Ongoing Compliance

From the outset, corporations face different requirements from other business entities. They come into existence by means of a state filing, and they incur formation fees. Corporations then face unique compliance requirements, such as annual directors' and shareholders' meetings, issuing shares, and so on, throughout their existence. While some business owners may find the ongoing requirements associated with corporations to be a disadvantage, they are a small price to pay to maintain the limited liability that the corporation affords its shareholders.

> *Major topics covered: This chapter contains information on the federal, state, and local requirements that corporations face. It also addresses corporate compliance issues such as annual meetings of directors and shareholders, includes an annual requirement checklist, and outlines steps for dissolving a corporation, should you face this necessity.*

Many of the annual federal, state, and local requirements that corporations face are similar to, but not the same as, those faced by other business entities. For example, most businesses are required to pay taxes annually, but the steps that corporations must take differ from those for most other business entities, particularly partnerships and sole proprietorships, where the owners are legally considered the same as the business. Separation of business and owner is a cornerstone of the corporate entity, and the rights associated with it should be protected. This chapter outlines the steps you need to take in order to keep your corporation in good standing and to protect the limited liability currently afforded to your shareholders.

FEDERAL REQUIREMENTS

At the federal level, paying annual income taxes to the Internal Revenue Service (IRS) is the primary requirement facing corporations. As individuals, we are all familiar with the need to pay income taxes. April 15 is a date that is ingrained in our minds. In terms of filing annual tax returns, corporations are no different, except that the due date for corporations differs from that for individuals.

Federal Income Taxes

All corporations must file tax returns with the IRS. If you keep April 15 in your mind as the date your corporate income tax return must be filed, you will almost certainly miss your deadline, since "Tax Day" for corporations differs from that for individuals. Corporate tax returns must be filed with the IRS by the fifteenth day of the third month after the end of the corporation's tax year. For example, if your corporation is a calendar-year taxpayer, your corporate tax return will be due by March 15 every year. After you hold your initial meeting of directors and determine the tax year for your corporation, you may wish to note on a calendar the date when your federal corporate income tax return will be due.

As you now know, there are differences between C corporations and S corporations in terms of taxation. One commonality is that the time frame for filing tax returns for both types of corporations is the same. Even though C corporations must file Form 1120 and S corporations must file Form 1120S, the returns are due at the same time. Note that the IRS has taken steps to prohibit S corporations from selecting fiscal years that do not coincide with the calendar year. S corporations have found it advantageous to have a fiscal year that ends early in the calendar year, and the IRS has now lengthened the processing time for S corporation elections that select a non–calendar-year fiscal year, and may impose a fee on these applications. (Additional information on this can be found in the instructions for IRS Form 2553 on the IRS web site.) The IRS now requires a compelling reason, such as the seasonality of a business, in order to grant a non–calendar-year fiscal year for an S corporation.

With C corporations, not only are corporate income tax returns filed, but taxes are also paid at this level. With S corporations, the tax return is filed, but the profit or loss of the S corporation is passed through to the shareholders and reported on their personal tax returns. Taxes are then paid at the individual level.

It is important to remember that a profitable C corporation will be required to pay some amount of tax each year. The IRS has rules and regulations in place governing estimated corporate income tax payments, which are made on a quarterly basis. You can think of this as being similar to having federal and state taxes as well as social security contributions withheld from your paycheck. As most of us know, a substantial portion of our paycheck each month goes to taxes. In theory, this keeps us from having to face a substantial tax payment when we file our individual tax returns each spring. The concept is similar for corporations. Profitable corporations make estimated tax payments to the IRS quarterly in order to decrease the amount of federal income tax that must be paid at the time the corporate income tax return is filed. The amount and timing of these payments depend upon the specific circumstances of your business.

Chapter 3 provided some insight into the basics of corporate taxation; however, this is a complex subject. A number of books have been written that address only this topic, so in the interest of keeping this book to a reasonable length, we will not dive into the specifics of corporate taxation. The IRS web site (www.irs.gov) includes detailed information on corporate taxation requirements and procedures, as well as allowing you to download the necessary forms and publications. As we outlined at the end of Chapter 3, there are a number of organizations that can offer assistance on tax matters to small business owners, or you can contact an accountant or tax adviser.

Payroll Tax Requirements

Payroll tax requirements deserve a separate mention in this book because of the severity of the consequences of not complying with these requirements and the penalties for failing to comply. All taxing authorities require payroll withholdings for your employees. Payroll withholdings apply not only at the federal level, but at the state and often the city or municipality level as well.

The federal government requires employers to withhold, and remit directly to the government, a portion of the employee's federal tax liability and both the employer's and the employee's portion of FICA and Medicare taxes. Employee income tax withholdings are based upon the employee's expected earnings and stated exemptions. There are very specific rules promulgated by the federal government regarding the amounts of these withholdings. Both employer and employee FICA and Medicare withholdings are based on prescribed withholding rates and, in the case of FICA, a maximum threshold. To learn more about these mandates, visit the IRS web site or contact the IRS directly for additional information on payroll tax withholding requirements.

The state governments' withholding requirements often mimic federal requirements with regard to income tax withholding; however, state income tax regulations vary significantly from state to state. Several states charge no income tax, and therefore withholding is not required. City and locality taxes may also be charged in certain areas. Check with both your state and local government taxing authorities to determine how these withholdings affect your business.

As previously mentioned, not complying with payroll tax withholding requirements can have severe consequences. Failure to pay payroll taxes results in the officer or employee who has this responsibility for the corporation being personally liable. The importance of determining the specific federal, state, and local payroll tax requirements for your business cannot be overstated.

The Business Owner's Toolkit web site includes good information on payroll tax requirements. It helps to address the types of compensation that are taxable, which payroll taxes apply, and outlines record keeping requirements. You can find this information at www.toolkit.cch.com/text/P07_1000.asp.

STATE REQUIREMENTS

Corporations are creatures of the state. They are created by state filings, are subject to state statutes, and face a number of state requirements. Each state's requirements for companies incorporated in that state and for those that are foreign-qualified to transact business in the state differ. Most states require an annual statement, which allows the state to keep its information on your corporation current. Most states also have franchise tax and/or state income tax requirements for corporations. These items are discussed later in this section.

Another possible annual state requirement that you should be aware of is the need to renew any state-issued business licenses. Some states require certain types of businesses to obtain licenses at the state level in addition to the local or county level. It may be that your particular state issues business licenses that are valid for a period of 2 or maybe 5 years. It could also be that licenses must be renewed annually. The last thing you want is to have your business licenses expire, so be sure to note when they must be renewed.

Annual Statements

The annual statement is typically used by the state to keep the information on your corporation in the state's records accurate. The annual statement is often a relatively short report or form on which you must verify or complete information on your corporation. The information varies by state, but information that is commonly requested on the annual statement includes the corporation's legal address, the names and addresses of directors, and the names and addresses of officers. Some states may also ask for stock information or information on shareholders that own more than a certain percentage of your corporation's shares.

If certain information for the corporation has changed, most states allow you to correct that information when you file the annual statement, instead of contacting the secretary of state when the change occurs. In order to change information that is included in your articles of incorporation, you typically must file a certificate of amendment with the state and pay the necessary fees. Director information is one common exception to this. The states realize that a corporation's directors and their addresses can change fairly frequently. Most states that require director information to be listed in the articles of incorporation allow corporations to make changes to this information through the annual statement.

There is no set rule regarding when the states distribute their annual statements. Some states send them to all corporations at once, and other states send them to corporations around the anniversary date of their formation. For example, Delaware sends out its corporate annual statements around January, and they are due by March 1. Louisiana sends out its corporate annual statements a few months before the anniversary date of the corporation's formation, and they are due on that anniversary date.

Note that some states have different annual statement due dates for corporations and limited liability companies (LLCs). For example, Delaware sends out the annual statements for LLCs around April, and they are due by June 1. If you have a Delaware corporation and your friend Carol has a Delaware LLC, you'll want to track your annual statement due date separate from hers. When Carol tells you that annual statements are due by June 1, she is referring to the LLC deadline. Marking that date as your due date will cause you to miss the annual statement deadline for corporations, and a late fee will be imposed.

Most states mail annual statements to the corporation's registered agent; however, a few states send these documents to the corporation's legal address. If you utilize a registered agent service provider, it is this provider's responsibility to forward annual statements and other important state documents to your corporation. If you act as the registered agent for your own corporation, state documents will be sent to the registered agent address you specified in your articles of incorporation.

Annual statements typically have a fee associated with them, and if you miss the deadline, most states impose a late fee. The late fees that states impose can often more than double the amount of your annual statement fee. Failing to file your annual statements and pay the necessary fees on time, or not filing your annual statements at all, causes your corporation to be not in good standing with the state. Not being in good standing basically means that your corporation is not fulfilling its obligations as a business incorporated within that state. If your corporation remains not in good standing long enough, it can be administratively dissolved by the state. When this happens, your business is no longer recognized as a corporation in that state, and the advantages of being a corporation are lost. States have varying time frames before they will administratively dissolve corporations. These time frames range from a few months to a number of years.

Note that the annual statements that the states send to corporations and the corporations return are different from the annual reports you may have received from publicly traded companies. If you own stock in a publicly traded company, you should receive its annual report every year. The Securities and Exchange Commission (SEC) requires public companies to report their financial results quarterly and to send their results for the fiscal year to shareholders in the form of an annual report. Annual reports are filed with the SEC, mailed to all shareholders of record, and also made available to prospective new shareholders. The annual reports of public corporations are extensive documents that often run anywhere from 25 to 100 pages in length. They fully outline the corporation's financial results, and they often provide a narrative account of the year the corporation had. They routinely outline industry trends, highlight significant changes in or additions to the company's products and services, and discuss events that transpired for each of the corporation's business units, if it has multiple units.

Until you take your company public (if this is a step you are considering), you will not have to worry about annual reports—only annual statements. To learn more about the annual statement requirements for your state of incorporation, see the detailed state pages on Business Filings' web site.

Franchise Taxes and State Income Taxes

There are different types of annual state taxes that your corporation may incur. Franchise taxes are taxes that are assessed on corporations and LLCs by the states for the mere privilege of being formed and/or transacting business in that state. State income taxes are taxes that businesses pay on the profits earned in that state. Some states have only income taxes, and some have only franchise taxes. To make it more confusing, some have both, and some have neither. To find out whether your state of incorporation has franchise and/or state income taxes, see the detailed state pages at www.bizfilings.com/learning/detailedstateinfo.htm.

Like federal income taxes, state income taxes are often calculated as a percentage of your taxable income. A number of different formulas are used for calculating franchise taxes. Some states base the tax on the corporation's capital. Others base it on the total number of authorized shares and par value.

Throughout the book, we've made references to Delaware's franchise taxes. Delaware is a state that bases the franchise tax on the number of authorized shares the corporation has, and in some cases on par value as well. The Delaware franchise tax for companies with a low number of authorized shares is quite straightforward. Currently, if you have 3000 or fewer authorized shares (regardless of their par value), your annual corporate franchise tax is $30. If you have more than 3000 authorized shares, Delaware allows you to use either the authorized shares method or an alternative method that includes your total gross assets, number of issued shares, stated par value, and number of authorized shares in the equation.

For example, if your corporation has more than 10,000 authorized shares, you can use either of these calculations for figuring your franchise taxes.

1. *Authorized shares method.* The current tax is $90 for the first 10,000 plus $50 for each 10,000 shares or part thereof over 10,000. For example, if Fast Boating Incorporated has 35,000 authorized shares, its franchise tax would be $240 if it used the authorized shares method.

2. *Alternative method.* Divide total gross assets by total issued shares, carrying the result to six decimal places. This is your "assumed par." If the assumed par is the same as or greater than the stated par value (the par value listed in your articles of incorporation), multiply the assumed par by the total authorized shares. This is your assumed par value capital. If your assumed par value capital is greater than $1,000,000, round up to the next million and multiply by $200 per million (e.g., $10,002,000 = 11 × $200). Should your assumed par be less than your stated par value, multiply the total authorized shares by the stated par value and continue with the calculation. Each no-par share must be considered to have a value of $1. The minimum tax is $30, and the maximum tax is $150,000.

For companies with a high number of authorized shares, the authorized shares method would probably end up producing a very high annual tax amount. The alternative method helps to lower the annual franchise taxes. Because the alternative method includes par value in the formula, having a higher par value can also lead to an increase in your franchise taxes. Keeping the par value low is another way to help keep your franchise taxes lower.

In the case of Delaware, on the franchise tax statement, you will figure your tax amount based on the authorized shares method. If you believe the alternative method will produce a lower tax, you can include the necessary data (number of shares issued and total gross assets) on the form and utilize the alternative method to calculate the tax due.

In some states, the concepts of franchise tax and income tax are combined. For example, California's franchise tax is based on net income, but there is also a minimum tax amount. The current California tax rate for corporations is 8.84 percent of net income, but there is an $800 minimum tax. So, even if your corporation has no net income, it must still pay the $800 minimum. The minimum tax does not need to be paid during the corporation's first year; however, if your corporation has net income during its first year, taxes based on net income do have to be paid.

As mentioned in earlier chapters, Nevada is one state that does not have state income or franchise taxes; however, Nevada does impose annual statement fees on corporations. Corporations that are physically located in Nevada and that transact business there may find paying no state income or franchise taxes to be quite advantageous.

Franchise tax statements are often sent concurrently with the annual statements and have the same deadline. Delaware is an example of a state that does this. The annual statement fee is included on the franchise tax form, and is paid when franchise taxes are paid. In states where franchise tax statements are sent separately, they are also typically sent to the registered agent for your corporation. As with annual statements, not paying your corporation's franchise taxes will cause your corporation to be deemed not in good standing with the state.

If your head is not yet spinning, it may be when you study the franchise and/or income tax information for your state of incorporation. In states that base the tax calculation on net income, it is difficult for business owners to estimate the amount of taxes they will owe, particularly in the company's first year of existence. For questions regarding franchise and state income taxes for your specific business, it is best to contact an accountant or tax adviser.

LOCAL REQUIREMENTS

Some municipalities impose taxes on businesses that are physically located there. You should be aware of the requirements and all payment deadlines imposed by your county, city, and/or municipality. Also, if your particular business requires a city or county business license, or possibly both, you should be aware of the term of these licenses. If they must be renewed annually, it's advisable to note this on a business calendar and transfer it to each new calendar you purchase for your business.

In addition, many localities impose a property tax on real and/or personal property. Examples of real property include land and buildings. In this case, personal property does not refer to the property of the shareholders. Instead, it refers to tangible and movable items of property, such as inventory, office furniture, equipment, or other such assets. (As a side note, examples of items that are not considered to be personal property include stock certificates, certificates of deposit, and intellectual property, which are typically viewed as intangible assets.) Filing deadlines and taxes assessed vary significantly from state to state or between municipalities. Some tax the value of personal property as of a specific day each year. (You may have seen inventory closeout sales at the local shopping mall; those businesses are typically trying to decrease their inventory prior to the specific day on which inventory is taken for calculating the tax amount.) Some states or municipalities offer exemptions for specific types of property, such as computers, to encourage business investment. Some charge no property taxes at all. Also, the time of year when the property tax is assessed varies, and these tax returns must typically be filed with the city or possibly the state government. For more information on your city's property tax requirements, it is best to contact your city government.

ONGOING CORPORATE COMPLIANCE

Corporations face a number of ongoing requirements that are unique to this type of business entity. Other types of entities, such as partnerships and sole proprietorships, do not have stock, directors, or shareholders. Therefore, items such as issuing stock, recording stock transfers, and holding directors' and shareholders' meetings do not apply to them. This chapter seeks to provide you with a general list of steps you need to take in order to keep your corporation in compliance with corporate requirements.

As previously mentioned, the benefits that corporations provide to their shareholders are not automatic. You must take a number of actions in order to keep your corporation valid and in good standing with the state. You need to properly capitalize your corporation, comply with the state's formation and annual requirements, issue shares, hold meetings, record corporate actions, and so on. If you do not consistently do all of these things, you risk losing your corporate status. This is where the concept of piercing the corporate veil comes into play.

Piercing the Corporate Veil

Piercing the corporate veil is the legal term for a corporation's shareholders losing the limited liability that corporations provide. This is a concept that all small business owners should understand. Closely held corporations often do not comply with all of the required corporate formalities; however, the importance of complying with these formalities cannot be overstated. It's highly likely that one of the main reasons you decided to incorporate was the limited liability that corporations offer their shareholders. Maybe some of your other reasons were the advantage of establishing credibility for your business and the tax-deductible nature of certain corporate payments. Whatever the case, these benefits will no longer exist should you pierce the corporate veil.

Piercing the corporate veil can be accomplished in a number of ways. If the shareholders of your corporation engage in illegal or fraudulent acts, this may not only cause a piercing of the corporate veil, but also result in your shareholders being convicted of crimes and possibly sent to jail. A corporation does not provide protection from liability to shareholders, directors, or officers who commit criminal acts. Needless to say, engaging in such acts would ruin your corporate image and possibly the business itself.

Inappropriate or inadequate capitalization of the corporation is another way to lose limited liability. As Chapter 16 outlined, consistent commingling of business and personal assets can lead to piercing the corporate veil. For example, if a corporation's shareholder consistently deposits corporate checks into his or her personal checking account, the separation between owner and corporation can be lost. If a judge cannot distinguish between what belongs to the owner and what belongs to the corporation, he or she may determine that the corporation was acting like a sole proprietorship, and therefore revoke its corporate status. Proper financial records should also be kept, and appropriate accounting steps should be taken. In addition, not providing the corporation with adequate start-up capital, or providing it with adequate start-up capital but draining that capital very quickly for salaries, dividends, and personal loans, could lead to a determination that the corporate veil has been pierced.

As previously mentioned, corporations must also comply with formalities that are unique to this entity. For example, stock certificates should be issued to all shareholders when the corporation is formed. Any changes in ownership should be documented by both issuing or retrieving stock certificates and recording all stock transfers in the stock transfer ledger. Directors' and shareholders' meetings need to be held and documented. This includes the initial meetings for both of these groups and the annual meetings held thereafter. All actions taken at these meetings should be properly documented, and the minutes kept with the corporate records.

Separation of the business and its owners and keeping good records are key to ensuring that your corporation maintains its corporate status. While there is no official body that polices corporations to ensure that they comply with the necessary requirements and formalities, you never know when the need to produce records from the inception of your corporation may arise. A lawsuit against your business could cause a judge to subpoena your corporate records. It's advisable to keep good records all along, instead of scrambling when you need to prove that your business has been carrying out its corporate responsibilities.

In summary, here are ways in which you can help to prevent piercing of the corporate veil and thereby protect the limited liability the corporate entity affords to shareholders:

- Do not commingle business and personal assets. Keep business assets, including bank accounts, equipment, and property, completely separate.
- Document all corporate actions, including the issuing of shares; record director resolutions; and create and keep minutes of all directors' and shareholders' meetings.
- Keep your corporation adequately capitalized.
- Let people know of your corporate status. Contracts should be in the name of the corporation, invoices that you receive should be paid by the corporation, and invoices that you send to customers should be from the corporation. Maintain a distinct separation between the corporation and its owner(s).

Annual Meetings of Directors and Shareholders

As previously mentioned both in this chapter and in earlier chapters, corporations are required to hold annual meetings of directors and shareholders. There is a common misconception that this is unnecessary for closely held corporations where the shareholders are very involved in the management of the business. However, whether or not you feel that annual meetings are useful for your corporation, holding them is a requirement that is imposed on all corporations, no matter how large or small they may be. Despite their importance, annual meetings are one of the corporate elements that are most often disregarded; however, holding and documenting your annual meetings is a relatively easy way to demonstrate that your corporation is carrying out its responsibilities.

In their traditional corporate roles, directors are not involved in the day-to-day activities of the company, and therefore virtually all business decisions that need the directors' approval are addressed during the initial, annual, and any special meetings. The annual meeting is typically the time when directors review the state of the business, vote on items needing their approval (including any proposed amendments to the corporation's bylaws), and help establish the direction and goals for the corporation for the coming year. Special meetings of directors may be called to address urgent corporate business that cannot wait until the next annual meeting to be addressed.

In most closely held companies, all or the majority of the directors are also officers and shareholders of the corporation. They are fully aware of the company's direction and goals, and the steps they would like the company to take in order to achieve those goals. Closely held corporations often utilize the vehicle of unanimous written consent of directors for approving items that need a vote of the directors. This often is a time saver for the directors and is a relatively easy way to comply with the annual directors' meeting requirement.

For example, Jeff and Tammy are the sole directors, officers, and shareholders of Complete Health Limited. Both Jeff and Tammy are employed by the company and are very involved in the day-to-day management of its affairs. Since Jeff and Tammy are involved in all business decisions related to their corporation, they may feel that an annual meeting of directors is unnecessary. That is untrue, and in reality they can meet this requirement relatively easily. When Jeff and Tammy make corporate decisions that necessitate board approval, they can document that the decisions were made by unanimous consent of directors in lieu of holding a meeting. If Tammy is the secretary of the corporation, she should create the unanimous consent document, both she and Jeff should sign and date it, and then she should store it with the corporate minutes and records. The requirement has then been satisfied.

If Complete Health Limited has a third director, Stacy, who is not an employee of the corporation, it may be best for formal meetings to be held. This is an opportunity for the three directors to meet, discuss the current state of the corporation and where it's going, and vote on any decisions that must be made. Since Stacy is not an employee of the corporation, it is likely that she is not fully aware of the business logistics; therefore, regular meetings may be particularly helpful for Stacy. Depending on the guidelines established in the bylaws of Complete Health Limited, this meeting could happen by electronic means, such as via teleconference, making it easy to fit the meeting into the schedules of the three directors.

We are not trying to paint a picture of the annual meeting as a negative experience. Many directors view this meeting as an opportunity and look forward to each year's meeting. In many closely held companies, directors who are not involved in the day-to-day affairs of the company are friends or family members of those who are. The annual meeting provides a reason for the directors to get together outside of the office once a year (maybe over dinner, or maybe on the beach). Where and how you hold your annual meeting is up to you and your fellow directors. The important thing is the fact that you hold it and document it.

The primary points of business at the annual meeting of shareholders are electing directors and voting on any actions that need shareholder approval. With closely held corporations, the annual meeting of shareholders presents a situation similar to that of the annual meeting of directors. Shareholders are often very involved in the day-to-day affairs of the business, and often also act as directors and officers. Nonetheless, either an annual meeting of shareholders or approval of all items by unanimous or majority consent in lieu of holding the annual meeting is required.

Let's return to the example of Jeff, Tammy, and Stacy, where all three are both directors and shareholders of the corporation. It is possible, and actually quite common, to combine the annual meeting of directors and the annual meeting of shareholders. If Jeff, Tammy, and Stacy decide to meet in the mountains for a ski weekend, they could set the date, time, and place of both meetings to be over that weekend. Over dinner one night, the three can discuss and vote on the items needing board approval and then the items needing shareholder approval. Alternatively, the three may decide to hold the annual meeting of directors followed by the annual meeting of shareholders via teleconference one morning from their respective homes or offices. In either case, the outcome of these meetings should be noted in the meeting minutes, and those minutes stored with the corporate records.

Holding annual directors' and shareholders' meetings and documenting the outcome can also prove important in the event of internal disputes. To return to the example of Jeff, Tammy, and Stacy, suppose that at their annual meeting they agree to purchase $10,000 of new equipment for their business. This decision is documented in the meeting minutes and kept with the corporate records. Six months later, the company is not doing so well financially, and Tammy claims that she never agreed to the decision to purchase the new equipment. The minutes would document that she was present at the meeting in question and would list the vote by which the decision was approved. If the vote was unanimous, the record from this meeting would demonstrate that she had indeed approved the equipment purchase.

Calling, Holding, and Documenting the Annual Meetings

The process for calling and documenting annual meetings is similar to the process for calling and documenting the initial meetings, which was discussed in Chapter 13. Notice of the date, time, and place for the annual meeting of directors should be sent to all directors. Likewise, similar notice should be sent to all shareholders for their annual meeting. In the case of Jeff, Tammy, and Stacy, who agree to hold the meetings on their ski weekend, they could waive notice of the meeting and include the waiver document with their corporate records.

Having a standard agenda for your annual meetings can help them go as quickly and smoothly as possible. A sample agenda for the annual meeting of directors could include:

- Roll call (to ensure that a quorum exists)
- Reading and acceptance of the preceding meeting minutes
- Reports from committees or officers
- Report on the financial status of the corporation
- Performance of any officer reviews
- Addressing of any unfinished business
- Discussion and vote on new business items
- Adjournment

A sample agenda for the annual meeting of shareholders could include:

- Documenting of attendance (to ensure that a quorum exists)
- Reading and acceptance of the preceding meeting minutes
- Reports from officers or directors
- Report on the status of the corporation
- Election of directors
- Addressing of any unfinished business
- Discussion and vote on any new business items
- Adjournment

Documenting the decisions made at these meetings is very important. This provides a formal record that these corporate acts are taking place on an annual basis, and also provides a written record of the business decisions made at these meetings. If an actual meeting is held either in person or by teleconference or videoconference, the secretary of the corporation should prepare and sign the minutes, and then keep them with the corporate minutes and records. Minutes should include the date, time, and place of the meeting; record who attended; and document all decisions made. If items are approved during the meeting, such as new vendor contracts or leases, copies of these documents should also be kept with the meeting minutes.

If the decisions are made by unanimous (directors) or majority (shareholders) consent in lieu of holding a meeting, a formal document should still be prepared and kept with the corporate records. For directors, the document should state that the actions were taken by means of unanimous written consent in lieu of holding an annual meeting. For shareholders, the document should state that the actions were taken by means of majority written consent in lieu of holding a meeting, and the consent document should be promptly provided to all nonconsenting shareholders. Like meeting minutes, the unanimous and majority consent documents should outline the business decisions made and include copies of any documents approved. They should then be signed by all directors or shareholders, whichever the case may be, and kept with the corporate records.

Keeping Corporate Records

We have mentioned a number of times that certain items should be kept with your corporate records. Maybe by now you are envisioning a safe within your office that contains years of meeting minutes, copies of contracts, and copies of directors' and shareholders' resolutions. That is a bit extreme, but keeping these documents in a safe place is a good idea. Records are commonly kept in the corporate kit or in a binder that is used solely for corporate documents. If you are ever required to produce your corporate records and/or minute book, it will save you a lot of time if these documents have been kept together all along.

The corporation's president or secretary often keeps corporate records, such as the articles of incorporation and bylaws. IRS documentation, such as your employer identification number and your S corporation election approval, are often also kept with these records.

Traditionally, the secretary of the corporation is responsible for keeping the corporate minutes, as he or she is typically responsible for creating and signing the minutes of directors' and shareholders' meetings. The corporate minutes are often kept in a binder with tabs separating the minutes of directors' meetings from the minutes of shareholders' meetings, or in separate binders for directors' and shareholders' meetings. You should also attach any supporting documents for business decisions made at these meetings, such as copies of contracts, to the minutes and keep them with the minutes in the minute book. If the directors or shareholders make decisions by unanimous or majority written consent in lieu of holding a meeting, the formal consent documents, and any supporting documentation, should also be kept in the minutes book.

The corporation's treasurer typically keeps the financial records. Keeping financial records goes beyond keeping quarterly and annual revenue and expenditure numbers. As Chapter 17 indicated, it is advisable to keep all bills, invoices, receipts, and check records for a period of 7 years. Records such as salary and retirement information, deeds, titles, and federal and state tax returns should be kept indefinitely.

A number of states have statutes requiring that corporate records be kept at the principal address for the corporation. While our constant talk about keeping certain items with your corporate records may have sounded simply like good advice, in reality doing so is required by law in a number of states. The state pages on Business Filings' web site outline the corporate record requirements imposed by the states, if they have statutes governing the items that corporations must keep and where the corporations must store these records.

Regardless of who in your corporation is in charge of keeping your corporate records, you'll want to ensure that your company keeps the following items:

- A copy of your articles of incorporation and any amendments
- A copy of your bylaws and any subsequent revised and amended copies
- Your corporate seal
- A stock transfer ledger recording all transfers of your corporation's stock
- Copies of all meeting notice documents sent to directors and shareholders
- Copies of all director and shareholder resolutions
- A corporate minute book with minutes from all directors' and shareholders' meetings and copies of all documents approved during those meetings, and/or all unanimous or majority written consent documents

Including any written correspondence with shareholders is also recommended; however, this may apply to a lesser degree in closely held corporations. When the shareholders are also directors and officers of the corporation, written communications, such as notices of meetings, may not be sent. The shareholders may opt to waive notice, and instead select the date, time, and place. However, if your corporation does have any written correspondence to shareholders, it is advisable to keep that correspondence with the corporate records.

Tools for Helping with Formalities

As mentioned, small business owners often wear a number of hats, particularly in companies with only one or a few employees. Remembering the annual requirements and formalities that your business faces may not be at the top of your to-do list, so having assistance with this task may be beneficial for you.

A corporate kit includes a number of items necessary for carrying out corporate formalities. Corporate kits, which were introduced to you in Chapter 11, routinely include a binder customized with your corporate name (which can double as a corporate record and minute book), a custom corporate seal, custom stock certificates, a stock transfer ledger, and sample meeting minutes. If you did not obtain a corporate kit at the time you incorporated, you can order a corporate kit for your corporation from an incorporation service provider, even if you did not utilize that provider's services for preparing and filing your formation documents. You may also be able to purchase a corporate kit from a legal supply store, although in this case the corporate kit may not be customized with your corporate name.

Each time your corporation issues shares of stock, a stock certificate should be issued to that shareholder. The transaction should also be recorded in the stock transfer ledger. Likewise, if your corporation buys back shares of stock from a shareholder, the certificate or certificates should be collected from the shareholder, and the transaction recorded.

The sample minutes included with the corporate kit can help you to create a standard format for your own meeting minutes and facilitate the consistent documentation of corporate decisions made by directors and shareholders. Also, if you used an incorporation service provider when you formed your business, this provider may have customizable forms for minutes, resolutions, and notices. Attorneys can provide versions of these documents that are specifically customized for your business and the particular meeting or situation.

Keeping a corporate calendar specifically for noting deadlines and keeping reminders of corporate formalities is also advisable. The next section includes a checklist of annual requirements and corporate formalities. This list can help you create your corporation's annual compliance calendar. You should research which of the items on the checklist apply to your specific type of corporation, and note a deadline date next to each item to help you remember when you need to address each of these items.

Finally, in addition to formation services and customizable forms, many incorporation service providers have compliance offerings for small business owners. Even if you did not utilize the services of an incorporation service provider when you formed your company, you may be able to utilize a provider's compliance offering. Research the offerings of Business Filings Incorporated and other incorporation service providers to find the tools best suited to your needs.

CHECKLIST

Figure 18-1 gives a checklist to help you remember the annual requirements and formalities that corporations face. For each requirement, the checklist includes a blank line where you can write in the deadline for taking this step. While this checklist may not cover all the requirements for your specific type of business, you can use it as a foundation for creating an all-inclusive list that is specifically tailored to your business.

DISSOLVING A CORPORATION

There may come a point in the life of your business where you will need to dissolve your corporation. Dissolution is not always a negative event. It could be that your corporation is being acquired, and so it will be dissolved and become part of the acquiring company. It may be, however, that your business did not achieve the success you had hoped, and so ceasing operations is your best option. While we want this book to provide you with the information necessary to start and run a successful business, we feel that it is important to address dissolution, should you ever face the need to take this step.

Voluntary versus Involuntary Dissolution

There are two types of dissolution: voluntary and involuntary. With voluntary dissolution, the shareholders vote to dissolve the corporation. This type of dissolution can happen for a number of reasons: the company is being acquired, the shareholders decide that they no longer want to own the business but cannot find a buyer or buyers for it, or the shareholders realize that the corporation does not have the capital necessary to

F I G U R E   18-1

Annual Requirements and Ongoing Compliance Checklist

Item	Deadline
Federal, state, and local requirements	
___ File federal income tax return	_____
___ If C corporation, pay necessary corporate income taxes	_____
___ If S corporation, report profit/loss on shareholders' tax returns	_____
___ File state income tax return (if applicable), pay taxes	_____
___ Pay state franchise taxes (if applicable)	_____
___ Complete annual statement and pay necessary fee	_____
___ Comply with state sales and use tax obligations	_____
___ Comply with payroll tax obligations	_____
___ Comply with property tax obligations	_____
___ Pay county or city taxes (if applicable)	_____
___ Renew state, county, city, and/or municipality business licenses	_____
Ongoing compliance items	
___ Send proper notification of annual meeting of directors	_____
___ Hold annual meeting of directors • Document all actions of the meeting • Keep minutes of the meeting with corporate records	_____
___ Send proper notification of annual meeting of shareholders	_____
___ Hold annual meeting of shareholders • Elect directors • Document all actions of the meeting • Keep minutes of the meeting with corporate records	_____

ONGOING REQUIREMENTS - Keep these items with your corporate records

___ A copy of your articles of incorporation and any amendments

___ A copy of your bylaws and any subsequent revised and amended copies

___ A stock transfer ledger recording all transfers of your corporation's stock

___ Copies of all meeting notice documents sent to directors and shareholders

___ Copies of all directors' and shareholders' resolutions

___ Minutes from all directors' and shareholders' meetings and copies of all documents approved during those meetings

___ Your corporate seal

continue in existence beyond a certain point. Whatever the reason for voluntary dissolution, the correct steps for dissolving the company are typically followed, which is not always the case with involuntary dissolution.

Involuntary dissolution happens when the corporation is dissolved by the secretary of state or a state court, without the approval of shareholders. For example, the state can administratively dissolve a corporation that is not in good standing, which typically happens after the corporation has not filed annual statements and paid the necessary annual statement fees and franchise taxes for a certain period of time. The courts also have the authority to involuntarily dissolve a corporation, even though this rarely happens. For example, if a corporation obtained its articles of incorporation through fraudulent means, making its existence technically fraudulent, a court may dissolve the corporation.

Financial Steps

Financially speaking, when you dissolve your corporation, you need to file final federal and state tax returns and pay all necessary taxes. You need to pay all necessary annual statement fees and franchise taxes to your state of incorporation. You also need to pay all creditors the amounts still owed to them and then divide the remaining assets among your shareholders. If you are ceasing operations because of bankruptcy, the process may differ. You should follow the procedures outlined by law for bankruptcy filings.

Business- and State-Related Steps

Since corporations are brought into existence by means of a state filing, it makes sense that they cease to exist by means of a state filing. If you want to voluntarily dissolve your corporation, you will need to file a certificate of dissolution with the state. Often, there is a fee associated with this filing. Most states recognize that if a business is closing its doors, it does not have much money for state filing fees, so the states typically keep this cost low. Also, any state franchise taxes owed by your corporation will typically need to be paid at the time of dissolution.

From the standpoint of your business, you should notify your employees (if you haven't done so already), notify your customers (particularly if they have an ongoing contract or relationship with you that will be disrupted by your closing), and notify vendors and partners that your corporation is closing.

In summary, starting and running a business is an exciting, yet stressful, experience for entrepreneurs. It won't always be easy, but hopefully it will prove to be very rewarding. As there are over 25 million small businesses in the United States, you are not alone in the challenges you face. Remember that there are a number of resources available today to help small business owners with all facets of their businesses. As your business continues to grow, we hope you will share your experiences with other entrepreneurs who are just starting their businesses, helping them to start off on the right foot.

We wish you success with your business.

501(c)(3) The section of the Internal Revenue Code that allows for tax-exempt status for nonprofit corporations organized for some religious, charitable, educational, literary, or scientific purpose.

1244 stock *See* Section 1244.

affidavit of mailing notice A written declaration made under oath that notice of a meeting has been properly sent to the shareholders or directors.

agent A person authorized by another to act on his or her behalf. Thus, an agent can enter into contracts and other such legally binding agreements on behalf of another. A corporation's officers usually act as agents of the corporation.

aggregate par value The par value of a share multiplied by the number of authorized shares. This amount is important in determining initial fees and annual franchise taxes in many states.

amendment A filing with the proper state authority to make an addition or change to the provisions contained in the articles of incorporation.

annual meeting of shareholders A yearly meeting of shareholders at which directors are elected and shareholders are able to vote on other major corporate issues.

annual statement A required yearly state filing that typically contains information concerning the directors and officers and basic corporate financial information. Also called the annual report.

apostille A method of certifying a document for use in another country pursuant to the 1961 Hague Convention. With certification by apostille, a document is entitled to recognition in the country of its intended use, and no certification or legalization by the embassy or consulate of the foreign country in which the document is to be used is required.

apparent authority Authority based upon the appearance to reasonable persons that the agent is authorized to act on behalf of the principal.

articles of incorporation A corporation's primary legal document; they serve as a corporation's constitution. Articles of incorporation, which are filed with the state government to begin the corporation's existence, contain the basic information on the corporation as required by state law. Also called a certificate of incorporation or a charter.

articles of organization The primary formation document for limited liability companies (LLCs). The articles of organization are very similar to a corporation's articles of incorporation. The incorporation document for corporations in Massachusetts is also called the articles of organization.

asset Anything owned, tangible or intangible, that has monetary value.

authorized shares/authorized stock The total number of shares a corporation is authorized to issue. This number is specified in the articles of incorporation. Not all of the authorized shares need to be issued to shareholders. Corporations can have unissued shares that can be issued at a later date.

basis An accounting term that is important for tax purposes. The basis of stock is the amount you paid for the stock or the fair market value of property contributed in return for the stock. When you transfer or sell your stock, your gain or loss will be determined by comparing your transfer price to your basis. If the sale amount is more than your basis, you will have a gain; if the sale amount is less than your basis, you will have a loss.

bearer shares Corporate stock certificates that are owned simply by the person who holds them, the "bearer," as with a check written to bearer.

board of directors *See* directors.

business entity An organization that has a separate existence for tax purposes. Some types of business entities are corporations and foreign corporations, business trusts, limited liability companies, and limited partnerships.

business judgment rule The rule that states that the directors of corporations will not be held personally liable for unwise business decisions provided that the directors made an informed decision and that the decision was not tainted by self-interest.

business purpose What your business does or will do. Corporations are required to list their basic purpose in their articles of incorporation. Most states allow for a general-purpose clause, such as "all lawful business purposes."

buy-sell agreement An agreement between the shareholders of a corporation in which the surviving owners or the entity agrees to purchase the ownership of a withdrawing or deceased owner.

bylaws The rules and regulations governing a corporation's internal affairs. This document is adopted at the initial meeting of directors, and usually contains provisions relating to shareholders, directors, officers, and general corporate business.

capital gains or losses Gains or losses realized from the sale or exchange of capital assets. The amount is determined by calculating the difference between an asset's purchase price and its sale price.

capitalization The assets invested in a business, whether they be cash or other items, to provide working capital or a means to start the business.

capital stock *See* authorized stock.

C corporation A standard business corporation. It is called a C corporation because it is taxed under subsection C of the Internal Revenue Code.

centralized management A fundamental characteristic of a corporation; shareholders elect directors to represent their views.

certificate of authority A document issued by the proper state authority to a foreign corporation granting the corporation the right to do business in that state.

certificate of incorporation *See* articles of incorporation.

certified copy A copy of a document filed with the state that is signed by an officer of the state and certified as being a true copy.

charter *See* articles of incorporation.

close corporation A corporation that elects in its articles of incorporation to be registered under the close corporation statutes of its state. In order to make this election, the corporation must have the following traits: a small number of shareholders, no ready market for the corporation's stock, and substantial participation by the majority of the shareholders in the management of the corporation. A close corporation is also called a statutory close corporation.

closely held corporation A corporation whose stock is not traded on a public stock exchange. In a closely held corporation, the shareholders are typically active in the conduct of the corporation's business.

common stock The primary stock of a corporation. This stock gives shareholders the right to participate in electing the directors of the corporation and to receive a proportionate share of any assets distributed.

compensation committee A committee created within a corporation's board of directors that is responsible for setting the salaries for the corporation's executives and management; one of the most common committees of the board.

consideration The inducement to enter into a contract. Consideration must be something of value to the people who are making the contract.

corporate kit The corporation's record book, which typically contains copies of the articles of incorporation, the bylaws, minutes of the initial and subsequent directors' and shareholders' meetings, and a stock transfer register.

corporate record book *See* corporate kit.

corporate seal A device use to imprint certain corporate information, such as the name of the corporation and the state of incorporation, on corporate documents. Corporate seals may be required when a corporation attempts to open a bank account.

Court of Chancery The Delaware court that oversees matters involving Delaware's general corporate law. It uses only judges appointed for their knowledge of corporate law.

cumulative voting A method of voting that allows shareholders to aggregate their votes in favor of fewer candidates than there are slots available. This method of voting is intended to create adequate representation of minority shareholders.

D&B D-U-N-S number A unique nine-digit identifier assigned to businesses by D&B (formerly Dun & Bradstreet) for authenticating, validating, and establishing business credentials. Reports generated on a company with a D&B D-U-N-S number are often used by companies and government agencies when evaluating whether to do business with that particular company.

deemed dividend payment A salary payment to an owner that is reclassified by the IRS as a dividend payment because the IRS considers the salary payment to be unreasonable.

directors The people who manage or direct the affairs of a corporation, but do not handle the day-to-day operations. Typically, the directors make only major business decisions and monitor the activities of the officers. Directors are elected by the shareholders.

dissolution The termination of a corporation's legal existence. A number of things may cause a corporation's dissolution, including failure to file annual reports, failure to pay certain taxes, bankruptcy, or voluntary dissolution of the corporation by the shareholders and directors.

distribution A transfer of money or property from a corporation to a shareholder.

dividend An optional distribution of money or property that the corporation pays to shareholders out of the corporation's profits.

doing business as (DBA) A DBA is a name, other than the legal name, under which business is conducted. For individuals, sole proprietorships, and partnerships, the legal name is the name on the owner's birth certificate, social security card, etc. For corporations, the legal name is the name shown on its articles of incorporation. A DBA filing does not change the official name; however, it allows the individual or company to use additional names. DBAs are typically filed at the county level with the county recorder's office. Also called assumed name or fictitious name.

domain name The unique identifier used to locate a web site on the World Wide Web.

domestic corporation A corporation in the state in which it is incorporated.

double taxation The situation that occurs when C corporations pay taxes at the corporate level and then distribute profits to shareholders in the form of dividends, on which the shareholders must pay personal income tax.

employer identification number (EIN) The number assigned to a corporation or other business entity by the IRS for tax purposes. Banks generally require an employer identification number to open a business bank account. Also called EIN or federal tax identification number.

equity The shareholders' ownership in a corporation.

executive committee A committee created within a corporation's board of directors that is responsible for performing the functions of the entire board in between meetings; one of the most common committees of the board.

expedited state filing A filing made in a faster manner upon payment of an additional filing fee; most states allow expedited filing of corporate documents.

express authority Permission to act that is given explicitly, typically in writing or orally.

federal tax identification number *See* employer identification number.

fiscal year Any 12-month period used by a business as its fiscal accounting period.

foreign corporation A corporation in all states other than the state in which it is incorporated.

foreign qualification *See* foreign-qualify.

foreign-qualify The process by which a corporation that is "transacting business" in a state other than the one in which it is incorporated registers for a certificate of authority to transact business in the other state; if such a corporation does not do so, it can lose access to that state's courts and face fines. This process "foreign-qualifies" a corporation to transact business in a state other than its state of incorporation.

franchise tax A tax on the privilege of carrying on business as a corporation or limited liability company in a state. The amount of the franchise tax may be determined by the corporation's earnings, the total value of its capital or stock, or the amount of business it does.

general partnership *See* partnership.

general-purpose clause A business-purpose statement in the articles of incorporation that is not specific, but simply provides for "all lawful business purposes."

hybrids Members of a corporation's board of directors who have ties to the company, but are not employed by the company.

identity materials Material that displays the name and the trademarks of a corporation or other business entity, such as letterhead and business cards.

implied authority Authority that is inherent in the office. For example, the president of a corporation has the implied authority to sign ordinary contracts on behalf of the corporation. The president would not need a resolution granting him the express authority to sign such ordinary contracts.

incorporation service provider A business that provides incorporation or LLC formation services along with ancillary corporate products such as corporate kits and registered agent services. Business Filings Incorporated is an example of an incorporation service provider.

incorporator The person or entity that prepares, files, and signs the articles of incorporation.

indemnify To reimburse or compensate. Directors and officers of corporations are often reimbursed or indemnified for all the expenses they may have incurred during the incorporation process. Also, the articles of incorporation may provide for the indemnification of directors for any breach of their fiduciary duty to shareholders.

informal action An action of shareholders or directors done by unanimous or majority written consent in lieu of holding a formal meeting.

initial meeting of directors *See* organizational meeting.

initial meeting of shareholders A meeting that typically takes place after the organizational meeting of directors at which the shareholders ratify the directors' actions taken at the organizational meeting.

insiders Members of a corporation's board of directors who are employed by the corporation.

IRS Form SS-4 The form required by the Internal Revenue Service to apply for an employer identification number.

IRS Form 1023 The form required by the Internal Revenue Service to apply for tax-exempt status.

IRS Form 2253 The form required by the Internal Revenue Service to apply for S corporation status.

legal address (of a company) Typically, the main or headquarters address of the corporation.

liabilities Things for which a person or business entity is responsible or liable. A debt or obligation is often called a liability.

limited liability A restriction on the level of liability shareholders have with regard to the obligations of a business. The shareholders of a corporation are typically not personally responsible for the debts and liabilities of the corporation because the corporation is an entity that exists separately from the shareholders. Their liability is typically limited to the amount they invested in the company.

limited liability company (LLC) A business entity formed upon filing articles of organization with the proper state authority and paying the necessary state fees. LLCs provide limited liability to their members (owners) and are typically taxed like a partnership, preventing double taxation.

limited partnership A business entity created by a state filing that includes both limited partners and general partners. The limited partners have limited liability for the debts of the partnership but cannot participate in management. The general partners have unlimited personal liability and are able to participate in management. If a limited partner participates in management, he or she risks being treated as a general partner with unlimited personal liability.

manager In a limited liability company (LLC), one of a group of people who act much like a board of directors. If the LLC is to be controlled by managers, this fact is typically stated in the articles of organization.

member A person or entity that is an owner of some or all of a limited liability company. Members make the business decisions of the LLC, unless the articles of organization provide that the LLC will be controlled by a manager or managers.

membership interest A member's ownership in a limited liability company; similar to a partner's interest in a partnership and a shareholder's stock in a corporation.

merger The process by which two corporations join together into one, with one corporation surviving and the other disappearing. The assets and liabilities of the entity that disappears are absorbed into the surviving entity.

minutes A written record detailing the events and actions that take place at a corporate meeting, such as a directors' meeting or a shareholders' meeting. Minutes should be kept in the corporation's record book.

name availability search A search conducted at the state level to determine that a corporate name is available and is not already in use by another corporation, LLC, foreign corporation, or foreign LLC in that state.

name ending The word *Corporation, Incorporated, Company,* or *Limited,* or an abbreviation of one of these words, used to show that your business is incorporated. Most states require a corporate name ending.

name reservation A state action allowing the intended name of a business to be reserved for a specific period of time and prohibiting any other business entity from forming in the state using that exact name. A name can be reserved, usually for up to 120 days, by applying with the proper state authorities and paying a fee.

nominating committee A committee created within a corporation's board of directors that is responsible for nominating people to fill vacancies on the board; one of the most common committees of the board.

nonprofit corporation A corporation formed for some charitable, civil, or other social purpose that does not entail the generation of profits for shareholders. These corporations can apply for tax-exempt status at both the federal and state levels. Nonprofit corporations must file not-for-profit articles of incorporation with the state. Also called not-for-profit corporation.

no-par-value stock Stock with no minimum value. Most states allow no-par stock. If the stock is no-par, then the amount of stated capital is an arbitrary amount assigned by the board of directors.

notice of litigation *See* service of process.

notice of meeting(s) A written notice informing shareholders and directors of meetings, typically sent 60 to 100 days before the meeting is to be held. A notice is not required if a corporation is holding a meeting by unanimous written consent.

officers People who oversee the day-to-day activities of a corporation. A corporation's board of directors appoints the officers, which usually consist of a president, vice president, treasurer, and secretary. In most states, one person can hold all of these posts.

organizational meeting The initial meeting of a corporation's directors, at which the formation of the corporation is completed. A number of initial tasks take place at this meeting, such as ratifying the articles of incorporation, issuing initial shares of stock, electing officers, approving the bylaws, and passing a resolution authorizing the opening of a bank account.

OSHA (Occupational Safety and Health Administration) The federal agency that deals with safety standards in the workplace. OSHA requires employers to provide a safe workplace by informing employees about potential hazards, training them to deal with hazards, and recording workplace injuries.

outsiders Members of a corporation's board of directors who have no direct affiliation with the corporation.

partnership An association of two or more persons to carry on as co-owners of a business for profit. In contrast to a corporation, a partnership can come into existence without the need to file any formal papers with any state official. Also called a general partnership.

par value The stated minimum value of a share of stock. Stock must be sold for at least this value or the owner of the stock can face liability. With low-par-value or no-par-value stock, this liability is minimized.

pass-through taxation The situation in which the income of the business entity is not taxed at the entity level. The entity does complete a tax return; however, the income or loss shown on this return is "passed through" the business entity to the individual shareholders or interest holders, and is reported on their individual tax returns. S corporations and LLCs are both pass-through tax entities.

piercing the corporate veil A corporation's losing limited liability for shareholders. Not following corporate formalities is one common cause of piercing the corporate veil.

pooling agreement *See* voting agreement.

preemptive rights Rights delineated in the articles of incorporation granting shareholders the first opportunity to buy a new issue of stock in proportion to their current equity percentage. The shareholder has the right to buy the new issue of stock, but is not required to make the purchase. If the shareholder elects not to exercise this right, the shares can be sold on the open market.

preferred stock Stock that generally provides the shareholder with preferential payment of dividends or distribution of assets upon dissolution of the corporation but does not carry voting rights. If a corporation is to have preferred stock, this fact must be stated in the articles of incorporation.

principal office The main office or headquarters of the corporation. The principal office is sometimes listed in the articles of incorporation.

privately held corporation *See* closely held corporation.

professional corporation A corporation that is organized for the purpose of engaging in a learned profession such as law, medicine, or architecture. Professional corporations must file articles of incorporation with the state that meet the state's specific requirements for professional corporations.

professional limited liability company (professional LLC) An LLC that is organized for the purpose of engaging in a profession that requires a license, such as law, medicine, architecture, accounting, or engineering; similar to a professional corporation.

pro rata Proportionately. For example, a pro rata distribution to shareholders would be proportionate to their ownership interest.

proxy A grant to another person of the power to vote on behalf of the shareholder. If a shareholder cannot attend a meeting, the shareholder is often allowed to vote by proxy.

publication fee The fee paid to a newspaper for the publication of a notice of incorporation. Some states that currently require publication of a notice of incorporation are Arizona, Georgia, and Pennsylvania.

publicly traded corporation A corporation whose stock is traded on a public stock exchange, such as the New York Stock Exchange or NASDAQ.

public record Documents kept by a governmental unit to which the public has access. For example, articles of incorporation that have been filed with the state are a matter of public record.

quorum The minimum attendance required in order to conduct business at a meeting. Usually, a quorum is achieved if a majority of the directors are present (for directors' meetings) or a majority of the outstanding shares are represented (for shareholders' meetings).

record date The date on which a person must be registered as a shareholder in the corporation's stock transfer ledger in order to receive a dividend or be eligible to vote.

registered agent The agent named in the articles of incorporation who is responsible for receiving service of process and other important documents on behalf of the corporation. The registered agent must be located in the state of incorporation.

registered office The office named in the articles of incorporation. The registered office must be where the registered agent is located; it need not be the principal office or place of business of the corporation.

resolution A formal decision of the corporation that has been adopted by either the shareholders or the board of directors.

S corporation A corporation that has elected subchapter S tax treatment by filing IRS Form 2553. This tax treatment allows the corporation to not be a separately taxable entity. Instead, the income of the corporation is treated like the income of a partnership or sole proprietorship; the income is "passed through" to the shareholders. Thus, the shareholders' individual tax returns report the income or loss generated by an S corporation. An S corporation election may also be required at the state level.

S corporation election *See* S corporation.

Section 1244 The section of the Internal Revenue Code that allows for special treatment of losses on "small business corporation" stock. This section allows individuals to deduct as ordinary losses any losses that result from the sale or exchange of small business corporation stock. The ordinary tax treatment is also allowed if the stock becomes worthless. The maximum amount of this deduction is currently $50,000 ($100,000 if a joint return is filed) in any one year. If stock is not qualified under Section 1244, the losses can only be subtracted from capital gains.

service of process The paperwork that begins a lawsuit. With corporations, service of process is made or served on the corporation's registered agent. Also called notice of litigation.

share An ownership interest in a corporation. The total ownership of a corporation is measured in shares of stock.

shareholder Any holder of one or more shares in a corporation. A shareholder usually has evidence that he or she is a shareholder in the form of a stock certificate. Also called a stockholder.

shareholder agreement *See* buy-sell agreement.

sole proprietorship A business carried on by the owner as an individual. The owner of a sole proprietorship is personally and fully liable for all business debts; thus, the owner's personal property can be taken to pay business debts.

stated capital The par value of shares multiplied by the number of shares outstanding. The amount of stated capital may affect the ability to pay dividends.

state filing fees Fees that the state requires to be paid when corporate documents, such as articles of incorporation, amendments, or dissolutions, are filed with the state.

statement by incorporator A statement required if the directors are not named in the articles of incorporation. The initial directors are named in this document, thereby allowing the directors to hold the organizational meeting of the corporation. Also called action of incorporator.

statute A law enacted by a legislature.

statutory close corporation *See* close corporation.

stock An equity or ownership interest in a corporation, measured in shares. Ownership of shares is demonstrated by stock certificates.

stock certificate A written instrument that shows ownership of shares in a corporation.

stockholder *See* shareholder.

stock transfer book/ledger A record book that lists the owners of shares of stock in a corporation, how many shares each of them owns, and the dates of all stock transfers.

trademark A word or mark used by a business to identify a product and distinguish it from the products of its competitors. If the business uses such a name or logo to identify a service, it is called a service mark.

transacting business A term that is important in the determining whether a corporation or LLC needs to foreign-qualify its business in a state outside of the state of formation. If a corporation or LLC is transacting business in a state, it is required to foreign-qualify. Typically, a company is transacting business in a state if it has substantial and continuous contacts with that state.

transferability of interest The ability to sell or otherwise transfer one's ownership in a corporation or other business entity.

unanimous written consent A process by which directors and shareholders can act without a meeting if they each give their consent to specific corporate actions in writing; it is allowed by nearly all states.

unlimited life One of the fundamental characteristics of a corporation; it provides that a corporation's life will continue regardless of what happens to its owners. This is unlike the situation facing a partnership or sole proprietorship, where the life of the business is tied to its owners.

venture capital Funding for companies. Venture capital typically entails some investment risk; however, the potential return may be greater than average.

voting agreement An agreement by two or more shareholders to vote their shares in a particular manner. Voting agreements are most typically used for the election of directors.

waiver of notice The voluntary relinquishing of the right to notice of a meeting of shareholders or directors.

INDEX

The authors of this book come from two companies that provide information and services to help small business owners with the often overwhelming process of starting and running a small business. Business Filings Incorporated, an incorporation service provider, has been helping entrepreneurs form corporations, limited liability companies, and nonprofit corporations online since 1996. CCH Incorporated, the developer of the CCH Business Owner's Toolkit, is a leading resource for entrepreneurs who need help in answering business, tax, and legal questions and getting practical tips that help them work smarter, save money, and stay in compliance with the law.

Karen B. Nathan

Karen Nathan is the director of marketing and business development for Business Filings Incorporated (www.bizfilings.com), with 10 years' experience in various facets of marketing. Helping to create articles and content geared toward small business owners has become a primary focus of hers. Through her experience with Business Filings, Karen has insight into the issues faced and questions raised by entrepreneurs who are evaluating whether to incorporate their businesses and those who are undertaking or have just completed this process. With her fondness for writing, Karen brought to this project the goal of making the often complex and intimidating process of incorporating a business both understandable and manageable.

Alice H. Magos

An accountant and certified financial planner, Alice Magos is a small business analyst with over 35 years of small business operations and finance experience. Alice is a key member of the team that created CCH's award-winning Business Owner's Toolkit (www.toolkit.cch.com), an online service that helps small office/home office business owners, as well as CCH's Personal Financial Planning Toolkit (www.finance.cch.com). She is the Business Owner's Toolkit online advice columnist, "Ask Alice," offering direct, practical advice on starting, financing, managing, and marketing small businesses. In addition, Alice has edited a number of small business books for CCH.

Alice offers a comprehensive understanding of the finance, operations, human resources, and legal issues faced by small businesses and invaluable insight into strategies for building and maintaining a successful enterprise.